THE MAKING OF PIERS PLOWMAN

The Making of Piers Plowman

Malcolm Godden

LONGMAN
London and New York

Longman Group UK Limited,
Longman House, Burnt Mill, Harlow,
Essex CM20 2JE, England
and Associated Companies throughout the world.

Published in the United States of America
by Longman Inc., New York

© Longman Group UK Limited 1990

First published 1990

British Library Cataloguing in Publication Data
Godden, Malcolm
 The making of Piers Plowman.
 1. Poetry in English. Langland, William. Piers
 Plowman – Critical studies
 I. Title
 821'.1

ISBN 0-582-05924-0 CSD
ISBN 0-582-01685-1 PPR

Library of Congress Cataloging-in-Publication Data
Godden, Malcolm.
 The making of Piers Plowman/Malcolm Godden.
  p. cm.
 Includes bibliographical references.
 ISBN 0-582-05924-0. — ISBN 0-582-01685-1 (pbk.)
 1. Langland, William, 1330?–1400? Piers the Plowman. I. Title.
PR2015.G64 1990
821'.1 — dc20   89-37583
                                                 CIP

Set in Linotron 10/12 pt Bembo

Produced by Longman Singapore Publishers (Pte) Ltd
Printed in Singapore

Contents

Preface

Piers Plowman is a great poem but a very complex one, and this book is an attempt to explain its workings and elucidate some of its complexities. The approach reflects my own gradual recognition that one cannot hope to understand the poem without trying to comprehend the ways in which it developed and altered over many years and, still more, the ways in which the author's thinking developed. Since the main evidence for these developments is the poem itself in its various versions, the analysis inevitably depends, in large part, on a critical interpretation of the poetry. If the emphasis, even so, is on the author and his relation to his age rather than on that necessary figment of twentieth-century criticism, the poem as an autonomous creation, this stems from a conviction that the poem itself is a record of the poet's own story and that some of its most striking moments reflect major shifts in his thinking. Chapters 2–4 deal with the A version and its relation to the Z text; chapters 5–9 discuss the writing of the B version; and chapter 10 examines the revision which produced the C version.

In attempting to discuss the range of Langland's writing I am conscious of the enormous number of critical and historical studies which have influenced my thinking or which touch in various ways on my argument. To mention all the points of agreement, and still more to explain in detail why I am not convinced by the points of disagreement, would have doubled the size of the book; I have therefore noted only those instances where a reference to a particular study seems especially useful.

I am aware of debts to all those with whom I have discussed the poem, including several generations of students at Liverpool University and Oxford. I would like to thank especially Hugh White of University College, London, who has done his best to bring rigour to my thinking in our many discussions of Langland; Charlotte Brewer of All Souls College, Oxford, who not only proved a remarkably tolerant host to my ideas in her Langland reading group but went on to lend a receptive ear to my later thoughts and painstakingly read and criticised the whole book in draft; Mark Anderson of Longman, whose interest and criticism have been much valued; and Julia Briggs of Hertford College, Oxford, who was a constant stimulus during my work on Langland, read successive drafts with a sharp eye, and provided the sympathetic but non-specialist reader that the book needed.

The four versions

The table shows the extent of the four successive versions of *Piers Plowman*, from Z to C. Small Roman numerals are the passus numbers.

	Z	A	B	C
Vision I The field and Lady Mede	Prologue, i–v	Prologue, i–v	Prologue, i–iv	Prologue, i–iv
Vision II The confessions and plowing	v–viii 92 (unfinished)	vi–viii	v–vii	v–ix
Vision III Do-wel and knowledge	—	ix–xi, xii? (unfinished)	viii–xii	x–xiv
Vision IV Patience and Haukyn	—	—	xii–xiv	xv–xix
Vision V Charity and the Samaritan	—	—	xv–xvii	
Vision VI The Passion and Harrowing of Hell	—	—	xviii	xx

A note on texts

References to the Z text are to the only edition: *William Langland: Piers Plowman, the Z Version*, eds A. G. Rigg and C. Brewer (Toronto, 1983). The A text is cited from *Piers Plowman: the A Version* ed. G. Kane (2nd edn, London, 1988), the B text from *The Vision of Piers Plowman: a Complete Edition of the B Text*, ed. A. V. C. Schmidt (London, 1978), and the C text from *Piers Plowman by William Langland: an edition of the C Text*, ed. D. A. Pearsall (London, 1978). Text-references cite the version (Z, A, B or C), the passus number in that version (i–xxii) and the line numbers within the passus. Reference is also made to *Piers the Plowman: a Critical Edition of the A-Version*, eds T. A. Knott and D. C. Fowler (Baltimore, 1952), and *Piers Plowman: the B Version*, eds G. Kane and E. T. Donaldson (2nd edn, London, 1988). Schmidt partially modernises the spelling, but Kane and Pearsall reproduce the spelling of their respective manuscripts (a particularly idiosyncratic spelling in the case of the C version). To avoid unnecessary difficulty and inconsistency I have modernised the spelling of quotations from the A and C versions to match that of Schmidt's edition, substituting modern forms for þ and ȝ, following modern practice with i/j and u/v, replacing y with I for the pronoun and adding capitals. I have also modernised in the same way quotations from other Middle English texts where appropriate. Biblical quotations are taken from the Revised Version.

We make out of the quarrel with others, rhetoric, but of the quarrel with ourselves, poetry. Unlike the rhetoricians, who get a confident voice from remembering the crowds they have won or may win, we sing amid our uncertainty; and, smitten even in the presence of the most high beauty by the knowledge of our solitude, our rhythm shudders.

[W. B. Yeats, *Per Amica Silentia Lunae*, Anima Hominis v; from *Mythologies* (London, 1959), p. 325]

For Janet, Ruth, Lucy and Eleanor

Chapter One

The poem and the poet

*P*iers Plowman was one of the great literary successes of the Middle
Ages. More than fifty manuscripts of it have survived from the late
fourteenth and the fifteenth centuries, compared, for instance, with only
one of *Sir Gawain and the Green Knight* and one of Malory's *Morte d'
Arthur*. Its influence is apparent on Chaucer and on a whole series of
later poems and political tracts; it inspired the leaders of the Peasants'
Revolt in 1381; in the sixteenth century it had the distinction of being
banned by Parliament, and when the ban was lifted in 1550 it rapidly ran
through several editions (see pp. 17–19). The poem explores a great range
of topics: the nature of society and its proper aims; the role of kingship;
the best way of life; the virtues and dangers of learning; predestination
and the salvation of the righteous heathen; the ideals of poverty and asceticism; the nature of Christ's redemption of mankind and how far it
can be reconciled with notions of justice and merit; the decline and corruption of the Church and Christianity. Behind these issues lie still
larger questions about the purpose of life on earth and the relationship
of man and God. Throughout the poem Langland presents these as issues on which different views can be cogently, even passionately, held
and yet which desperately need resolution.

The verse shows the same kind of range in quality and manner. At
moments it is marked by an intensely lyrical quality that goes beyond
intellectual argument. At other times it sinks to the prosaically laboured
exposition of points of doctrine. Langland can use colloquial language
and vivid detail to create energetic portraits of the contemporary scene;
but he can also produce language of the purest simplicity to charac-
terise his ideals. The exposition of abstract notions can suddenly find

1

expression in moments of almost comic visual imagination, as when Abraham's claims to have comforted and protected the souls of the just are vividly dramatised, by way of the traditional notion of Abraham's bosom as a term for limbo, in the dreamer's sight of Lazarus playing with patriarchs and prophets in Abraham's lap (B xvi 253–6).

For all the poem's success, the range of subject and variety of approach have always proved a challenge to readers and been productive of disagreement about its nature and meaning. The sixteenth-century reformers hailed Langland as a precursor of the Protestant Reformation,[1] while many twentieth-century commentators have read him as an orthodox Catholic – 'the most Catholic of Englishmen' as one critic puts it.[2] At the beginning of this century J. M. Manly found such variations of view within the poem that he came to the conclusion that it was the work of five different poets.[3] A recent critic has concluded that 'the poem, however skilfully annotated and explicated, seems to lack a convincing controlling *idée*'[4] Even Langland's defenders can acknowledge the difficulty: 'It is the merit of Langland's poem that we share the sense of confusion and apparent repetition of experience.'[5]

One factor in particular that has made the poem a challenge and a puzzle is its gradual evolution through successive versions. None of the numerous manuscripts of the poem is in Langland's own hand or likely to have been copied under his supervision or checked by him, and they preserve many different forms of the text. Out of the multiplicity of manuscripts, however, the late-nineteenth-century editor Walter Skeat was able to distinguish three successive versions of the poem, A, B and C,[6] and most contemporary opinion now accepts that all three are by Langland. Recent work has tentatively identified a fourth version, or perhaps a draft, earlier than them all, the Z text.[7] In its final form, in C, the poem is thus the record of several successive stages of writing, themselves reflecting the poet's own thinking and imagination at different stages of his life. The gradual and at times agonised development of the poem presents an obvious problem for the reader and the critic: where and what *is* the text, the essential and authentic form of the poem? To concentrate attention on any particular one of the extant versions means excluding some of Langland's distinctive writing, often some of his best writing, and attempting to understand passages which originated in quite different contexts from the version in question. The other major factor which has affected the poem's reception is the multiplicity of dreams and authority-figures. The ultimate model for this kind of poetry was probably something like the *Consolation of Philosophy* of the sixth-century Boethius, who presents a single vision in which an authority-figure called Philosophy instructs the narrator. In Piers, however, we have a multiplicity of dreams – eight in the B version, as well as two dreams within dreams – and within those dreams we often find several opposing authority-figures taking different views. This is already evident in the very earliest vision, where Holy Church and Theology are opposed, and finds its culmination in the sixth vision where the four 'wenches' called Mercy, Truth, Righteousness and Peace quarrel like fishwives. The poem's techniques, and Langland's talents, are essentially dramatic, using a variety of characters to give energetic voice to opposing views, no doubt in large part because the poet himself could feel the attractions and strengths of both sides. He had a kind of negative capability which, aligned with an honesty of vision, insisted on registering the conflicts that he saw. Much of the poem's power lies in the tension between the poet's desire to articulate a vision of unity and his honest recognition of the complexity of the issues he set out to resolve. An increasing concern of the poetry, indeed, is an epistemological problem: how can one discover the truth? Is it a matter of innate understanding, or the study of learned authorities, or a flash of divine enlightenment?

If we are to understand Langland and the complexity of his reception, what the poetry demands is an analysis which follows the poet through from the earliest stage in the Z and A versions to the last revisions in the C version, and takes full account both of the variety of authorial views and dramatic structures in the poem and of the developments in Langland's own thinking as he wrestled with the great social and intellectual issues of his time. This book is an attempt at such an analysis.

The development of the poem

The story of *Piers* began soon after 1362, when Langland produced a short, fairly straightforward poem consisting of two closely linked visions – the Z text. In the first of these visions, the poet/narrator sees a field full of people which is explained to him by a woman clothed in white called Holy Church; a marriage is arranged between Lady Mede and Fals but is forestalled by Theology; Mede is brought before the king and eventually discredited by Conscience and Reason. The narrator wakes briefly and then dreams again of the same field. Conscience preaches repentance, the sinners confess and set off to find Truth, Piers the Plowman describes the way and then sets them to work on his half-acre, and Truth sends them his pardon promising salvation. The poem ends, apparently unfinished, with the description of the terms of the Pardon, without reporting the end of the dream.[8] It is a neat, relatively simple, allegorical poem, offering a critique of contemporary society and an imaginative vision of how it might be morally transformed.

Some short time later Langland produced a new version of the poem, known as the A text. He revised what he had written earlier, completed

3

the second vision with a few more lines of action and dialogue (including the tearing of the Pardon by Piers) and a waking period, and then added a third vision. In this, the dreamer meets a series of personifications – Thought, Wit, Study, Clergie and Scripture – who explain to him the nature of Do-wel, Do-bet and Do-best. Although the sequel takes its primary subject, Do-wel, from the end of the preceding vision, its mode of action is very different, with the dreamer engaged in dialogue rather than merely being an observer of action, and the area of concern begins to shift from the nature of society to the intellectual problems of contemporary theology, especially the role of learning. This version too breaks off incomplete, without concluding the third dream.

Around 1380 Langland produced the B version of the poem. He again revised what he had written before, completed the third vision and then added five more visions (there is also an inner dream within the third vision and another within the fifth). The first of these new visions takes up the issues of knowledge and the good life which were raised by the third vision of the version and by its continuation in the B version: the dreamer participates in a meeting with Clergie, Conscience and Patience which culminates in the repudiation of Clergie, and then observes the meeting of Patience and Conscience with Haukyn the active man, which similarly culminates in the rejection of Haukyn's life of labour in favour of that embodied by Patience the hermit. But the remaining visions shift the interest again into a quite different, and more historical, area, the life of Christ and the creation of the Church, with the dreamer once more becoming primarily an observer of the action. In the fifth vision the dreamer sees the Tree of Charity and watches as its fruit falls and is stolen by the devil, and then observes a re-enactment of the parable of the Good Samaritan involving Abraham and Moses; the two episodes function as a symbolic commentary on the Fall of Mankind and its redemption by Christ's sacrifice. The sixth vision presents the Crucifixion and Harrowing of Hell in imaginative terms. In the seventh, Christendom and the Church are created by Piers the Plowman and then attacked by Pride. And the eighth describes allegorically how the Church succumbed to corruption, and ends with Conscience departing to seek Piers the Plowman.

The final version of the poem, C, was probably produced about 1390. Langland again thoroughly revised the whole poem, adding new material at various points, deleting some earlier passages and moving others. He preserved the basic structure created in the B version, but reduced the visions from eight to seven. The last two passus are not changed at all, probably because Langland did not complete the intended revision.

The Z version is extant in only one manuscript and it may not have been deliberately circulated by Langland, but the other versions exist in numerous copies – there are about seventeen of each – and must all have been widely disseminated in Langland's own time. While these four versions stand out, it is likely enough that the process of rethinking the poem and recasting it was a continual one, perhaps associated in part with recitation. There are some signs in the manuscripts of an abortive attempt to continue the A version, and Donaldson suggests that the A, B and C texts may just be accidental survivals of a whole series of forms:

> I sometimes wonder whether the C-text, the B-text and even the A-text are not mere historical accidents, haphazard milestones in the history of a poem that was begun but never finished, photographs that caught a static image of a living organism at a given but not necessarily significant moment of time.[9]

The history of the poem is in part a story of progress through conflict, moving forward by challenging what has gone before. When Langland resumed the poem in the A version his first act was to write a scene in which Piers tears up the Pardon with which the Z version had ended. When he later came to produce the B text, he began the continuation with Scripture mocking the poet for the arguments with which he had ended the A version. And when he produced the C version some of the new passages seem to have been conceived as critiques of salient arguments in the B version. Langland was driven on to revise and continue his poem by a kind of creative dissatisfaction with what he had written before, a dissatisfaction which he worked out by energetic writing rather than deletion. At the same time, there is an evident and deep reluctance to destroy what his imagination had conceived at an earlier stage. He respected the autonomy of his poetry, and tended to look for new meaning in the earlier scenes and characters, rather than changing the substance. The prime example of this is Piers himself, introduced initially in the Z version as a model of the honest worker but following the development of the poet's concerns, and the poem's, to become first an eremitic figure and then a kind of Messiah in subsequent versions.

The identity of the poet

The only contemporary information that survives about the author of *Piers Plowman* is a note in one manuscript of the poem that his name was William Langland and that he was the son of Stacy de Rokayle, a minor landowner of Shipton-under-Wychwood in Oxfordshire.[10] The information is probably right. Stacy de Rokayle certainly existed, though little else is known about him,[11] and the identification of the poet's name is supported by a pun in the B version:

'I have lyved in londe,' quod I, 'my name is Longe Wille.'

(B xv 152)

A sixteenth-century tradition that he was born at Cleobury Mortimer near the Malvern Hills[12] may also be accurate. The Malvern Hills are where Langland sets his opening dreams, and the dialect of the poem, as witnessed by the alliteration and supported by the language of many of the manuscripts, confirms that this was his place of origin.[13]

If we are to go beyond these bare details we have to turn to the picture which Langland gives of himself within the poem, though with the proviso that these references seem at times contradictory and may in part be fictional. The opening lines suggest already both the fictive quality and the fundamental equivocation:

In a somer sesoun whanne softe was the sonne
I shop me in-to a shroud as I a shep were;
In abite as an ermyte, unholy of werkis. (A Prol. 1–3)

That is, he is dressed like a shepherd[14] and also like a hermit. The opening lines of the third vision show that the clothing referred to here is russet:

Thus, yrobid in rosset, I rombide aboute. (A ix 1)

Russet was the simple, untreated woollen cloth worn by peasants; hence the notion of being dressed like a shepherd. But russet was also often adopted by hermits and friars as a sign of simplicity and austerity. The significance is well put by a caustic comment in the contemporary poem *Pierce the Ploughmans Crede*:

Thei usen russet also . somme of this freres,
That bitokneth travaile . & trewthe opon erthe.[15]

Langland turns this into a sign of ambivalence: he is dressed like a layman and a worker but also like a cleric and hermit, without quite identifying himself with either. A little later Holy Church addresses him as if he were a minstrel or performer:

'Love is the levest thing that oure lord askith,
And ek the plante of pes; preche it in thin harpe
Ther thou art mery at mete, yif men bidde the yedde;
For in kynde knowyng in herte ther comsith a might.'

(A i 136–9)

The ambiguity in the narrator's status is evident again in the third vision. The narrator meets two learned friars, addresses them politely 'as I hadde ylernid' and they in turn address him paternally as 'my sone', as if he were a layman, but he quickly takes on the role of a learned cleric:

'*Contra*', quath I as a clerk and comside to dispute. (A ix 16)

The ambivalences remain in the B version. The reference to the narrator as minstrel is deleted, but two new passages take up the question of the narrator's role as poet. Following a scene highly critical of friars the dreamer ponders aloud whether he dare make known his dream, and the character Lewte (justice or fidelity) replies that it is proper for laymen to tell the truth about such things but not for priests and bishops, and urges him therefore to continue berating worldly sin in his poetry (B xi 86 – 106). In the next passus the character Imaginatif rebukes the dreamer for wasting his time writing poetry when he ought to be praying for others:

'Thow medlest thee with makynges – and myghtest go seye thi
   Sauter,
And bidde for hem that yyveth thee breed; for there are bokes
   ynowe
To telle men what Dowel is, Dobet and Dobest bothe.'

(B xii 16–18)

The point seems to be that the narrator's proper work is prayer, that he is therefore a man of the Church, or at least trained as one, but lacks a benefice or other office, living instead from the offerings of others – 'that yyveth thee breed'. Both passages invite us to identify the dreamer with the poet, but while the first implies he is a layman the second suggests that he is at least potentially a cleric. The beginning of the next passus describes him, with perhaps deliberate ambiguity, wandering 'in manere of a mendynaunt' (B xiii 3), meaning either like a beggar or like a member of a religious mendicant order, such as a friar (the cautious, qualified 'in manere of' recalls the language of the opening lines of the poem). Passus xv, xviii and xx similarly begin by presenting the narrator as a destitute wandering figure, while in passus xx the character Nede takes up the question of the narrator's destitution, arguing that poverty is an ideal state. The close of his speech recalls the arguments offered by contemporary friars justifying their life of begging.

'Forthi be noght abasshed to bide and to be nedy,

7

Sith he that wroghte al the world was wilfulliche nedy,
Ne nevere noon so nedy ne poverer deide.' (B xx 48–50)

(See p. 163 on this passage.) Yet the implication that the narrator is a friar
or hermit is undermined by other references indicating a domestic life
with a wife and daughter. In the B version passus xviii (hereafter B xviii)
Langland refers in passing to a wife Kytte and daughter Calote:

> And right with that I wakede,
> And called Kytte my wif and Calote my doghter. (B xviii 428–9)

In B xx he refers rather bawdily to the onset of impotençe under the assaults of Elde (Old Age) and his wife's disappointment at the loss of
sexual pleasure:

> And of the wo that I was inne my wif hadde ruthe,
> And wisshed wel witterly that I were in hevene.
> For the lyme that she loved me fore, and leef was to feele –
> On nyghtes, namely, whan we naked weere –
> I ne myghte in no manere maken it at hir wille,
> So Elde and heo hadden it forbeten. (B xx 193–8)

The contrast between the two pictures, wandering ascetic and settled
layman, comes to a crisis in a new episode in the C version. The narrator describes himself living with his wife Kitte in a cottage in Cornhill,
writing poetry critical of idlers and false hermits, himself able to do
manual work but unwilling to do so (C v 1–9). The character Reason
rebukes him for his idleness and taking him, not surprisingly, for a
layman proposes a series of manual labours for the community (though
he also suggests the duties of a priest). In defence the narrator offers a
very different account of himself from the one he had just given:

> When I yong was, many yer hennes,
> My fader and my frendes fonde me to scole,
> Tyl I wyste witterly what holy writ menede . . .
> And fond I nere, in fayth, seth my frendes deyede,
> Lyf that me lykede but in this longe clothes . . .
> And so I leve in London and opelond bothe;
> The lomes that I labore with and lyflode deserve
> Is *paternoster* and my prymer, *placebo* and *dirige*,
> And my sauter som tyme and my sevene psalmes.
> This I segge for here soules of suche as me helpeth
> And tho that fynden me my fode fouchen-saf, I trowe,
> To be welcome when I come, other-while in a monthe,

Now with hym, now with here; on this wyse I begge
Withoute bagge or botel but my wombe one. . . . (C v 35–52)

Thus he claims to be educated and a cleric of some kind (the long robes
indicate a man of religion of any type); his occupation is the religious
work of prayer, but he seems to be without benefice or other post,
presenting himself as a beggar wandering from place to place and dependent on the support of those for whom he prays. The old tradition
that Langland is here describing the life of a chantry priest, retained to
say prayers for the dead, is probably wrong. The prayers which he mentions are indeed elsewhere specified as the equipment of a chantry
priest appointed to say daily masses for the souls of the dead, but
Langland himself mentions them earlier as the proper equipment of all
priests and parsons (C iii 463–4), and the narrator's point is that he prays
for the 'soules of such as me helpen', not the souls of the departed.
E. T. Donaldson visualises Langland, on the basis of this account as 'a sort
of itinerant handyman, like a modern neighbourhood gardener who
performs odd jobs for a whole suburban block – except, of course, that
Langland's odd jobs were prayers'.[16] The difficulty with this view is that,
whatever the reality of Langland's own life, the narrator speaks of his
reliance on the voluntary offerings of others, not on payments for work.
What he is apparently describing is the life of a religious mendicant of
some kind, aspiring to the ideal of voluntary poverty but lacking the
formal status of the more familiar representatives of that ideal, the friars
and the monks, as Conscience goes on to point out:

'Forthy rebuke me ryhte nauhte, Resoun, I you praye,
For in my consience I knowe what Crist wolde I wrouhte.
Preyeres of a parfit man and penaunce discret
Is the levest labour that oure lord pleseth . . .'.
Quod Consience, 'By Crist, I can nat se this lyeth;
Ac it semeth no sad parfitnesse in citees to begge,
But he be obediencer to prior or to mynistre.' (C v 82–91)

'Preyeres and penaunce' is the term which Langland habitually uses for
the way of life followed by hermits, anchorites, friars and monks (see
p. 54).

The contrasting pictures are very hard to reconcile. Clerics in minor
orders could be married, and there are even contemporary references
to married hermits,[17] but the passages still seem to be describing two
very different ways of life. How much can be true of Langland himself?

The poet's wife Kitte and his daughter Calote figure in most accounts of Langland's life, and the latter became the heroine of a Vic-
torian historical novel about the poet,[18] but the probability is that both

are fictions and meant to be understood so by readers. Kitte seems to be a type-name for a sensual woman: it is used in C vii 304 for the wife of the character Actif, a woman 'wanton of manners' who so cleaves to him, and complains of his absence, that he cannot follow Piers' directions for the road to Truth. Calote is otherwise unknown as a personal name, but occurs frequently as an ordinary noun, in various spellings.[19] In the sixteenth century it is common as a term of abuse for women, apparently meaning 'whore', 'loose woman', 'beggar's female companion': 'contemptuous base-born callet as she is' says Queen Margaret of Duke Humphrey's wife (2 Henry VI, I. iii. 86). That it was already current in the fourteenth century in a similar meaning, though perhaps not in quite such a pejorative sense, is evident from Hoccleve's phrase 'Lewd callets', directed at women who dare to argue about Scripture when they should be content to spin.[20] The sense 'whore' is perhaps too derogatory to fit Langland's use, but the word presumably implied something like 'slut'. The source of both names is probably the epithet 'Kit callet', widely used as a term of abuse in the sixteenth century and no doubt current earlier.[21] It would seem that the name Kitte prompted in Langland's mind the name Calote for a daughter, the two names together suggesting a rather earthy and ignorant woman.

The implications of the names are borne out by the context. The wife in B xx is a literary stereotype drawn from an anti-feminist tradition exemplified by the Wife of Bath's Prologue and the characters of Dunbar's *Twa Mariit Women*[22]: she is a model of sensuality, wishing her husband dead when he is no longer up to the sexual activity which she had loved him for. The Kitte of C v is part of the narrator's supposed life of self-indulgence, when he loved nothing but idleness and easy living. The other Kitte of C vii clearly reflects the same notion. The names and the characters go together as part of the poet's mocking presentation of himself as a low-life figure with a low-life family; together they represent unredeemed humanity. If Langland actually had a wife and daughter they could not have been called Kitte and Calote and his wife could not have resembled the picture which he draws of Kitte. These two are clearly invented for particular local literary needs, however, and there is no need to suppose they have any parallels, more respectable and differently named, in reality. The representations of the dreamer as a married man, as an idle sensualist and as a naive fool all cohere as parts of the same fiction. An instructive parallel is to be found in a slightly earlier French allegorical poem, the *Pèlerinage de la vie humaine* by Guillaume de Deguileville: the author was himself a monk but represents his persona in the dream as a layman.[23]

If one version which Langland gives of his narrator's life is a fiction, the same may be true of the other identity, as a cleric and wandering as-

cetic. The account of himself as a flawed exemplar of religious poverty in C v has a thematic function at that point and in so far as he specifies
prayer as his occupation and says nothing of poetry, it is evidently not
a full account of the poet himself. It is, too, perilously close at times to
the pictures of the false hermits whom the poem elsewhere satirises.
Yet the theological learning and knowledge of Latin displayed in the
poem show that the clerical training described in C v must be a fact, and
the consistency with which he represents himself as a kind of eremitic
figure, living an unsettled life and dependent on others for food and
shelter, suggests there may be some resemblance to reality here. There
was probably, indeed, a surprising degree of similarity between the life
of the religious poet and that of a hermit. Minstrels often led wandering lives, receiving shelter and support from the wealthy for the sake of
their talents and in respect for their main patrons (cf. C ix 128ff).
Langland would probably not have called himself a minstrel – he does
not refer to his work as minstrelsy and his own references to minstrels
are slightly distanced, even condescending – but his way of life may at
times have been similar, sojourning at the houses of various patrons and
being called on to recite at meals. Hermits too seem often to have led
rather peripatetic lives in this period, in close contact with the rest of
society rather than living in seclusion, and a hermit living in a
benefactor's house might be called on to address his guests.[24] A
religious poet and a quasi-eremitic cleric may have been difficult to
distinguish, at least externally. It would perhaps not always have been
clear whether Langland's patrons or protectors sheltered and supported
him for the sake of his poetry or for his piety.[25]

A useful parallel is the earlier-fourteenth-century mystic Richard
Rolle.[26] Rolle went from Yorkshire to be a student at Oxford but
dropped out in disgust at its worldliness and became a hermit, though
he probably never took priest's orders and had no formal status in the
Church; he became a man of religion simply by abandoning the paren-
tal home and stealing his sister's dresses to provide the appropriate long
clothes. For the rest of his life he resided with a series of patrons, male
and female, devoted much of his time to writing verse and prose (some
of it aggressively polemical rather than contemplative), was often involved in controversy and engaged in the affairs of others, and could be
called on to meet his patron's guests and address them. Although he
was accepted by most of his contemporaries as a hermit and wore the
appropriate dress some held him to be a layman. Langland was not a
mystic, and was more satirical and social in his literary concerns, but he
may well have been in other ways a similar figure to Rolle; while in
some respects resembling a minstrel and therefore a member of secular
society, he could also claim to resemble a hermit and exemplify the ideal
of religious poverty. The dialectic of Langland's poetry no doubt en-

couraged him to exploit and exaggerate the ambiguities of his own position, which become emblematic of the conflict running through the poem between material and spiritual, secular and heavenly, but as the opening lines of the poem suggest, he probably did indeed occupy a shadowy borderland in the medieval social scene, between layman and cleric, impoverished worker and exemplar of voluntary poverty.

Langland tells us little about his intended audience or readership. It is now a familiar point that the late fourteenth century saw the growth of a reading public for the vernacular, and that while Chaucer's early poetry seems to assume an audience of listeners, his *Canterbury Tales* presuppose readers – 'turn over the leef and chese another tale'.[27] A similar shift in cultural expectations is evident in the alliterative poetry closest to Langland's. The narrator of *Winner and Waster* around 1350 speaks proudly of the superiority of poetry that is found in no books, but fifty years or so later *Mum and the Sothsegger* ends with the narrator pulling out of a bag a whole series of written poems (see p. 13 for details of these poems). Langland himself was perhaps caught up in the shift from public listening to private reading. In the A version there is Holy Church's reference to the dreamer reciting at meals to the accompaniment of the harp, but in the B text this reference is dropped; Imaginatif now speaks of the narrator writing books, and the narrator himself begins to talk of writing his dreams down. In the B version too Langland begins to use more numerous Latin quotations, including lines or passages extraneous to the verse itself. The latter at least suggest readers, and rather educated readers at that. The multiplicity of manuscripts, even of the A text, indicates rapid dissemination of the poem in writing from an early stage, and the owners we know of are priests and lawyers, who were probably concerned with private reading, rather than secular lords, who might have provided occasions for public recitation. Langland possibly thought of himself as writing in a tradition of poetry for public recitation but found in practice that his appeal was to those who wanted copies for private reading, and increasingly wrote for them.

The literary background

Langland drew on a variety of literary models. There are some signs of the influence of the thirteenth-century French *Romance of the Rose*, with resemblances in allegorical method and some similarities of content.[28] Another possible influence was contemporary drama. In his scene-settings and presentation of conflict, especially in the Prologue and in B xviii on the Passion and Harrowing of Hell, Langland shows strong resemblances both to the morality plays and the mystery cycles (see pp. 30 and 144). Surviving examples are later than Langland, but both types were current in his time. The major influence, however, and the most important for understanding his development, was the poetic tradition of his own region of England. The Malvern Hills, on the borders of Herefordshire and Worcestershire, are the right place of origin for Langland's poetry. He comes from a tradition of radical, populist, anti-intellectual alliterative verse closely associated with the West, especially the South-west Midlands. Its earliest surviving products are two short poems in alliterative verse found in a collection of poetry put together at Hereford around 1340.[29] Though fairly sophisticated in language and style, these two poems speak in the voice of the common man against the oppression of king and Church. *The Song of the Husbandman* articulates the complaints of the peasant as producer against the taxation of king, barons and officials, while *The Satire of Consistory Courts* speaks for the ordinary layman crushed by the Church's legal machinery for enforcing its moral code. The theme is taken up a little later by *Winner and Waster* (c. 1350).[30] Here clergy, lawyers and merchants form the army of Winner, dedicated to the accumulation of wealth, while Waster's army is composed of the conspicuous consumers, particularly the landowning gentry, it seems, who neglect their farms and fell their woodlands, creating a wasteland of their estates, in the pursuit of feasting and display. The perspective is that of the provincial from the West Country, viewing the life of London and the South with increasing alarm and taking the side of the ordinary producer, despoiled by both classes. The poem's satire turns finally against the king too (here identifiably Edward III), initially set up as judge between the two sides but ending by acknowledging his dependence on both, particularly for making war.

The same anti-Establishment stance is evident in *Pierce the Ploughmans Crede*,[31] written after Langland's poem but not necessarily dependent on it, where the narrator seeks truth unsuccessfully among the four orders of friars, who instead try to blacken each other, and finds it eventually in the words of a poor but honest plowman. *Richard the Redeless* (1399)[32] belongs to the same literary tradition. Cast as an address to the deposed king, it attacks his counsellors, the corruptions of the lawcourts, the extravagance of the nobility and their use of private armies of followers to intimidate. The poet writes of the need to speak out at this moment of crisis, despite the risks. Sharpest of all, and most comprehensive in its satire, is the early-fifteenth-century *Mum and the Sothsegger*,[33] the latest and best of these poems. The poet searches in vain for a *sothsegger* or truth-teller in court, universities, convents, abbeys, churches and palaces but finds everywhere Mum, the principle of self-serving silence, the refusal to speak out against corruption; eventually, in a dream, he meets a mysterious gardener who offers him the beehive as an image of society (he is killing the drones) and tells the poet that the soothsayer is only to be found in his own heart; the poet, encouraged, draws out of his bag an endless stream of satires against all the branches of the contemporary Establishment.

These poems have much in common. They all use the alliterative metre and poetic diction characteristic of the West Midlands and North, in a less heightened and esoteric form than that found in romances such as *Sir Gawain and the Green Knight* and the *Morte Arthure*. Their stance is consciously provincial and populist, speaking for the common man (and often in his voice) against the establishment of the Church and State, although their sophistication of technique and range of allusion belie a lower-class origin. They are closely engaged with the issues and figures of their day; Edward III and Richard II are readily identifiable, and the satire is very specific. They also show a surprising self-consciousness about the poet's role, insisting on his duty to speak and his independent authority for doing so, without feeling any need to invoke patron or audience. *Richard the Redeless* is clearly intended to be circulated anonymously, and perhaps this is true of some of the other poems.

Langland uses the same metre and language as these poets, and sets his opening dream in the Malvern Hills, at the heart of the region from which they spring. Like them he chooses a simple peasant, Piers, as his authority figure (compare the husbandman, the plowman in the *Crede*, and the gardener in *Mum and the Sothsegger*) and engages with specific issues and personalities of the time (Edward III, Richard II, the French wars, perhaps Alice Perrers, Edward's mistress) He sees himself as an outsider and yet speaks at times with confident authority. He discusses the justification for his satiric poetry, and insists on its need. He may well have known *Winner and Waster*, which shows striking similarities with his opening section. Some of the other poems are later than *Piers* but they do point to a thriving literary tradition of populist, radical, politically engaged poetry which must have prompted him, and imply a readership for this kind of writing. In time Langland perhaps moved away from this tradition. By the C version he is describing himself as cleric rather than poet or satirist, and as Londoner rather than a provincial, and the poetry becomes less political and more religious in spirit and subject as it goes on; but Langland's starting-point and birthplace is the radical poetry of the South-west Midlands.

The intellectual background

The intellectual background for Langland's poetry is harder to identify. His knowledge of the Bible, of biblical commentary, and of theology indicates a degree of education, though not necessarily at a university. His poetry shows a response to some of the great intellectual issues of his time: predestination and free will, the salvation of the heathen, the ideal of poverty. Commentators have argued for St Augustine, St Thomas Aquinas and the fourteenth-century Franciscan *moderni*[34] in turn as the key theologians for an understanding of Langland's ideas, but Langland seems to have been eclectic in his use of the theological tradition absorbed at school or university, and often strikingly resistant to the standard views of his time. His character Imaginatif proves peculiarly difficult to relate to the usual definitions of the *vis imaginativa*, for instance.[35] His use of the key term 'active life' is quite different from the *activa vita* of Aquinas, Augustine, Gregory the Great and other authorities, though there is a near parallel in the Wyclifite tracts (see p. 48). His view of the Redemption as a battle with death and Hell rather than a propitiatory sacrifice to God the Father is out of the normal current of the time, though it can be traced back through Grosseteste to the earlier Middle Ages (see p. 141). Owst's claim for popular preaching as a major influence on Langland is overstated,[36] but the far older claim that Langland was a Wyclifite deserves a degree of respect. Parallels between Langland and the works of John Wyclif himself are slight and outweighed by the differences, but there are some striking similarities with the vernacular tracts and sermons which are traditionally attributed to Wyclif though probably written by his followers.[37] A favourite saying in these tracts is the line 'A simple paternoster of a plowman in religion is better than a thousand massis of covetous prelatis and veyn religious [i.e. monks].'[38] Apart from the general resemblance here to Langland's elevation of Piers the Plowman above priest, pardoner and palmer in the second dream of the Visio, it is strikingly close to the lines with which he ended the A text:

> Arn none rathere yravisshid fro the righte beleve
> Thanne arn thise kete clerkis, that conne many bokis;
> Ne none sonnere ysavid, ne saddere of consience,
> Thanne pore peple as ploughmen, and pastours of bestis,
> Souteris and seweris; suche lewide jottis,
> Percen with a *paternoster* the paleis of hevene,
> Withoute penaunce, at here partyng, into the heighe blisse.
>
> (A xi 306–13)

Langland's image of the Pardon sent to Piers and his companions by Truth in A viii (B vii), given by God for good living in contrast to the paper pardons sold by the Church, is again very close to a Wyclifite dictum:

> Ther cometh no pardon but of God for good lyvynge and endynge in charite, and this schal not be bought ne solde as prelatis chaffaren thes dayes; for who is in most chairite is best herde of

God, be he schepeherde or lewid man, or in the chirche or in the field; and who kepith wel the hestis of God schal have pardon and the blisse of hevene, and noon othere for creature under God.[39]

More generally, the pervasive anticlericalism and anti-intellectualism of the vernacular Wyclifite texts have much in common with Langland, expecially the A text third vision; the belief in true poverty as a condition of the priesthood seems to be shared by Langland; and the Lollard insistence that the individual layman can achieve salvation without the mediation of priest and Church seems implicit in the presentation of Piers.

This is not to say that Langland would have thought of himself as a Wyclifite or Lollard. In some important respects he differs from them. He shares their hostility to friars, but not to monks. His gradual development of a contemplative ideal of poverty and prayer is quite foreign to the Wyclifite insistence on the primary duty to preach. In any case Langland's first version of the poem was almost certainly produced before Wyclif had gained any influence outside Oxford or directed his argument to the common people. One of the unexplained oddities of Lollardry is that the beliefs expressed by Lollards on trial and in their vernacular writings often bear very little relation to the views expressed by Wyclif himself in his Latin writings.[40] Equally, Lollardry was a popular movement among the laity and the vernacular Lollard writings show a strong anti-intellectualism and a concern with grass-roots religion, whereas Wyclif himself devoted his efforts mainly to intellectual disputation in the schools and seems to have been little interested in grass-roots religion. Yet the Lollards revered him as their *doctor*. It looks as if what we call Lollardry was to a large extent an amalgam of radical religious attitudes already current, whose adherents took Wyclif as their spokesman just as they later revered Sir John Oldcastle. The anti-intellectualism is also to be found in the mystics of the period, and Langland's contemporary John Gower has something rather similar to the 'simple plowman' theme:

It were betre dike and delve
And stonde upon the ryhte feith,
Than knowe al that the bible seith
And erre as somme clerkes do.[41]

The links between Langland and Lollards probably reflect not his adherence to a recognised movement but the influence of a largely unrecorded tradition of religious radicalism which occasionally surfaced elsewhere. One sign of the links between Lollardry and other movements which influenced Langland or appealed to him is the career of

William Swinderby, who was at one stage a hermit but became one of the wildest and most popular of the Lollard preachers.[42]

The reception of the poem

The radicalism of Langland's poetry achieved one striking and perhaps unexpected effect when it furnished a rallying cry for the leaders of the Peasants' Revolt in 1381, recorded in a letter written by John Ball to his fellow-conspirators:

> Iohon Schep, som tyme Seynte Marie prest of York, and now of Colchestre, greteth wel Iohan Nameles, and Iohan the Mullere, and Iohon Cartere, and biddeth hem that thei bee war of gyle in borugh, and stondeth togidre in Godes name, and biddeth Peres Ploughman go to his werk, and chastise wel Hobbe the Robbere, and taketh with yow Iohan trewman, and alle his felawes, and no mo, and loke schappe you to one heved, and no mo.
> Iohan the Mullere hath ygrounde smal, smal, smal;
> The Kynges sone of hevene schal paye for al.
> Be war or ye be wo;
> Knoweth your freend fro your foo;
> Haveth ynow, and seith 'Hoo';
> And do wel and bettre, and fleth synne,
> And seketh pees, and hold you therinne;
> and so biddeth Iohan Trewman and alle his felawes.[43]

The use of the name Piers Plowman could be a coincidence, but the phrase 'do wel and bettre' shows that Ball was indeed thinking of Langland's poem. The letter is cryptic and difficult to interpret, but suggests that already by 1381 Langland's Piers had become a symbol of apocalyptic revolution: he is for John Ball a figure of authority associated with God and with images of the second coming, but also a representative of peasant power. The letter captures a genuinely radical and apocalyptic quality in Langland's poetry, but seems to be unconscious of the poem's social conservatism. If the leaders of the Peasants' Revolt were indeed quoting, as the chronicles claim, the familiar jingle

> When Adam delved and Eve span
> Who was then the gentleman?

they had not noticed that Langland had already given an answer to the question in his first passus, where Holy Church claims that King David

17

'in his dayes dubbide knightes' and that there had been knights even before that, and before Eden:

> And Crist, kingene king, knightide tene,
> Cherubyn and seraphyn, such sevene and another;
> Yaf hem might in his mageste, the meryere hem thoughte,
> And over his meyne made hem archaungelis. (A i 103–6)

One might compare too the passage on envy and communism in the B version:

> Envye herde this and heet freres go to scole
> And lerne logyk and lawe – and ek contemplacion –
> And preche men of Plato, and preve it by Seneca
> That alle thynges under hevene oughte to be in comune.
>
> (B xx 273–6)

The revolt probably came soon after Langland completed the B version where the apocalyptic note of coming revolution is still strong; compare, for instance, B x 314ff, added in the B version. When he revised the poem again, perhaps ten years later, he shows no evident response to the revolt and its use of his poem. The C version is in some respects a little less radical, but only as a continuation of a trend already apparent in the B version. Langland was perhaps neither surprised nor sorry that his prediction of disaster had come true. The apocalyptic passages and the egalitarian ideals remain, with no clear sign that Langland felt they had been misinterpreted.

The other important contemporary response is Chaucer's. He never refers to Langland or his work, but his portrait of the plowman in the General Prologue to the *Canterbury Tales* (ll. 529–41) is probably based on Langland's presentation of Piers.[44] The choice of a plowman as an image of moral perfection seems to owe much to Langland, and the details of digging and threshing and tithe-paying, together with the general honesty of labour, seem to come from him too. What Chaucer saw in Langland was not revolution or apocalypse but an image of the sanctity of human labour, the peasant remaining socially in his station but rising above friar, monk and pardoner in his moral perfection.

Others at the time responded similarly to the poem without seeing any threat in it. It was widely read among the book-owning classes in the fifteenth century, with a very large number of manuscripts surviving. Copies are mentioned as bequests in the wills of a wealthy cleric from York Minster, a country rector, a lawyer.[45] But the dangerous radicalism was certainly recognised in the sixteenth century when *Piers Plowman* became an influential and highly controversial work caught up in the Protestant Reformation.[46] It was on the list of books banned by Parliament until 1550, presumably because of its anticlericalism. John Bale (antiquarian and Protestant polemicist) refers to it early in the sixteenth century as the work of one Robert Langland, a disciple of Wyclif 'writing against the open blasphemies of the Papists and prophesying many things which came to pass in our days'. Once the parliamentary ban was lifted three editions came out in rapid succession, the first two by Robert Crowley, a Reformist pamphleteer and printer who saw the poem as essentially Protestant in spirit (though helping his argument by censoring the most obviously Catholic elements in the poem). Piers himself became a symbol of radical satire in political tracts of the sixteenth century, such as *Piers Plowman's Exhortation, The Plowman's Complaint*.[47] The poem's element of radical fervour was clearly recognised by those with a receptive ear.

After the excited response to the poem in the sixteenth century interest seems to have subsided and there were no new editions until the nineteenth century, though Pope owned a copy of Crowley's edition and Thomas Warton discussed *Piers* in his *History of English Poetry* (1774): it has, he said, 'much sense and observation of life'.[48] In the nineteenth century, however, the poem was caught up again in religious and social controversy. Thomas Whitaker published an edition of the C version in 1813 and devoted much of his introduction to a demonstration that the author was a good Catholic, though he also commented on the quality of the poetry: 'When aroused by the subject, he has a wildness of imagination, and a sublimity (more especially when inspired by the great mysteries of revelation) which has not been surpassed by Cowper.'[49] Others accused Whitaker of suppressing from his text 'all the passages relating to the indecent lives and practices of the Romish clergy'.[50] Numerous commentators drew attention to the poem's apparently prophetic references to the Reformation, and pointed out similarities between Langland's social and religious ideals and those of nineteenth-century Anglicanism.[51]

Modern responses to the poem and the question of unity

Skeat's demonstration that there were three successive versions of the poem led to Manly's argument, at the beginning of this century, that they were the work of several different authors,[52] and although multiple authorship, after decades of discussion, has now generally been dismissed the controversy was one of the factors which caused twentieth-century criticism to be particularly engaged with the search for a coherent design and unified argument in the poem. Langland himself had imposed a variety of structuring devices on the poem as it developed. At the lowest level there is the passus (literally meaning a step): there are eight in the Z version, eleven in A, twenty in B and twenty-two in C (plus a prologue in each case). These seem to be simply convenient ways of dividing up the text, often at a significant change in the action but not always; the dividing point between one passus and the next sometimes varies between versions. Then there is the division into visions: two in the Z version, three in A, eight in B and seven in C. Some of these divisions correspond to stages in the history of the poem. Thus the second vision in A and in subsequent versions closes just a few lines after the point where the poem had ended in the Z version, and in the B version Langland introduces a dream within a dream at precisely the point where the A text had ended. No doubt other visions end at points where Langland had reached the end of an argument or issue and wanted to pause and take stock of his thoughts. In some cases, though, the action and argument continue from one vision into the next, and the division seems to be a device to cover a lapse of dream-time, as with visions five and six of the B version, or to introduce a relevant waking sequence, as with visions seven and eight of the B version.

Further distinctions are provided by the titles given to parts of the poem in the manuscripts. In the only manuscript of the Z version there are no titles apart from prologue and passus numbers. In the A version, however, titles mark a distinction between the first two dreams, called the Visio of Piers Plowman, and the third dream, entitled the 'Vita of Do-wel, Do-bet and Do-best according to Wit and Reason' (though Reason does not in fact appear). The titles thus distinguish between the part of the poem preserved from the Z version and the sequel new to the A version. In the B version this two-part structure is replaced by a four-part division. The term 'Vita' is dropped but in some manuscripts at least the triad of Do-wel, Do-bet and Do-best is extended to cover the whole of the poem after the Visio: thus Do-wel now covers the third and fourth visions (passus viii–xiv), Do-bet the fifth and sixth visions (passus xv–xviii) and Do-best the seventh and eighth visions (passus xix and xx). The same fourfold structure is repeated at approximately the same points in manuscripts of the C version, even though the fourth and fifth visions (that is, the last in Do-wel and the first in Do-bet) are now merged into one.[53]

The fourfold structure suggested by the titles was used as the basis for what became for many years the dominant theory of the thematic structure of the poem, initially proposed by H. W. Wells in 1929.[54] He argued that Do-wel, Do-bet and Do-best stood for the active, contemplative and mixed lives, and that the Visio section described the active life and its virtues, the Do-bet section the contemplative life and the Do-best section the mixed life which combined the two, while the Do-Wel section offered a more general discussion of all three lives. (On the

active and contemplative lives see p. 48.) The difficulties of this theory
have increasingly been recognised in recent years. The terms 'active'
and 'contemplative' carried a variety of different meanings in the period,
rather than forming a clear and familiar pattern which Langland could
expect his readers to supply; although the Visio deals mainly with the
active life it also touches on others, and there is no evident concen-
tration on the other lives in the later sections; and the concept of the mixed
life as the highest mode of existence is a rare and unlikely one. The
terms 'active' and 'contemplative' are important keys to understanding
the poem in places but it is difficult to see them as having quite the
centrality that Wells had proposed.[55]

In recent years the view that has come to figure most prominently
as an explanation of the poem's central concerns and organisation is
the argument that the poem is an account of the spiritual progress or
growth in understanding of the dreamer, usually called Will for this purpose. The poem is thus to be seen as a kind of *Pilgrim's Progress* adapted
to the first person, in which the dreamer functions as an everyman-
figure undergoing an exemplary ascent from sin and ignorance to
enlightenment. Characteristic expressions of this view are: 'this is substantially a poem about Will and his attempts to find out the truth about
the human condition'; 'the story of Will's growth in knowledge and understanding provides the poem's one consistent thread of narrative';
'Will's development through his dreams and waking vicissitudes gives
the poem linear progression'; 'the sequence depends for its continuity
on the character of the dreamer; Will's presence alone holds this poem
together. The quest for salvation is his personal quest'.[56]

The difficulty with such views, as has several times been pointed out,[57]
is that they require a fair degree of extrapolation from occasional details
in the poem. Though dream poems are common in the Middle Ages,
Piers Plowman is unique in employing a series of dreams, and the inter-
relationships of the poet with his various personae are corresponding-
ly complex. As we have seen above, Langland plays with varied and at
times contradictory pictures of his persona's status and way of life. There
are also important distinctions to be made in the authorial voice and
stance. Thus in formal terms one can distinguish between the I-figure
who is a character within the dreams, involved in the dream action and
engaged in conversation with other characters in the dream – the
dreamer – and the I-figure who has the dreams, reports them to the
reader, comments on them himself, and acts and speaks outside the
dreams – the narrator. The dreamer's main role is to question authority-
figures and he is therefore presented fairly consistently as a naive and
ignorant character, but his degree of prominence in the visions varies.
In the first vision of the A version he questions Holy Church about the

scene before him and acts as object for her teaching, but in the whole of the second vision he figures only in the single line reporting that he read the Pardon:

> And I behynde hem bothe beheld al the bulle. (A viii 92)

In the third he argues with a series of authority figures about the definition of Do-wel and finds himself the object of Study's criticisms. In the continuation of the third vision in the B version Langland begins with an account of the dreamer's life and makes him briefly the protagonist of a kind of fable or morality-play plot, as an exemplary sinner. The dreamer seems initially to be the protagonist of the fourth vision too, but he soon becomes a peripheral figure, with no role in the second half of the vision, and in the subsequent visions he reverts to a subordinate position, questioning authority-figures and guides about the vision and occasionally responding to events with emotion. In the final vision he is attacked by Elde and passes through penance to the House of Unity, but these moments seem incidental to the main concerns of the vision. Where the dreamer figure of *The Romance of the Rose* has the consistent aim of winning the rose and the figure in *Pearl* a consistent aim of understanding his daughter's situation, the dreamer in *Piers* takes his cue from events as they unfold. His questions vary from 'what is false?' in the first vision to 'what is Do-wel?' in the third and fourth and 'what is charity?' in the fifth.

The narrator is in some respects very like the dreamer: there is little difference, for instance, between the narrator questioning the friars about Do-wel in the prologue to the third vision and the dreamer questioning Thought and Wit within the vision. The representation of the narrator in the B version as 'witless' (B xiii 1) and 'a fool' (B xv 3) chimes well with the presentation of the dreamer as naïve and ignorant within the dreams. But often the narrator speaks with much more authority, as if on behalf of the poet himself, both inside and outside the visions. The earliest example is a comment in the Prologue on the corruption of the friars:

> But holy chirche and hy holden bet togidere,
> The moste meschief on molde is mountyng up faste.
>
> (A Prol. 63–4)

This direct address by the narrator to the reader, warning of disaster if Church and the friars remain divided, clearly belongs to a quite different personality from the one sharply rebuked for his stupidity by Holy Church only a little later:

'Thou dotide daffe,' quath heo, 'dulle arn thine wittes.' (A i 129)

The narrator in the Prologue reflects the views of the poet, as revealed by the whole poem, rather than the stupidity of a straw man. Other examples of this authoritative voice are the description of the contents of the Pardon in the second vision and the commentary on the vision, some of the interventions in B xi (e.g. ll. 153ff), the passage on sloth at B xiii 409–56, the passage on the clergy at B xx 277–94, the address to Reason on the clergy and the state of society in C v. Thus while the narrator is sometimes represented as a naïve and foolish figure somewhat like the dreamer, at other times, both within the dream descriptions and outside them, he can address the reader directly in an authoritative voice, commenting on the issues on behalf of the author. At times, and no doubt for reasons linked with the poet's own uncertainties, it is difficult to tell which of these voices or masks Langland is using; the closing speech of the A version, for example, is assigned by one editor to the dreamer, by others to the narrator.

This complex interweaving of authorial personae and voices is something we are now familiar with from Chaucer: in *Troilus and Criseyde* too the narrator can speak as a *faux-naif* sympathising with Criseyde, as a poet struggling with his art and as a stern moralist condemning both his characters. A similar mix of voices is to be heard in the Pardoner's tale and the Merchant's. Langland's awareness of what he is doing, and pleasure in it, is nowhere more evident than in the witty lines in the A text version of the Pardon, where the merchants, delighted to find themselves included in the document, reward Will for writing it:

> Thanne were marchauntis merye; many wepe for joye,
> And yaf Wille for his writyng wollene clothis;
> For he copiede thus here clause, thei couden hym gret mede.
> (A viii 42–4)

Will appears here as a character in the dream-world with the merchants, but the person who has written the crucial clause of the Pardon is neither the dreamer, who has merely observed it, nor the narrator, who has merely dreamed about it, but William Langland the poet.

The I-figure contributes much of the sense of drama and debate, rather than mere exposition, which characterises the poem, but both within the dream and in the waking state he remains as full of questions and uncertainty at the end as he is at the beginning, and his own remarks and responses provide little evidence of a growth in understanding. Indeed, as the discussion above shows, he is really a complex of different identities and voices rather than a single personality. Those who see the poem as the story of Will seem in fact to be thinking of an imaginary figure lurking behind the action rather than the explicit I-figure. Thus Derek Pearsall writes in a recent study, 'the poem ends, full circle, with the dreamer going out once more in search of Piers Plowman.'[58] In fact it is not the dreamer but the character Conscience who sets off to seek Piers; indeed, despite the 'once more' there are no instances at all in the poem of the dreamer seeking Piers. A. V. C. Schmidt implicitly recognises that problem and corrects Pearsall when he says of the dreamer 'whilst at his final awakening it is not he but Conscience who sets out as a pilgrim, it has become clear that Will has advanced from identification with the folk of the field and later with their representative, the Active Man Haukyn, to a real if implied identification with Conscience'.[59] The argument has a kind of cogency but the Will who is described here is not the figure called 'Will' or 'I' in the poem but a rather more hypothetical figure corresponding to the critics' own reconstructions of the poem's development.

If there are problems in making the story of the dreamer serve as the thematic centre and organising principle of the poem, it is admittedly hard to offer anything else in its place. Indeed, the desire to find such coherence may itself be a hampering modern obsession which distracts attention from the real strengths and attractions of the poem. It is at the moments of radical change in direction and thought that the poem is at its imaginative best. What the history of the poem suggests is that the successive versions and the individual visions grew gradually out of each other, not from any preconceived design but from a continued and intensely imaginative engagement with the issues of the time and the tensions of the poet's aspirations. As Langland himself tells us, if he had known the answers when he started he would not have written the poem:

'If ther were any wight that wolde me telle
What were Dowel and Dobet and Dobest at the laste,
Wolde I nevere do werk, but wende to holi chirche
And there bidde my bedes but whan ich ete or slepe.'
(B xii 25–8)

The topics which Langland confronts were of vital importance for his time, and the whole tone of the poetry indicates a poet who cared passionately about them. If we can detect an overall pattern or progress in the later versions of the poem, it is because they record the development of Langland's own arguments with himself.

Notes and References

1. See J. N. King, 'Robert Crowley's editions of *Piers Plowman*: a Tudor apocalypse', *Modern Philology* **73** (1976), 342–52.
2. C. Dawson, 'William Langland', in *The English Way*, ed. M. Ward (London, 1933), p. 160.
3. J. M. Manly, '*Piers Plowman* and its sequence', *The Cambridge History of English Literature*, eds A. W. Ward and A. R. Waller (Cambridge, 1908), II, 1–42.
4. J. Norton-Smith, *William Langland* (Leiden, 1983), p. 126.
5. J. Lawlor, 'The imaginative unity of *Piers Plowman*', *Review of English Studies* NS **8** (1957), 125–6.
6. The three versions were printed in parallel in *The Vision of William concerning Piers the Plowman, in Three Parallel Texts*, ed. W. W. Skeat, 2 vols (Oxford, 1886). Full details of the editions of the versions of *Piers Plowman* are given in the Note on Texts and the Bibliography.
7. See Rigg and Brewer's edition.
8. In the one surviving manuscript of the Z version, the original scribe completed his work at this point. Another scribe subsequently continued writing out the poem, but for the rest of the vision he seems to have drawn on a copy of the A version and after that on a copy of the C version.
9. E. T. Donaldson, 'MSS R and F in the B-tradition of Piers Plowman'. *Transactions of the Connecticut Academy of Arts and Sciences*, **39** (1955), 211.
10. The note, in a hand of about 1400, is in Trinity College Dublin MS D.4.1. For discussion see George Kane, *Piers Plowman: the Evidence for Authorship* (London, 1965).
11. The fullest discussion is by S. Moore, 'Studies in *Piers Plowman*', *Modern Philology* **12** (1914), 19–50. Moore, however, argues against the authenticity of the note.
12. Kane, *Evidence*, p. 38.
13. See M. L. Samuels, 'Dialect and grammar', in *A Companion to Piers Plowman*, ed. J. A. Alford (Berkeley, 1988), pp. 201–22.
14. Some manuscripts read *scheep* meaning 'sheep' but this seems a less likely reading (see my article 'Plowmen and Hermits in Langland's *Piers Plowman*', *Review of English Studies*, **35** (1984), 129n).
15. *Pierce the Ploughmans Crede*, ed W. W. Skeat (Early English Text Society OS 30, London, 1867), ll. 719–21.
16. E. T. Donaldson, *Piers Plowman: the C-Text and its Poet* (New Haven, 1949), pp. 218–9.
17. R. M. Clay, *The Hermits and Anchorites of England* (London, 1914), p. 88.
18. Florence Converse, *Long Will: a Romance* (London, 1903).
19. See under *callet* in the Oxford English Dictionary and *callot* in the Middle English Dictionary, and the excellent discussion of the two names by T. F. Mustanoja, 'The suggestive use of Christian names in Middle English poetry', in *Medieval Literary and Folklore Studies in Honor of F. L. Utley*, eds J. Mandel and B. A. Rosenberg (New Brunswick, 1970), pp. 51–76.
20. 'To Sir John Oldcastle', l. 147; in *Hoccleve's Works, The Minor Poems*, ed. F. J. Furnivall, vol. 1 (Early English Text Society ES 6, London, 1892).

21. Sir Thomas More uses it abusively of Luther's wife in 1532: 'Frere Luther and Cate Calate his nunne, lye luskyng together in lechery' (*The Complete Works of Sir Thomas More*, eds L. A. Schuster, R. C Marius, J. P. Lusardi and R. J. Schoeck, vol. VIII (New Haven and London, 1973), Part I, p. 181, line 3. The glossary suggests 'strumpet' as the meaning of the name. In one of John Heywood's works a character uses it as a derogatory term for a scandal-monger and backbiter,' a false flatryng fylth' called Alice: 'Kyt Calote my coosyn sawe this thus far on' ('A Dialogue containing Proverbs', I.x.181., in *John Heywood's Prose Works and Miscellaneous Short Poems*, ed. B. A. Milligan (Urbana, 1956), p. 41). And in a Ben Jonson masque a gypsy reminds his captain how often they had entertained him with depictions of Kit Callet: 'Ever at your solemn feasts and calls We have been ready with th'Egyptian brawls, To set Kit Callet forth in prose or rhyme.' The other activities mentioned are drinking and theft, so that the reference is probably to something fairly disreputable; the most recent editor glosses the name 'a gypsy version of Maid Marian, and cant for a whore' ('The Gypsies Metamorphosed', l. 247, in *Ben Jonson: the Complete Masques*, ed. Stephen Orgel (New Haven, 1969)).

22. *The Riverside Chaucer*, ed. L. D. Benson (Oxford, 1988), pp. 105–16; *The Poems of William Dunbar*, ed. W. M. Mackenzie (London, 1932), pp. 85–97.

23. See the recent edition of the Middle English version of this work, *The Pilgrimage of the Lyf of the Manhode*, ed. Avril Henry, vol. I (Early English Text Society 288, Oxford, 1985), p. xxvii.

24. See Clay, *Hermits*, and Hope Emily Allen, *Writings ascribed to Richard Rolle, and Materials for his Biography* (New York and London. 1927).

25. See the excellent account in A. V. C. Schmidt. *The Clerkly Maker* (Cambridge, 1987).

26. For Rolle's life see Allen, *Writings*.

27. *The Canterbury Tales*, Fragment I line 3177, in *The Riverside Chaucer*.

28. See D. Owen, *Piers Plowman: a Comparison with some Earlier and Contemporary French Allegories* (London, 1912).

29. The collection is Harley MS 2253 in the British Library. The two poems are edited by R. H. Robbins in *Historical Poems of the XIVth and XVth Centuries* (New York, 1959), pp. 7–9 and 24–7.

30. Edited by I. Gollancz (London, 1920).

31. Edited by Skeat (see note 15).

32. Skeat thought this poem, which survives in fragmentary form, was by Langland and included it in his Clarendon Press edition of *Piers Plowman* (Oxford, 1886). Langland's authorship was subsequently dismissed and the poem was then identified as part of the same poem as another fragmentary piece in alliterative verse known as *Mum and the Sothsegger*, and the two were edited together under that title by M. Day and R. Steele (Early English Text Society OS 199, London, 1936). In fact the two are almost certainly distinct poems by different authors.

33. Edited by Day and Steele.

34. See especially M. Goldsmith, *The Figure of Piers Plowman* (Cambridge,

1981); T. P. Dunning, *Piers Plowman: an Interpretation of the A Text* (Dublin and London, 1937), 2nd edn revised by T. P. Dolan (Oxford, 1980); and J. Coleman, *Piers Plowman and the Moderni* (Rome, 1981).

35. See H. R. B. White, 'Langland's Ymaginatif, Kynde and the *Benjamin Minor*', *Medium Ævum* **55** (1986), 241–8, and the earlier studies cited there.

36. G. R. Owst, *Literature and Pulpit in Medieval England* (Cambridge, 1933; 2nd edn, Oxford, 1961).

37. *Select English Works of John Wyclif*, ed. T. Arnold, 3 vols (Oxford, 1869–71); *The English Works of Wyclif hitherto unprinted*, ed. F. Matthew (Early English Text Society OS 74, London, 1880). On the possible relations of Langland to Wyclif and the Lollards, see Pamela Gradon, 'Langland and the ideology of dissent', *Proceedings of the British Academy*, **66** (1980), 179–205 and separately. Connections are stressed by D. A. Pearsall in the introduction and notes to his edition of the C version.

38. Matthew, *Wyclif*, p. 274.

39. Ibid., p. 238.

40. G. Leff, *Heresy In the Later Middle Ages*, 2 vols (Manchester, 1967), comments on the differences between Wyclif and Lollardry (II, 535–7).

41. *Confessio Amantis*, Prologue, ll. 346ff, in *The English Works of John Gower*, ed. G. Macaulay (Early English Text Society OS 81, London, 1900).

42. See Leff, *Heresy*, II, 589.

43. In *Fourteenth-Century Verse and Prose*, ed. K. Sisam (Oxford, 1921), piece XIVd.

44. N. Coghill, 'Two notes on *Piers Plowman*', *Medium Ævum*, **4** (1935), 92. See further J. A. W. Bennett, 'Chaucer's contemporary', in *Piers Plowman: Critical Approaches*, ed. S. Hussey (London, 1969), pp. 310–24, and Jill Mann, *Chaucer and Medieval Estates Satire* (Cambridge, 1973), pp. 208–12.

45. J. A. Burrow, 'The audience of *Piers Plowman*', *Anglia*, **75** (1957), 373–84, reprinted in his *Essays in Medieval Literature* (Oxford, 1984), pp. 102–16, and Anne Middleton, 'The audience and public of *Piers Plowman*', in *Middle English Alliterative Poetry and its Literary Background*, ed. D. A. Lawton (Cambridge, 1982), pp. 101–23.

46. King, 'Robert Crowley's editions of *Piers Plowman*'.

47. Gradon, 'Ideology'; and Helen C. White, *Social Criticism in Popular Religious Literature of the Sixteenth Century* (New York, 1944), Ch. 1.

48. Thomas Warton, *History of English Poetry*, 3 vols (1774–81), I, 266.

49. The comment is quoted by Skeat, *Piers Plowman*, II, p. xliv.

50. See Skeat, *Piers Plowman*, II, p. lxxix n. 3.

51. See, for instance, the comments excerpted by Skeat, *Piers Plowman*, II, pp. xxxviii–ix, xlvii–liii.

52. See above, n. 3.

53. Some doubt has been expressed about the authenticity of these rubrics recently (see especially R. Adams, 'The reliability of the rubrics in the B-text of *Piers Plowman*'. *Medium Ævum*, **54** (1985), 208–31) but the agreement of the B and C MSS remains a strong argument in their favour.

54. H. W. Wells, 'The construction of *Piers Plowman*', *Publications of the Modern Language Association of America*, **44** (1929), 123–40.

55. The theory seems to have been effectively killed off by an essay by S. S. Hussey, 'Langland, Hilton and the three lives', *Review of English Studies*, NS **7** (1956), 225–37 .

56. M. Goldsmith, *The Figure of Piers Plowman* (Cambridge, 1981), p. 2; J. F. Goodridge, *Langland, Piers the Ploughman* (Harmondsworth, 1959), p. 12; A. V. C. Schmidt, *Piers Plowman*, p. xxiii; E. Vasta, *The Spiritual Basis of Piers Plowman* (The Hague, 1965), p. 26; this is also the approach of J. Lawlor, *Piers Plowman: an Essay in Criticism* (London, 1962).

57. B. Palmer, 'The guide convention in *Piers Plowman*', *Leeds Studies in English*, NS **5** (1971); A. Middleton, 'The idea of public poetry in the reign of Richard II', *Speculum*, **53** (1978), 94–114; D. Mills, 'The role of the dreamer in *Piers Plowman*', *Piers Plowman: Critical Approaches*, ed. S. S. Hussey (London, 1969), pp. 180–212.

58. D. A. Pearsall, *Old English and Middle English Poetry* (London, 1977), p. 178.

59. Schmidt, *Piers Plowman*, p. xx.

Chapter Two

The first vision: wealth and society (A, Prologue, i–iv)

The poet, wandering in the Malvern Hills, falls asleep and dreams. He sees a plain full of people, set between a tower on a hill and a castle keep in a valley: there are plowmen, hermits, minstrels, merchants, ecclesiastics of all kinds, lawyers and tradesmen. As he stands puzzled by this confused mass of social types, a woman in white, identified as Holy Church, descends from the tower and explains the scene to him: the tower is the home of Truth, the prison keep the home of Wrong, and the 'field' a maze in which contemporary society pursues its ends regardless of those principles of Truth and Love which should guide it. Asked by the poet to show him 'the false', she directs his gaze to a crowd surrounding a beautifully dressed woman identified as Mede (that is, meed or reward, but coming to stand for the corrupting power of wealth, and especially rewards and bribes). Mede is to be married to False, it appears. The marriage is resisted by Theology and reported to the king, who summons Mede to the court. He attempts to marry her to his knight Conscience but the latter refuses and a fierce debate develops between the two. Conscience summons Reason to his support and Mede is eventually discredited by her attempts to influence the trial of Wrong; the dream ends with Reason and Conscience installed as the king's chief advisers, inaugurating a new era of Utopian peace [1].

The poet begins in the time-honoured way of dream-poems, describing himself falling asleep and seeing a vision. The general scheme of the vision is clear. Society is a chaotic mass of competing individuals, oblivious of the poles of Truth and Wrong (who are also God and the devil). The real dominating force in this society is Wealth, and the poet envisages the king first trying to harness wealth to the good society and then excluding it altogether, invoking the human faculties which can reorganise society in place of the appetite for wealth. The society which Langland depicts is the England, and especially London, of his own time. Conscience and Mede argue about the conduct of the recent wars in France; the king himself is clearly Edward III, with his son the Black Prince beside him, and Mede has resemblances to Edward's mistress, Alice Perrers. The situation which he describes was probably nothing very new. A money-based, mercantilist economy had hit the largely agricultural society of Western Europe two centuries earlier, producing urban growth and, as many thought, corrupting Church and the law.[2] The uneasy grafting of administrative bureaucracy on to the feudal system, the creation of offices without commensurate salaries, and the attempts to raise money by enforced gratuities rather than statutory taxation, had created a situation in which government and justice seemed to be up for sale, in Church as well as State.[3] But every society is inclined to think itself the first in which fundamental human principles of good faith and justice have been replaced by money payments.

What gives the poetry a deeper significance and sharpness is the underlying concern with larger questions of the nature of man and the purpose of his existence, and in particular the interplay of secular and religious views of society, an interplay mirrored most clearly in the rivalry of Holy Church and Mede. That conflict is already present in the poet's opening description of himself dressed as a shepherd and as a hermit. As we have seen, the point makes literal sense but its formulation is deliberately provocative and polarising. To dress as a shepherd is to take on the role of one of the world's workers (and this is perhaps even true if we take shepherd as a metaphor for pastor, a spiritual teacher of the flock); to take on the garb of a hermit is to reject the world in favour of a spiritual isolation and dedication. Such polarities are then developed in the description of the field full of folk.

The field contains society as it is, unordered, in a maze as Holy Church later puts it. The technique is one of displacement and disorientation. Society is lifted unaware from its normal setting of town and village to a field below the Malvern Hills between a tower and a castle, the homes of Truth and Wrong, with the poet, and reader, looking down upon it. The justifying context of familiar actuality, of social traditions and pressures, gives way to a context of moral absolutes. The scene closely resembles that of the contemporary morality plays, where the human characters act out their roles in a central arena surrounded by the raised stages or scaffolds on which sit God, the World and the devil. There is a particularly close parallel in the staging of *The Castle of Perseverance*, which has the scaffold of God in the east of the circle, the scaffold of

the devil in the north and that of the World in the west[4]; so in the poem
the tower where God lives is to the east of the field and the dreamer is
told to turn to his left, that is northwards, to see False. Theatre in the
round here serves not to merge the actors with the audience but to
deprive the actors of the protection of the stage and scenery and the
back wall and thus to emphasise the nakedness of the human characters removed from the flux of reality. The important difference from
the morality plays is that whereas they present a central figure who
stands for man in general–Humanum Genus, Mankind, Everyman–
Langland presents all the myriad types of people in society–plowmen,
anchorites, merchants, minstrels and so on. This remains so throughout
the first two visions, notably in the interweaving of Mede, Fals, Gile and
others with contemporary real figures such as sheriffs, summoners and
judges in the first dream, and of Sloth, Envy and Glutton with named
individuals or types in the second.

The field is offered initially as something merely observed, not ordered or explained, just as Chaucer was later to do with the vista of
society which he offers in the General Prologue to his *Canterbury Tales*.
The picture possibly owes something to the vision of contemporary
society in *Winner and Waster*, but there from the outset society is divided
and ordered under two banners. Yet Langland offers hints of a perspective, a way of evaluating this apparently random mass of social types.
Plowmen have pride of place at the head of the list, toiling for others
and experiencing few pleasures, in contrast to the idlers and sophisti-
cates who follow:

> Summe putte hem to plough, pleighede ful selde,
> In settyng and sowyng swonke ful harde;
> Wonne that thise wastours with glotonye destroiyeth.
> And summe putte hem to pride, aparailide hem thereaftir,
> In cuntenaunce of clothing comen disgisid. (A Prol. 20–4)

They are, of course, the only characters who naturally belong in a field.
The implied values of honest toil and simple, austere life are, however,
qualified by the presence of the hermits who come next, not toiling for
others but living very austere lives for a different purpose, to win heaven,
with no thought for 'likerous liflode':

> In preyours and penaunce putten hem manye
> Al for love of oure Lord lyvede wel streite,
> In hope for to have heveneriche blisse,
> As ancris and ermytes that holden hem in here cellis.
>
> (A Prol. 25–8)

The lines seem to question the virtue of the plowmen's lives. The problem of moral value proliferates with the merchants, who perhaps work for others but show no austerity, and the minstrels, who are innocent in their way but share neither the austerity nor the usefulness of the plowmen:

> And somme chosen hem to chaffare; thei chevide the betere
> As it semith to oure sight that suche men thriven.
> And somme merthis to make, as mynstralis conne,
> And gete gold with here gle giltles, I trowe. (A Prol. 31–4)

The difficulty of finding a social theory to cover all these is already apparent. Yet the Prologue goes on, more confidently, to concentrate on those clearly excluded by the values of austerity and useful toil initially implied: the japers who could work but do not, the beggars with only a pretence of austerity, the pilgrims dedicated to lies, the hermits who choose that way of life for ease rather than vocation, the friars, pardoners, parsons, lawyers and bishops who neglect their natural duties in the pursuit of wealth. The initial doubtfulness of the narrator's 'as it semeth to oure sight' and 'synneles I trowe' gives way to an authoritative, authenticating voice, a voice close to that of the poet rather than a naive narrator such as Chaucer uses:

> But holy chirche and by holden bet togidere,
> The moste meschief on molde is mountyng up faste. . . .
> Were the bisshop yblissid and worth bothe hise eris
> His sel shulde not be sent to disseyve the peple.
>
> (A Prol. 63–4, 75–6)

But the description then collapses back into uncertainty with the final, kaleidoscopic list of ranks and trades. The cries of the street-traders seem far removed from the stern questions of Truth and Wrong associated with *tour* and *donjon*.

Holy Church, who enters at this point, is the first of Langland's authority-figures, emblematic of the pure spiritual simplicities which often seemed the answer to all complexities. She belongs to the same tradition as Philosophia in Boethius's *Consolation of Philosophy* and the maiden in the *Gawain*-poet's *Pearl*. Clothed in white linen and descending from the tower of Heaven, she speaks for spiritual absolutes. Her role is to relate the folk of the field to the universals of Truth and Wrong. What she offers seems at first a thoroughly Heaven-directed philosophy by which only the hermits and anchorites would be justified:

32

A lovely lady of lire in lynene yclothid,
Com doun from that clyf and callide me faire,
And seide, 'Sone, slepist thou? sest thou this peple
How besy thei ben aboute the mase?
The most partie of this peple that passith on this erthe,
Have thei worsshipe in this world, thei kepe no betere;
Of other hevene thanne here holde thei no tale.' (A i 3–9)

But she goes on to develop a rather different argument which looks back to the origins of man and allows room for the plowmen and eventually other social classes:

'The tour on the toft', quath heo, 'Treuthe is thereinne,
And wolde that ye wroughten as his word techith,
For he is fadir of feith and fourmide yow alle
Bothe with fel and with face, and yaf yow fyve wyttes
For to worsshipe hym therewith whiles ye ben here.
And therfore he highte the erthe to helpe yow ichone
Of wollene, of lynene, of liflode at nede
In mesurable maner to make yow at ese.' (A i 12–19)

Holy Church thus identifies the inhabitant of the tower as Truth but immediately describes him in ways which identify Truth with God the Creator. In doing so, she perhaps suggests the fundamental identity of social morality and religion. Her choice of the term Truth for God, which becomes his main title for this vision and the next, turns out to testify to her belief that God is manifested in such social qualities as fidelity, keeping pledges, sustaining relationships (for truth carries not its modern meaning of fidelity to facts but its old meaning of fidelity to people, preserved in the form 'troth')[5]

Her argument that the Creator ordered the earth to give men the necessities of life implicitly justifies the plowmen and other labourers who make that divine dispensation possible by cultivating the earth. She goes on to justify knighthood by showing that it goes back to King David (l. 96), and further still to the creation of the angels (l. 103), and says that merchants and clergy are to be justified by their charity to others (l. 148–79). She is concerned, that is, to validate the basic structure of society by referring it back to God's creation of the world and his ordering of the necessities of life. There is no sympathy here with the common medieval view which saw the toil required to produce the necessities of life as symptomatic of a fallen world, emanating from God's curse on Adam when he had sinned.[6] Work, hardship and duty are part of the original dispensation in her account.

The argument is also concerned with human psychology and intellectual capacities. One of the central justifications for the contemporary sophistication of society and especially of the Church was the need for specialised, advanced knowledge in order to make salvation possible, just as one of the arguments that mystics and hermits offered for their way of life was the need for a special enlightenment in order to serve God fully (see pp. 70–72). Holy Church will have nothing of either view, insisting that man is provided with the five wits necessary to worship God, that the essential knowledge and instincts are present in man from the beginning, are in some sense 'kynde' or natural, and stem from the heart; cf. especially A i 127–31:

> 'Yet have I no kynde knowyng,' quath I, 'ye mote kenne me bet
> Be what craft in my cors it compsith, and where.'
> 'Thou dotide daffe,' quath heo, 'dulle arn thine wittes.
> It is a kynde knowyng that kenneth in thin herte
> For to love thi Lord levere thanne thiselve.'

Essentially, men can be valued not for their Heaven-directedness but for their conformity to the principles of Creation and nature. Despite the corruptions of the folk on the field and Holy Church's opening dismissal of the 'most part' of them, hers is an optimistic theory of man. She says nothing of fallen man or original sin, but sees a continuity between pre-Eden and post-Eden hierarchies and believes in the moral and intellectual capacities of natural man.

As the dreamer rightly points out, money is the major point of difference between the contemporary world and the theory which Holy Church sketches:

> 'Ac the mone on this molde, that men so faste holdith,
> Tel me to whom that tresour apendith.' (A i 42–3)

She at first evades the question by defining treasure as truth, but then takes it up in passus ii with her revelation of Lady Mede as the source of all corruption:

> 'Loke on thi left half, and lo where he standis,
> Bothe Fals and Favel and hise feris manye.'
> I lokide on my left half as that lady me taughte
> And was war of a womman wondirliche clothide,
> Ipurfilid with pelure, the pureste on erthe,
> Icorounid with a coroune, the king hath non betere;
> Alle here fyve fyngris were frettid with rynges
> Of the pureste perreighe that prince werde evere;
> In red scarlet robid and ribande with gold.
> Ther nis no quen queyntere that quyk is o lyve. (A ii 5–14)

As a term, *mede* (Modern English 'meed') is nearly always used in a good sense in Middle English, meaning reward or recompense; in using it to refer to a corrupting power Langland captures well the difference between ordinary human perspectives and an absolute moral one. Mede herself represents wealth, and her effect on society symbolises the corruption that its presence in the world causes. She includes in her ancestry the ambivalent Richesse of *The Romance of the Rose*, 'an high lady of gret noblesse' who 'bothe helpe and hynder may' according to Chaucer's version, and who is similarly dressed in purple robes adorned with gold and precious stones.[7] But she also derives from the Scarlet Woman, the Whore of Babylon, of the Book of Revelations, symbol of mercantile wealth:

> And the woman was arrayed in purple and scarlet colour, and
> decked with gold and precious stones and pearls, having a
> golden cup in her hand full of abominations and filthiness of
> her fornication. (Revelations 17: 4)

Holy Church is clear about the moral status of Mede and of the attractions of wealth. Mede is her rival, the child of Wrong, introduced in answer to the dreamer's request to be shown 'the Fals'. The two women are clearly opposites, the simple linen of the one contrasting with the colour and ornament of the other. In the magnificent mock-marriage charter that follows, all corruptions of the world are seen proceeding from the union of Fals and Mede. Yet a different and much more favourable view of Mede is suddenly offered by Theology:

> Thanne tenide hym Theologie whan he this tale herde,
> And seide to Cyvyle, 'Now sorewe on thi bokes,
> Such weddyng to werche to wraththe with Treuthe;
> And er this weddyng be wrought wo the betide!
> For Mede is molere of Mendis engendrit
> God grauntide to gyve Mede to Treuthe,
> And thou hast gyven hire to a gilour . . .
> And mede is a mulere, a maiden of gode;
> She mighte kisse the king for cosyn yif heo wolde.' (A ii 79–97)

That this is in direct and explicit conflict with Holy Church's view is indicated by the different account of Mede's paternity: Holy Church claims that her father is Wrong. Theology insists that he is Mendes (that is, Amends or Restitution). Theology's argument is, essentially, that Mede is a good force in society, destined by God for good ends but misapplied through the alliance with Fals; on this view, Mede herself is less the powerful courtesan that she appeared at first than an innocent led into bad company. It is a good argument, and the fact that Theology is its proponent suggests that for Langland it is not necessarily less sound or even less spiritual than Holy Church's more extreme view, although it may be that one of the distinctions which Langland has in mind here is between Holy Church as fundamental religious teaching and Theology as the more subtle arguments of the scholastic theologians who had developed a series of justifications for the role of money in society (see pp. 71 and 86 on the critique of theology). The argument voiced by Theology finds support in some aspects of Langland's presentation of the character Mede. Her name itself suggests her beneficial qualities. She is said to be a *mayde*, suggesting innocence, and introduced as such by Holy Church, for all the hints and later assertions of her sexual promiscuity. There are suggestions too that Mede is not a dominating whore but has herself been captured and seduced by Fals and his fellows:

> Thanne fette Favel forth floreynes ynowe,
> And bad Gile go gyve gold al aboute,
> 'And nameliche to the notories, that hem non faile;
> And feffe False-wytnesse with floreynes ynowe,
> For he may Mede amaistrien and maken at my wille.'
>
> (A ii 108–11)

This notion comes into particularly sharp focus in the scene at the end of passus ii, as Mede is abandoned by all her associates and left trembling and alone:

> Alle fledden for fer and flowen into hernis;
> Save Mede the maiden no mo durste abide.
> Ac trewely to telle, heo tremblide for fere,
> And ek wep and wrang whan heo was atachid. (A ii 195–8)

The fundamental question about the place of wealth in the good society is brilliantly captured in the ambivalence of Mede's own personality: beautiful innocent led astray by those around her, or magnetic courtesan cynically corrupting all she can reach?

It is Mede the victim figure that the king sees, as he implicitly adopts Theology's view and argues for Mede's marriage to a knight of his, Conscience. Under his control and allied to Conscience, the king feels, the magnetism of riches can be part of the good society. It is a view that gains weight from the hint that the king has been unaware hitherto of the misalliance but now knows the truth and has just acquired the help of Conscience – 'I have a knight hatte Consience, com late fro beyonde';

the union of Mede and Fals is perhaps the product of past neglect, not inevitable tendencies. This is a view firmly rejected by Conscience him-self who takes up Holy Church's role as the spokesman of simple spiritual absolutes:

Quath Consience to the kyng, 'Crist it me forbede!
Er I wedde such a wif wo me betide!
She is freel of her feith, fikel of hire speche . . . '
'Sessith,' seide the king, 'I suffre yow no lengere.
Ye shuln saughte, forsothe, and serve me bothe.
Kisse hire', quath the king, 'Consience, I hote!'
'Nay, be Crist,' quath Consience, 'cunge me rathere!'

(A iii 109–11, iv 1–4)

The practical view says that Mede can be governed by Conscience; the spiritual view says that Conscience will only be corrupted by Mede. The debate between the two is a real and serious one. Conscience's view of Mede as a corrupting and destructive force gains support from the description of her effect on the court and city, but Mede bases a powerful case on the argument that society and government, as a mat-ter of practicalities, simply do work through rewards and incentives. Hence her argument that it was she who made the king's French wars successful (presumably through bribery and the promise of plunder and ransom money) while Conscience weakened his efforts. In reply Con-science has to turn from practicalities to universals, arguing first that the only true 'meed' is the kingdom of Heaven, and when this fails to convince the king, calling in the aid of Reason.

For the crisis that eliminates Mede and enthrones Reason Langland abandons the marriage story and develops instead a legal case involv-ing Peace and Wrong – perhaps in part because he had come to see the corruption of justice as the major crime of Mede. Once again it is her surface plausibility that is striking. In so far as the plaintiff and defend-ant are two individuals, Mede's efforts to buy the former off so that he settles out of court seem justified and constructive; in so far as the dis-putants are Wrong and Peace, her intervention to reconcile them and save Wrong can be seen as a perversion of due order. Intertwined with the social and political issue is an epistemological one, with Reason and Conscience opposing Mede and Wit and Wisdom supporting her. As with Holy Church and Theology, we are faced with a disturbing dis-agreement of apparent authority-figures, though once again it reveals itself as a conflict between a kind of natural understanding and a sophis-tication of knowledge: Conscience and Reason seem to represent for Langland something like the *kynde wit* and *kynde knowyng* mentioned earlier by Holy Church, basic mental powers shared by all men and capable of recognising truth, in contrast to those intellectual powers which are possessed by some men only (particularly lawyers), which are fostered by wealth and used to disguise truth. This opposition between intuitive understanding and acquired knowledge came increasingly to disturb Langland, providing one of the main themes of the third vision.

The original idea of the king governing through a union of Mede and Conscience is now replaced by the Utopian vision of a kingdom governed by Reason and Conscience, aspiring to the love and truth preached earlier by Holy Church and marked by the qualities of the plowman, if only in metaphor:

'Rede me not,' quath Resoun, 'no reuthe to have
Til lordis and ladies loven alle treuthe . . .
Til clerkis and knightes be curteis of here mouthes,
And haten to here harlotrie other mouthe it;
Til prestis here prechyng preve it hemselve,
And do it in dede to drawe us to goode; . . .
I seighe it be myself, and it so were
That I were king with croune to kepe a reaume,
Shulde nevere wrong in this world that I wyte mighte
Be unpunisshit at my power for peril of my soule! . . .
And yif thou werche it in werk I wedde myne eris
That lawe shal ben a labourer and lede afeld donge,
And love shal lede thi land as the lef liketh.' (A iv 100–31)

The suggestion that in a society governed by Reason, with Mede eliminated, lawyers would become plowmen takes us back to the opening lines of the vision, where plowmen have first place.

Mede is at last expelled from society and Theology's favourable view of her is implicitly repudiated. By ending the dream with the king and his counsellors departing to church and then to a feast, Langland signals the successful conclusion of his argument. The climax is thus a rejection of the complex modern world of money and a return to the simpler society of the original Creation described by Holy Church. Yet the function of the conflict with Mede has not simply been to demonstrate the justice of Holy Church's arguments. What we have witnessed is, in some respects, a dialectic, with the thesis being offered by Holy Church and Conscience, the antithesis by Theology and Mede herself, and a synthesis coming out in Conscience's second speech. The idea of accepting the materialist element in human society and trying to build a better world on this basis has been abandoned, but not all of what Mede stands for is lost. Conscience takes over from her some aspects of reward, and accepts alongside the spiritual notion of heavenly meed the practical needs of society, claiming that what labourers and other poor workers receive from their masters is not meed but 'mesurable hire' and that what merchants make is not meed either but simple exchange. Similarly, Reason's Utopia is surprisingly close to the real world, a world of lords and ladies, knights and clerks, merchants and money. It is too a world governed by the human faculties, conscience, reason and *kynde wit*, not by Holy Church or Grace, God or Theology. There is here an insistence on saving society by returning it to its basic principles rather than opting out of it, following the path of the plow-men rather than the anchorities and hermits of the Prologue.

This fundamental belief in man perhaps explains the strength of Langland's feelings about Mede. Her appearance seems wonderful to the narrator, but the images of sexual promiscuity strike an unexpec-tedly bitter note:

'Theigh lerid and lewide hadde leighe be the ichone,
And theigh Falshed hadde folewid the this fiftene wynter,
I shal assoile the myself, for a sem of whete,
And ek be thi baudekyn, and bere wel thin arnede . . .'
'Is not a betere baude, be hym that me made,
Betwyn hevene and helle, and erthe theigh men soughte.
She is tykil of hire tail, talewys of hire tunge,
As comoun as the cartewey to knave and to alle,
To monkis, to mynstrelis, to myselis in heggis.'

(A iii 37–40, 118–22)

What horrifies Langland is her power to enslave men. Even Conscience has been known to hang on her neck, and others are driven to desperate acts in their lust for her. Her arrival at court brings sober judges and clerics dancing round her in comic imitations of young amorous squires (A iii 11–30). The really biting image is the picture of sheriffs turned into horses, with saddles and shoes, to carry this ravishing cour-tesan to London (A ii 126–44). The issue of Mede is associated in Langland's mind with questions of human dignity and freedom.

The poetry has presented the colourful flux of actuality in all its variety and vividness: the street-traders in the Prologue, the throngs of lawyers, notaries, sisours and summoners in passus ii, with the exquisite account of Liar's sojourn among prentices and traders, the crowds of judges, clerics, friars around Mede at court, the subsequent pictures of war and conflict at home. But the argument has hinged on the ability of the king to see through this complexity to the universals whose presence, in the shape of tower and dungeon, is noted in the Prologue by the poet but ignored by the folk; to see, that is, the engagement of Truth, Wrong, Fals, Meed and Peace in the daily flux of events. Where *Winner and Waster* apparently ends with a sardonic acknowledgement of a fallen world, Langland ends his vision of contemporary England with an idealistic picture of the king driving out the corrupting power of wealth and restoring a simpler society.

Notes and references

1. The plot and argument are much the same in the Z and A versions. In the analysis of detail, here and in Chapter 3, I have followed the A version since the exact status of the one surviving copy of the Z version remains somewhat uncertain and its readings in matters of detail may not always be authentic; but important differences of substance are noted in Chapter 3.
2. An excellent account of the problems is L. K. Little, *Religious Poverty and the Profit Economy in Medieval Europe* (London, 1978).
3. See J. A. Yunck, *The Lineage of Lady Meed: the Development of Medieval Venality Satire* (Notre Dame, 1963).
4. See the account in *The Macro Plays*, ed. M. Eccles (Early English Text Society 262, London, 1969), pp. xxi–iv.
5. See the entry under truth in the *Oxford English Dictionary*.
6. See for instance *Old English Homilies of the Twelfth Century*, ed. R. Morris (Early English Text Society OS 53, London, 1873), p. 181.
7. *The Romaunt of the Rose*, ll. 1033–128; in *The Riverside Chaucer*, ed. L. D. Benson (Oxford, 1988).

Chapter Three

The second vision: the world's work (A v–viii)

T he poet wakes and then falls asleep and dreams again. He sees
Conscience preaching to the field full of folk and urging them to
repentance. Representative sinners confess their faults and promise to
reform, and a thousand of them set off in a pilgrimage to Truth. Losing
their way they meet a plowman called Piers who describes the allegorical road to Truth and then agrees to be their guide if they will help him
finish plowing his half-acre field first. They set to work but Piers is
troubled by idlers who have to be driven back to work by Hunger. Truth,
approving of their efforts, sends a pardon promising Piers and his associates salvation for their labours, but a priest challenges it, claiming it
is not a pardon. Piers tears it up in anger, swearing to plow no more.
The quarrel wakens the dreamer, who muses on the mystery of the
dream.

The second vision is the most important and influential of all
Langland's poetry. It created the character after whom the whole poem
is named and from whom both Chaucer and the leaders of the Peasants'
Revolt took their inspiration. It also produced the crisis which changed
the whole current of Langland's poetry, and possibly of his thought.
The sudden eruptions of dramatic action (the thousand men setting off
to seek Truth, Piers thrusting out his head from his half-acre, Piers again
tearing the Pardon) and oscillations between the dynamic of reform
and the richly naturalistic pictures of the unchanging, irredeemable, and
at times comic incapacity of man to be other than he is – idle, sensual,
egotistic and misdirected – testify to the poet's intense engagement with
the development of the argument.

The first dream ends with signals of a successful conclusion. The

Prologue had emphasised the disorder of society, suggested by Holy Church's image of the maze and by the way in which all the different occupations seemed to be working or idling independently of each other, sometimes in conflict with each other. Mede herself had proved to be the magnet which gave direction to the different ranks and professions but in a fashion which only accentuated the crowding and the chaos and had eventually been discredited. The second vision begins with an attempt by the new political order which was launched at the end of the first vision to impose itself on the field full of folk, with Conscience returning to the field to preach. What Langland now seeks to present is his vision of a new social order, one made possible by the adoption of Reason and Conscience as counsellors. What, he asks, would a society governed by reason and conscience rather than the pursuit of wealth be like? Would it have an answer to Holy Church's opening criticisms – 'Of other hevene thanne here holde thei no tale'? The keynote of his social ideal is co-operative labour for the community, best symbolised by the plowmen who had been presented first in the Prologue and are then referred to obliquely as the image of the new order at the end of the first vision. At the same time, by asserting the fundamental spirituality of his ideal of labour Langland seeks to answer Holy Church's criticisms and the challenge represented by placing next to the plowmen in the Prologue the hermits and anchorites who took no thought for food.

As John Burrow has shown,[1] the structure of the second vision is based on a traditional religious pattern of penance: Conscience preaches to the populace, warning them of their sins and duties, the sinners confess and resolve to reform, then set off on a pilgrimage to Truth as a mark of their conversion and expiation of their sins, and eventually receive a pardon for their past sins, just as real pilgrims did when they arrived at Rome or Jerusalem. Langland was perhaps thinking of the kind of preaching to crowds and mass conversions which launched the Crusades. However, he uses this religious pattern as a means of structuring a process which is essentially secular and social: the guide for the pilgrims is a layman, Piers the plowman; the pilgrimage is eventually enacted by performing communal work under Piers, not by a spiritual journey; and the Pardon is given by Truth to those who work faithfully in their worldly occupations, not to those who leave them. The religious pattern turns out to be only a validating metaphor for a fundamentally secular activity.

Conscience begins his sermon with a call to wasters to work which echoes the beginning of the Prologue's description of the field:

> He bad wastour go werche what he best couthe,
> And wynne that he wastide with sum maner craft. (A v 24–5)

The sermon is of a traditional type, listing the duties of different ranks in society and urging the importance of each rank performing its appropriate duties. In medieval English the tradition stretches all the way from Ælfric in the tenth century to Thomas of Wimbledon in the fourteenth.[2] The rest of the vision is in one sense a working-out of the details of this sermon, but it is thoroughly characteristic of Langland to do so by questioning the basis of contemporary society and seeking to identify the universal values which should govern it.

The confession of the sinners which follows offers us as readers a curious challenge: energetic, lively, realistic satirical portraits that have been much admired and anthologised, yet strangely at odds with the scheme of the vision. This episode was originally a coherent part of the scheme. In the Z version it is fairly brief (72 lines), emphasising those qualities of excess and competitiveness which contrast best with the austerity and productive labour of the plowman, and all the sinners vow earnestly to repent. It is a convincing picture of the folk of the field genuinely repenting in response to Conscience's apocalyptic sermon and looking for a guide to reform their way of life. In the A version, however, the account of the sinners is vastly expanded to 226 lines, so that the sinfulness becomes more apparent than the penitence, and two of the sinners conspicuously fail to complete their repentance and reform. What is so striking about Langland's account of the confession of the sinners is that, much anthologised though it is, it increasingly fails to fit into the scheme of the poem. The pictures become longer and richer in detail, culminating in a Glutton seduced into his old haunt at the very moment when he is approaching the church to enact his reform, and able eventually to repent only because of the physical discomfort on the morning after. The very fact that the deadly sins are represented as ordinary men and women, unusual in itself, runs counter to the optimism about natural man manifested in the scheme of the vision; this is an altogether different vision of human nature. Yet it cannot be called a black vision: whatever may be suggested by Envy and Coveitise, the concluding portraits of Gluttony, Sloth and Robert the Robber have a mocking but genial quality far removed from the satire of Spenser or Swift. Langland clearly enjoyed this kind of satirical writing, and any suspicion that it might be a quasi-involuntary digression here is denied by the fact that he expanded it in the B and again in the C version. Alongside Langland's belief in the innate goodness of men and of the simple life, there is a contrasting sense of an essential colourful grotesqueness in humanity. It is perhaps a conflict between realism in the modern sense of the word, depicting the mundane actuality of human nature, and realism in the medieval philosophical sense, conceiving of man as he is in the mind of God. Digressiveness is a prevailing vice of Langland's writing, but here it seems to reflect something more, a powerful resistance to his own idealism.

Nevertheless, the movement to reform is picked up again immediately after the confessions, with a thousand men setting off on a pilgrimage to truth, as a mark of their conversion and perhaps an act of penance. Langland brings the folk back to the point where the poem had begun, wandering in a maze, though this time vaguely aware of an ideal of Truth:

> Ac there were fewe men so wys that the wey thider couthe,
> But blustrid forth as bestis over baches and hilles. (A vi 1–2)

Their problem now is ignorance rather than intransigence. Pilgrimages and quests are common motifs of medieval allegorical literature, and indeed of symbolic romance narratives such as the Quest of the Holy Grail, and one of their standard features is a guide to point the protagonist on his way. It is characteristic of Langland's rethinking of literary conventions that the pilgrims' first potential guide, the palmer, turns out to be entirely inadequate:

> 'Knowist thou ought a corseint, ' quath thei, 'that men callen
> treuthe?
> Canst thou wisse us the wey where that wy dwellith?.'
> 'Nay, so me god helpe,' seide the gome thanne.
> 'I saugh nevere palmere with pik ne with scrippe
> Axen aftir hym, er now in this place.' (A vi 20–4)

The palmer, a veteran of countless pilgrimages to distant shrines, is the representative of empty religious gestures; as a man living an exclusively religious life, a continual act of penance, he seems the proper guide for the pilgrims but knows nothing of Truth. It is the plowman living a secular life who knows Truth:

> 'Petir!' quath a ploughman and putte forth his hed,
> 'I knowe hym as kyndely as clerk doth his bokis.
> Clene consience and wyt kende me to his place,
> And dede me sure hym siththe to serve hym for evere;
> Bothe sowe and sette while I swynke mighte.
> I have ben his folewere al this fourty wynter;
> Bothe sowen his seed, and sewide hise bestis. (A vi 25–31)

Piers is initially introduced as a representative plowman, in contrast to the professional man of religion, the palmer, and he probably meant no more than that to Langland originally; his name is a simple type-name like those of Piers the Pardoner and Randolf the Reve earlier (A ii 73–

5), though Langland was eventually to discover further possible meanings in the name and the occupation. There is no need, at this stage at least, to invoke the New Testament use of the sower or the plowman as images for the preacher. From the beginning of the poem, plowmen have been mentioned alongside priests and bishops, not as metaphorical substitutes for them. Where the palmer knows saints' shrines and the clergy know books, Piers, as plowman, knows Truth (alias God) naturally and serves Him through his work.

Langland is here developing Holy Church's idea of a 'kind knowing' of Truth that is rooted in the heart, but now locating it in the heart of the ordinary peasant and explicitly contrasting it with the inferior knowledge of the professional religious. Piers is proving heir to a long tradition of medieval anti-intellectualism, a point which is developed further at the end of the vision and again in the following one. As in the later poem *Pierce the Ploughman's Crede* where the plowman knows what none of the orders of friars can tell the poet, it is apparently a simplicity of life and closeness to nature that fosters the knowledge of Truth.

Piers goes on to claim not only to know Truth as clerks and palmers do not but also to serve Him, through the nature of his work. It is a fresh appeal to the principles of Creation: by fulfilling his natural, God-given role on earth, Piers is serving God and knowing Him as the professional religious do not. Huizinga has rightly emphasised the novelty of what Langland was doing here: 'England, which, earlier than the other nations, became alive to the economic aspect of things, gave, towards the end of the fourteenth century, the first expression to the sentiment of the sanctity of productive labour in that strangely fantastic and touching poem.'[3] The notion that a man who faithfully fulfils the work to which he is called does enough (with due religious observances) to satisfy God, even if he is only a plowman, is not difficult to find elsewhere, but Langland suggests something more unusual, a direct and close relationship with God by virtue of sowing His seed and tending His beasts. Similarly, other writers saw manual labour for the necessities of life as the curse and punishment imposed on man at the Fall, but Langland will have none of this; when he later quotes God's words from Genesis, it is to emphasise the universal duty to work, not the curse:

> Go to Genesis the geaunt, engendrour of us alle:
> *In sudore* and swynke thou shalt thi mete tilien. (A vii 216–17)

In his contrast between empty religious gestures and virtuous toil Langland is perhaps closer to the slogans of the Lollards:

> A simple paternoster of a plowman that is in charite is better than
> a thousand massis of covetous prelatis or veyn religious.[4]

Or again:

> What lif that pleseth more to God is better prayer to God; as lif of
> a trewe plowman or ellis of a trewe heerde is betere preyere to
> God than prayer of any order that God loveth less.[5]

The significance of this issue is perhaps clearer if we recall that
Wyclif was charged with heresy for maintaining that friars should support themselves by the labour of their hands, and that a later follower
of his was accused, at his trial for heresy, of arguing that parish priests
should alternate their religious duties with earning a living by labour.[6]
There was an undercurrent of feeling that the professional religious
were to some extent parasites on the commonwealth and that moral
and even spiritual worth was to be associated with productive labour,
but it was a view seen in Langland's time to be threatening the Establishment: one manifestation of it was, after all, the couplet attributed
to the leaders of the Peasants' Revolt some years later:

> When Adam delved and Eve span
> Who was then the gentleman?

The allegorical route to Truth which Piers now describes for the
pilgrims is, appropriately, a moderate, practical, human way. In contrast
to, for instance, Deguileville's *Pilgrimage of the Life of Man* in the thirteenth century, or the fifteenth-century morality play *Everyman*, the
Church, clergy and sacraments play little part in this progress. Grace is
there near the end of the journey, but here is no Augustinian insistence
on the primacy of grace; Amende-you, the servant of grace, is present
too, and will gain the reformed sinner entrance. It is a journey which
men can make by themselves, and even the worst of sinners can find
mercy. It is therefore the parasites on society, pickpocket, street-
entertainer and waferer (on the nature of a waferer, see p. 110), who
draw back from the journey, not the down-to-earth workers:

> 'Be crist,' quath a cuttepurs, 'I have no kyn there.'
> 'Ne I,' quath an apeward, 'be aught that I knowe.'
> 'Wyte God,' quath a waffrer, 'wiste I that forsothe,
> Shulde I nevere ferthere a foote for no freris preching.'
>
> (A vi 115–18)

Langland may at one stage have intended to describe his pilgrims
following the route sketched by Piers, in the manner of a *Pilgrim's
Progress*, but already in the Z text it is described in too much detail to
bear the repetition of an actual journey. Piers proposes the plowing of

his half-acre initially as a task to be completed before the pilgrimage to Truth can be started but it soon becomes a replacement for the pilgrimage, as is clear from Piers' words:

'I wile worsshipe therewith Treuthe in my lyve,
And ben his pilgrym at the plough for pore menis sake.
My ploughpote shal be my pyk and putte at the rotis.'

(A vii 93–5)

The spiritual act of pilgrimage will after all be enacted by remaining at the plow, producing food for others. It is easy to see why this had to be so. Piers had come to know and serve Truth or God through his work in the fields, not through religious acts or spiritual exercises, and it was appropriate for others to discover Truth in the same way. Moreover the pilgrimage, even a metaphorical one, would necessarily have been a once-for-all journey, an image of a spiritual ascent, like Bunyan's Christian whose pilgrimage ends in death; Langland was interested in the idealism of a sustained way of life.

The pilgrims join Piers in his work and the co-operative labour on the half-acre gradually becomes an image of society at work, with the plowman as producer of food and clothing at the heart of the system, the knight protecting him from enemies and his crops from animals, the women sowing sacks for the wheat. It is an essentially secular world which is presented. Langland's knight, justified by his productive work in protecting plowmen from wasters and their crops from foxes, is a far cry from Chaucer's knight, devoting his life to fighting for the faith against the pagans. The religious exist on the fringes of this world, as recipients of charity:

'And ye loveliche ladies with your longe fyngris,
That han silk and sendel, sewith it whanne tyme is,
Chesibles for chappellis chirches to honoure.'. . .
'Ankeris and heremytes that holde hem in here sellis
Shuln have of myn almesse al the while I libbe.'

(A vii 18–20, 133–4)

Hermits, indeed, are seen as idlers who need Hunger to drive them to work:

An hep of heremites henten hem spadis
And dolven drit and dung to ditte out Hunger. (A vii 175–6)

It is productive labour which is central. At the same time, the pilgrimage imagery and the association of Piers with Truth are an assertion that this ideal of work for society has its own religious and spiritual value.

It is in this spirit that Hunger proclaims work as a universal ethic, with the twin authority of God and Nature:

'Kynde wyt wolde that iche wight wroughte
Other with teching, or telling, or travaillyng of hondis,
Actif lif or contemplatif; Crist wolde it alse.' (A vii 231–3)

Hunger here subverts a whole tradition of patristic and medieval polemic which sought to justify the religious life of prayer and contemplation as a way of life equal, and more often superior, to the work of the world, whether manual work or teaching. For most writers since the fourth century, active and contemplative meant two modes of religious life, usually the pastoral work of the clergy as opposed to the enclosed or secluded life of prayer and meditation followed by monks and hermits. The essence of the contemplative life was that it was not work; its great exemplar was that Mary who sat listening to Christ while her sister Martha did the duties of hospitality. Hunger identifies the two lives instead with manual labour and teaching, that is, presumably, with the work done for the community by laity and clergy respectively. The traditional justification of a life of prayer and meditation, superior to the working life though dependent upon it, which had been built on the active–contemplative distinction and the Gospel story of Martha and Mary, is here silently overthrown. Once again Langland is closely in tune with contemporary Wyclifite writings. They too define the active life as the ordinary work of the world:

This is clepid actif liif, whanne men travailen for worldli goodis and kepen hem in rightwisnesse.[7]

The Wyclifite treatise *Of Feigned Contemplative Life* similarly insists on preaching as the distinctive role of the religious, and dismisses the traditional ideal of the contemplative life of prayer and meditation as hypocrisy:

Thei [Antichrist's followers] seyn that men schulden cesse of prechynge and yeven hem to holy preiers and contemplacion for that helpeth more cristene men and is betre. Trewe men seyn boldly that trewe prechynge is betre than preiynge bi mouthe. . . . Lord, what charite is it to a kunnynge man to chese his owene contemplacion in reste, and suffre othere men goe to helle for brekynge of Goddis hestis, whanne he may lyghtly teche hem and gete more thank of God in litil techynge than bi longe tyme in suche preieris.[8]

Perhaps because of the implications of the word contemplation these texts tend not to use the term 'contemplative life' for the preaching work of the clergy, but Wyclif himself uses it in this sense in his Latin sermons.[9] Langland's alteration of this passage in the B version, and cancellation of it in the C version (see pp. 84 and 187), is one of the more interesting examples of him drawing back from the courageous novelty of his original ideas.

As the plowing gradually changes from a stage on the road to Truth into a symbol of life itself, it necessarily expands to include not only the reformed sinners with whom the scene began but the whole range of society, including idlers and wastrels. When the knight is incapable of forcing them to work, Piers has to summon Hunger. The need for Hunger's heavy-handed and merciless assaults certainly qualifies any sense of the plowing-scene as a Utopia but Langland is not, I think, envisaging the failure of Piers' ideal. Hunger's assaults are a way of testing the community, and an acknowledgement of what happens in the real world to those who will not respond to the demands of the work ethic. They are perhaps also a foretaste of future judgement, picking up echoes of the Gospel imagery of the harvest at the end of the world:

> At heigh prime Peris let the plough stande
> To oversen hem hymself; whoso best wroughte
> Shulde ben hirid thereaftir whan hervist tyme come.
>
> (A vii 104–6)

Compare Matthew 13: 38–9:

> 'The field is the world; the good seed are the children of the kingdom; but the tares are the children of the wicked one; the enemy that sowed them is the devil; the harvest is the end of the world; and the reapers are the angels.'

The co-operative labour is no longer the mark of an élite but a way of distinguishing the sheep from the goats.

Thus when the next passus begins with the words 'Treuthe herde telle hereof' what Truth has heard is not, probably, the failure of the ideal but the general endeavours of Piers and his fellows. Truth's message draws out the implications of the plowing episode in the light of the apocalyptic overtones that have developed, and promises salvation to all who work honestly in their duties to society:

> Treuthe herde telle hereof, and to Peris sente
> To take his tem, and tilien the erthe
> And purchacide hym a pardoun *a pena et a culpa*

> For hym and for hise heires, everemore aftir,
> And bad hym holde hym at hom and erien his laighes.
> And alle that holpen to erien or to sowen,
> Or any maner mester that mighte Peris helpen,
> Part in that pardoun the pope hath hem grauntid.
> Kinges and knightes that kepen holy chirche
> And rightfulliche in reaum rewlith the peple
> Han pardoun thorugh purcatorie to passe wel sone,
> With patriarkes in paradis to pleighe thereaftir. (A viii 1–12)

Since Piers has come to know Truth and serve him through his honest toil, it is right that Truth should promise him and those like him his protection, extending even beyond death through Purgatory to Paradise. Productive labour has become a sanctified way of life, not only substituting for pilgrimage as an act of spiritual merit but eventually taking on the identity of the good life which will be rewarded at the end of time with salvation. Just as literal pilgrimages are rewarded with papal pardons which free men from years in Purgatory, so the life of honest toil, as a metaphorical pilgrimage, is rewarded with Truth's Pardon which promises men salvation and a safe-conduct through Purgatory. As the details of the Pardon are revealed, the justification of honest toil is now extended by Truth to include not only plowmen but other productive trades ('any maner myster') and then kings, knights, bishops, merchants and even lawyers because of their work for the community (though the last two very grudgingly).

The helpless poor who cannot work present a difficulty in this system, but Langland saves them by drawing again on religious imagery: if work is in part a continuing act of penance which extinguishes the penalties of sin, serving thereby as an alternative to purgatory, then the hardships endured by those incapable of work may be seen as having a parallel role, as a kind of purgatory on earth:

> Ac olde men and hore that helpeles ben of strengthe,
> And wommen with childe that werche ne mowe,
> Blynde and bedrede, and broken here membris,
> That takith this meschief mekliche as myselis and othere,
> Han as pleyn pardoun as the ploughman hymselve;
> For love of here lough herte oure Lord hath hem grauntid
> Here penaunce and here purcatorie upon this pur erthe.
>   (A viii 82–8)

Other kinds of non-workers, however, whether false beggars or true hermits, are absent from the Pardon. What it offers is a justification of man that is expressed in both social and religious terms but is based on productive labour, with the plowman at the centre. The questions raised by the Prologue about the relationship of society to the tower of Truth have been answered in terms of the plowmen who work for others rather than the hermits who care only for Heaven. The story which had begun with the folk on the field oblivious of Truth finds a fitting climax with Truth rewarding them for the redirection of their labours.

The tearing of the Pardon

It is likely that Langland originally ended the poem with the lines just quoted. This is where the earliest known version of poem, Z, breaks off, at the end of the account of the Pardon (see Ch. 1). Whether Langland actually intended the poem to be recited and circulated in this form, or merely left it temporarily unfinished in frustration, is unclear, though the similarity between this ending and the last lines of the A version (A xi 306–13), itself breaking off abruptly and yet apparently circulated in this form, suggests Langland would not have found it impossible to allow the poem to be read in the Z form. It is certainly a fitting place to stop in terms of the development of the argument. What he has presented so far is a vision of contemporary society being purged of the corrupting power of wealth and restored to the fundamental simplicity of a primitive Golden Age society, like Eden but more hierarchical, primarily social and secular but with a spiritual sanctity and the blessing of God. Just as the first vision ended with the triumphant installation of Reason as the king's counsellor and the sealing ceremonies of church and banquet, so the second vision appropriately ended with Truth's promise of salvation for all his faithful followers. Yet something clearly made Langland dissatisfied with the ideal which he had imaginatively conceived. The dissatisfaction has been evident already in the persistent challenge to the ideal which he allowed himself to express in energetic language and colourful, boisterous characters: the palmer; the pickpocket, monkey-keeper and waferer who draw back from the journey to Truth; the wastrels on the field; and most of all the sinners who confess to Conscience. It is therefore not wholly surprising that when Langland resumed the poem it was to subvert all that he had so far written. The fact that the Z version stops short of this point suggests that this challenge to the Pardon was not a conscious part of his intentions when writing the plowing and Pardon scenes, but sprang from further reflection and reconsideration.

Langland resumes the poem with a new character, a priest. When the priest asks to see the Pardon it is found to contain just two lines in Latin, clauses from the Athanasian Creed:

'Piers', quath a prest tho, 'thi pardon muste I rede,

For I shal construe iche clause and kenne it the on englissh.'
And Peris at his preyour the pardoun unfoldith,
And I behynde hem bothe beheld al the bulle.
In two lynes it lay and nought o lettre more,
And was writen right thus in witnesse of Treuthe:
> *Et qui bona egerunt ibunt in vitam eternam;*
> *Qui vero mala in ignem eternum.*

'Petir' quath the prest tho, 'I can no pardoun fynde
But do wel and have wel, and God shal have thi soule;
And do evele and have evele, and hope thou non other
That aftir thi deth day to helle shalt thou wende.' (A viii 89–100)

The priest's intervention is a reiteration of the contrast between laymen who know and seek God instinctively and 'professional' men of religion who seek false gods, a contrast which has already been seen in the opposition of Piers and the palmer. The priest is offering to play his role of 'interpreting' (that is, adjusting, 'glosyng' as Langland calls it [Prologue 57]) the teaching of God. The two Latin lines are not, however, the priest's own rendering of the Pardon, for they are firmly there in the document, as the poet emphasises by including himself as observer. There is no need for us to make heavy weather of the passage by trying to account literally for the fact that the narrator has just given a long account of the contents of Truth's Pardon, covering some eighty-seven lines, and the Pardon itself is only now opened; it is a dramatic metaphor for the idea that the teaching of Truth, though spelled out in detail for the different ranks of society, can be summed up by those two lines from the Athanasian Creed. As a summary of the Pardon's message the Latin lines are not unreasonable. It does in some sense come down to the argument that those who do good will go into the eternal life and, by implication, that those who do evil will go into eternal fire, though in fact Truth had spoken of Purgatory rather than Hell. The Pardon, and all that preceded it, had merely sought to redefine 'doing good' in terms of a life of honest work for the community rather than specifically religious acts. The priest is right to say that the Pardon thus summed up is no pardon at all. A real pardon or indulgence dispensed a sinner from the punishment due for his sins, whereas Truth's Pardon dispenses those who live the good life. As the plowing had changed from a symbolic pilgrimage by sinners (and therefore an act meriting a pardon) to a metaphor for a whole way of life, so the notion of the plowing redeeming past sins fades from view and the Pardon which it achieves becomes a reward for a whole way of life rather than an act of forgiveness. This at least should be no surprise, although the formulation is dramatic: it has been clear since the beginning of the Pardon that Truth was offering a reward for living the good life rather than an escape from the penalties of an evil life, and Langland's preference for this over ordinary pardons is in line with his earlier elevation of Piers and his way of life over palmers and clerks who rely on religious gestures and forms. The Pardon's value and attraction for him is precisely that it judges the quality of a life rather than seeking to discount it. He goes on to make that point more cautiously and prosaically after the dream has ended:

> For-thi I rede yow renkes that riche ben on erthe:
> Upon trist of your tresour trienalis to have
> Be thou nevere the baldere to breke the ten hestis,
> And nameliche ye maistris, as meiris and juggis,
> That han the welthe of this world, and wise men ben holden
> To purchace pardoun and the popes bulles.
> At the dredful dom whanne dede shal arisen
> And come alle before Crist acountes to yelden,
> How thou leddist thi lif here and his lawe keptest,
> What thou dedist day by day the dom wile reherce.
>
> (A viii 165–74)

When Judgement comes, the actions of life will be counted, not the documents of the Church. Similar points are made by the Lollards:

> Ther cometh no pardon but of God for good lyvynge and endynge in charite, and this schal not be bought ne solde as prelatis chaffaren thes dayes; for who is in most charite is beste herde of God, be he schepeherde or lewid man, or in the chirche or in the feld; and who kepith wel the hestis of God schal have pardon and the blisse of hevene, and noon othere for creature under God.[10]

Yet if the priest's objection to Truth's Pardon should be no surprise to us, something in his words does seem to shake Piers himself, as he angrily tears up the Pardon and vows to give up plowing:

> And Piers for pure tene pulde it assondir
> And seide, '*Si ambulavero in medio umbre mortis*
> *Non timebo mala quoniam tu mecum es.*
> I shal cesse of my sowyng', quath Peris, 'and swynke not so harde,
> Ne aboute my belyve so besy be namore;
> Of preyours and of penaunce my plough shal ben hereaftir,
> And beloure that I belough er theigh liflode me faile.
> The prophet his payn eet in penaunce and in wepyng
> Be that the Sauter us seith, and so dede manye othere.
> That lovith God lelly, his liflode is the more:

Fuerunt michi lacrime mee panes die ac nocte.
And but yif Luk leighe he lerith us another,
By foules, that are not besy aboute the bely joye:
Ne soliciti sitis he seith in his gospel. (A viii 101–13)

The language here is of course ambiguous, and the ambiguity may reflect the poet's own uncertainties. The phrases 'not so harde', 'so besy', 'not besy', '*ne soliciti sitis*' seem to suggest an ideal of moderation or detachment, though it is difficult to see what value moderation in labour would have in the context of the second vision, which has stressed commitment in contrast to the idleness of *wastours*. R. W. Frank has pointed out that the text from St Luke's Gospel to which Piers refers ('take no thought for the morrow, for the morrow will take care of itself') was often taken by patristic and medieval commentators to be urging not that men should cease to labour for food and clothing but that they should free their minds from too exclusive an engagement with work and the world, and he suggests that this is what Langland is intending too.[11] Yet Langland seems to mean something sharper than that. Piers swears to cease from his sowing, dismisses his past concern with food as 'belly-joy' and insists that 'preyours and penaunce' will take over from his plow. The phrase 'preyours and penaunce' means more than might appear. It is the term which Langland uses in the Prologue for the way of life followed by the anchorites and hermits, and it appears again with reference to a similar way of life later in the poem:

Ancres and heremytes, and monkes and freres
Peeren to Apostles thorugh hire parfit lyvynge . . .
Hir preieres and hir penaunces to pees sholde brynge
Alle that ben at debaat, and bedemen were trewe. . . .
Preyeres of a parfit man and penaunce discret
Is the leuest labour that oure lord pleseth.
(B xv 415–16, 425–6, C v 84–5)

This use of 'penaunce' to mean not penance but the voluntary hardship and suffering undertaken by hermits and others like them is in fact very common in Langland and other writers of his time. The friars in *Pierce the Ploughmans Crede* claim to live a life of 'penance and poverty':

We haven forsaken the worlde . & in wo lybbeth
In penaunce & poverte . & precheth the puple.[12]

When Sir Lancelot and his fellow-knights become hermits, 'penaunce' is the word which Malory uses for their life of hardship:

And whan they sawe syr Launcelot had taken hym to suche per-
feccion they had no lust to departe but toke suche an habyte as
he had. Thus they endured in grete penaunce syx yere.[13]

In the Wyclifite writings 'penaunce' appears again and again with
reference to the life of voluntary poverty which should ideally be followed by bishops, priests and monks. One tract refers to bishops as 'thei
that schulden most lede the peple to hevene, bi trewe techynge of holy
writt and ensaumple of wilful poverte and mekenesse and bisy traveile
in praieres and devocions and penaunce'.[14] The treatise *On Clerkes Pos-
sessioners* (that is, monks) is particularly close to Langland, using
'penaunce' for the life lived by the apostles and ideally by monks, and
contrasting *discrete penaunce* with *wombe joie* (compare Langland's
penaunce discret (C v 84) and his *bely jove* (A viii 112); several manuscripts
of the A text actually read *wombe joie* here):

> [Possessioners] destroyen his ordinaunce that he made for clerkis,
> and in stede of mekenesse and wilful povert and discrete penaunce
> brengen in coueitise, pride and wombe joie and ydelnesse.[15]

> [Possessioners ought to enter their orders] to be dead to the world
> and to live in penaunce and streit povert as cristes apostils, and
> thus they suen this holy state of povert and penaunce for world-
> ly richesse and wombe joy.[16]

In swearing to cease from plowing and to devote his labours to prayer
and 'penaunce' Piers is abandoning the life of the plowman, with its
concern for material things, in favour of a religious life of prayer and
voluntary poverty like the hermit's. The implicit contrast of the opening lines, between plowmen toiling for food and hermits caring only for
Heaven, now at last comes into play.

Piers' action in tearing up the Pardon sent by Truth is startling; he
is the servant and follower of Truth or God, and the Pardon has
enshrined his own implicit ideals. Commentators have suggested that
Langland means something less startling than appears: that Piers is to
be understood as rejecting ordinary pardons by his action rather than
Truth's, or that tearing is really an act of acceptance, or that the tearing
refers not directly to Truth's Pardon but to the ending of man's damnation by original sin through the Redemption.[17] Yet it is clear enough
that Piers does reject Truth's teaching, for Truth has begun the passus
by instructing Piers and his fellows to remain at home and continue
their work of plowing, whereas Piers now swears to renounce the plow.
It is wholly consistent and right that Piers should by his actions reject
the Pardon which contained that teaching.

Geoffrey Shepherd has suggested that the tearing of the Pardon originated as a genuine dream or vision; an inner image that came suddenly and insistently to Langland's mind and seemed to him in some sense right and necessary, though he had difficulty in articulating, perhaps even understanding, quite why it was necessary.[18] If so, its deepest meaning may be Langland's rejection of his own poem. The Pardon represents not only the ideals held by Truth and Piers but also those which the poem itself had sought to express through much of the first two visions: the simple hard-working life of the plowman was an ideal for Langland himself. When the priest challenges it and Piers rejects it, we as readers are in no position to know where the poet himself stands; it is possible, that is, to read the tearing as a mistake by Piers, misled and abused by the more knowledgeable priest, and the narrator's subsequent criticisms of paper pardons would support such a reading. From the later development of the poem, however, especially in the B version, it becomes clear that the rejection is in some sense 'meant', that it answered to some deep-seated dissatisfaction in Langland himself with the ideals of the first two visions. Another writer might have destroyed or abandoned his poem in such a situation. Langland instead displaced his rejection on to Piers, whose tearing of the Pardon vicariously enacts the poet's tearing of his poem. Piers' action enabled Langland to go forward with the poem and develop the alternative to the Pardon's ideals more gradually.

What is involved in this rejection is in part a turning away from the work ethic and the whole concern with a spiritualisation of ordinary life and actual society to a more purely spiritual, ascetic and individual ideal, best symbolised by the hermit. This becomes clearer when one is able to consider Langland's reworking of the confrontation some years later, in the B text episode of Haukyn the waferer and Patience the hermit. But what may also be involved for Langland is an escape from an austere theology which puts all responsibility on man to a quieter, more submissive theology which puts faith in an omnipotent God. The old fifth-century conflict between the followers of Pelagus who asserted the centrality of individual merit in salvation and St Augustine who insisted on the primacy of divine grace, in comparison with which all human merit is insignificant, experienced a revival in the fourteenth century, with Thomas Bradwardine, Archbishop of Canterbury, reasserting the predominance of divine grace and complaining of the 'new Pelagians' of his time.[19] Bradwardine was probably thinking of William of Ockham and his followers, but there is a Pelagian strand in Wyclifite writings too:

For ech man that shal be dampned is dampned for his owne gilt, and ech man that shal be saved is saved by his owne merit.[20]

In this respect as well as in the choice of prayer as a way of life, Piers'
act represents a repudiation of positions occupied by Wyclifite writings. Thus Piers' first words on tearing the Pardon are a quotation from
the twenty-third psalm asserting his trust in God: 'though I walk in the
middle of the shadow of death, I shall fear none evil, since thou art with
me'. He goes on to invoke God as the universal provider:

'The foulis in the firmament, who fynt hem a wynter?
Whan the frost fresith foode hem behovith;
Have thei no garner to go to, but God fynt hem alle.'
(A viii 115–17)

This perhaps explains the critical role of the priest's words in prompting Piers' reaction. The priest is right in his summing-up of the Pardon and his denial that it is a pardon, and there is on the surface no
cause for surprise at this; he is speaking mainly from ecclesiastical *amour
propre*, demonstrating his professional expertise over Latin and pardons
but missing the spirit of the Pardon in his obsession with form. What
his words unconsciously point to, however, is the rigour which lies hidden in the Pardon: that it involves no mercy for failure, and that it relies
exclusively on men's actions. Langland does not want pardons in the
sense of ecclesiastical scraps of paper, but he finds that he does want
pardon in the sense of divine indulgence. This was in fact a note briefly
touched on at the end of Piers' account of the road to Truth:

'Mercy is a maiden there, hath might over hem alle;
And she is sib to alle synful, and hire sone also,
And thorugh the helpe of hem two, hope thou non other,
Thou might gete grace there so thou go be tyme.' (A vi 120–3)

This passage is, significantly, not present in the Z text but was added by
Langland when revising for the A version, and is in fact almost the only
reference to Christ or the Virgin Mary in the Visio in the A version,
which otherwise presents a sterner Old Testament God. The priest's
words are ultimately Langland's own acknowledgement of the austerity
of his Utopian vision; they express Langland's emerging doubts about
his social ideal, born in that gap between the Z and A versions. Hence
the violent revulsion to a different philosophy which puts faith in a
force beyond man and reduces man himself to a passive and submissive role.

It is tempting to suggest that this is really what being a hermit meant
for Langland: that the eremitic way of life is only a metaphor for an
inner, spiritual renunciation of the world and reliance on God. But in
Langland's poetry generally there are too many discussions of the prac-

tical issues of begging and poverty to discount his genuine interest in the eremitic way of life. The conflict between a social ethic which centres on work for the community and a religious ethic which emphasises individual perfection through poverty and prayer is a real and sustained dilemma for him. Even so, it is easy to see how the two aspects of *poverte*, external and internal, are intertwined in his mind here; it is equally evident in his later account of the hermit Patience, representative of both voluntary poverty and spiritual peace.

The gap between plowman and hermit, between the social ethic preached by Truth and the religious ethic now avowed by Piers, seems enormous at this point in the poem, and there is nothing to suggest possibilities of easy reconciliation. The very fact that it is the plowman Piers who renounces plowing for prayer is a warning to us against resorting to the easy argument that some are called to work and others to pray; though individuals in reality may not have to choose, Langland himself, through Piers, must. Equally, the violence of the choice denies any notion of a steady and deliberate progress through stages of existence. Yet there is just a hint here of common ground, as the dialogue between Piers and the priest continues:

> 'What!' quath the prest to Perkyn, 'Peter, as me thinketh,
> Thou art lettrid a litel; who lernide the on boke?'
> 'Abstinence the abbesse myn a b c me taughte,
> And Consience com aftir, and kennide me betere.'
>
> (A viii 118–21)

The priest as clerk and professional mocks Piers' appearance of learning, and Piers lays claim in reply to the kind of understanding that comes from innate powers (conscience) and the life of austerity (abstinence). He has a right, as plowman, to do so, but the word 'abstinence' reminds us that hermits could make the same claim to an understanding not based on books, and frequently did (see Ch. 4). Appropriately, therefore, in the continuation of the poem in the B version Patience the hermit is contrasted not only with Haukyn the exemplar of the active life but also with Clergie and the doctor, exemplars of learning. Piers has from the beginning been associated with a kind of natural understanding based on conscience which is different from the book-learning of *clerkes*, and this is preserved when he is translated to the life of prayer and penance; it is indeed what enables him to articulate the ideals of that life. Plowman and hermit do have in common such things as simplicity, austerity of life, and reliance on the understanding that comes from God and from the life of hardship rather than book-learning, and Piers and the poem are not leaving those qualities behind. What enabled Langland to continue the poem, and to retain Piers as his hero, was a half-conscious recognition, or belief, that the essential qualities of the plowman were not identified with his labour for the material needs of others.

The argument between Piers and the priest wakens the dreamer and ends the second vision. The narrator's discussion of the dream seems strangely unconscious of the drama with which it had ended. He discusses dream theory and in his emphasis on the prophetic dreams of the Old Testament as parallels seems to be making serious claims for his visions while at the same time evading responsibility for them. In his careful acknowledgement that papal pardons and bishops' letters do save, but at the Day of Judgement 'Do-wel' is superior, he draws out the implications of Truth's Pardon without showing any awareness that Piers has torn the Pardon up. The poet himself was perhaps still uncertain of the significance of that act, which had seemed to him imaginatively essential and yet contrasted violently with all that had preceded it. Certainly he developed it no further in the A version of the poem. The line with which he begins his reflections on the vision may be as true of the poet himself as of his persona:

Manye tyme this metelis han mad me to stodie. (A viii 131)

Notes and references

1. J. Burrow, 'The action of Langland's second vision', *Essays in Criticism*, 15 (1965), 247–68, reprinted in his *Essays in Medieval Literature* (Oxford, 1984), pp. 79–101.
2. *Ælfric's Catholic Homilies: Second Series, Text*, ed. M. Godden (Early English Text Society SS 5, London, 1979),pp. 183–9; *Wimbledon's Sermon*, ed. I. K. Knight (Pittsburgh, 1967).
3. J. Huizinga, *The Waning of the Middle Ages*, trans. F. Hopman, 2nd edn (Harmondsworth, 1972), p. 174.
4. *The English Works of Wyclif hitherto unprinted*, ed. F. Matthew (Early English Text Society OS 74, London, 1880), p. 274.
5. Ibid., p. 321.
6. J. J. Thomson, *The Later Lollards* (Oxford, 1965), p. 78.
7. *Select English Works of John Wyclif*, ed. T. Arnold, 3 vols (Oxford, 1869–71), I,384.
8. Matthew, *Wyclif*, p. 188.
9. *Iohannis Wyclif Sermones*, ed. J. Loserth, vol. I (London, 1887), Sermo vii, p. 49.
10. Matthew, *Wyclif*, p. 238.
11. R. W. Frank, 'The Pardon scene in *Piers Plowman*', *Speculum*, **26** (1951), 317–31. Cf. too T. P. Dunning, *Piers Plowman: an Interpretation of the A Text* (Dublin and London, 1937), 2nd end. revised by T. P. Dolan (Oxford, 1980), p. 116. This seems to have been a particularly Dominican

argument in the later Middle Ages, whereas the Franciscans argued for a literal interpretation.

12. *Pierce the Ploughmans Crede*, ed. W. W. Skeat (Early English Text Society OS 30, London, 1867), ll. 110–11.
13. *The Works of Sir Thomas Malory*, ed. E. Vinaver, 2nd edn (Oxford, 1967), III, 1254–5.
14. Matthew, *Wyclif*, p. 98.
15. Ibid., p. 117.
16. Ibid., p. 122.
17. Frank, 'The Pardon scene'; J. A. W. Bennett, *Langland: Piers Plowman* (Oxford, 1972), note to passus vii line III; R. Woolf, 'The tearing of the Pardon', in *Piers Plowman: Critical Approaches*, ed. S. Hussey (London, 1969), pp. 50–75.
18. G. Shepherd, 'The nature of alliterative poetry in late Medieval England', *Proceedings of the British Academy*, **56** (1970), 57–76.
19. G. Leff, *Medieval Thought* (London, 1959), p. 297.
20. Arnold, *Wyclif*, I, 350.

Chapter Four

The third vision: Do-wel and the problem of knowledge (A ix–xii)

T he narrator, wandering in search of Do-wel, meets two friars who claim he lives with them. He then falls asleep and dreams of Thought, who defines Do-wel, Do-bet and Do-best for him. They meet Wit who offers further definitions. Wit's wife, Study, intervenes to blame him for wasting his advice on a fool. She sends the dreamer on to her cousin Clergie, whose wife Scripture defines Do-wel yet further. The dreamer disagrees with her, and expresses his doubts. In a possibly un-authentic twelfth passus he is sent on a journey to meet Kynde Wit but dies before he reaches him.

The third and final vision of the A version is the least satisfactory of all Langland's work: muddled in its thought, uncertain in its tones, lacking in momentum or direction, inconsequential in its conclusion, if it con-cludes at all. It is difficult to avoid the suspicion that it is strongly autobiographical in origin. The dreamer becomes a more prominent figure than he has been before, or is to be again in subsequent versions. There is an intensely solipsistic element in the report that he disputed for three days with a character 'most like himself' – the poet never tells us the outcome of that argument, but it presumably ends in impasse. And given the subsequent development of the poem and its argument, the bruising failure of the dreamer's attempt to gain understanding from the representatives of higher learning seems painfully close to home. Langland's own intense engagement with the vision and dissatis-faction with it is evident from its textual history: he first abandoned it unfinished, then made an abortive attempt to continue it, then, in the B version, radically rewrote it, and again in the C version rewrote and abridged it. The failure to complete the A version of the poem perhaps stems from a struggle within himself which is reflected in the poetry.

Two different subjects become entwined in this vision: firstly, the nature of Do-wel, or the good life, and its relation to salvation; secondly, the problem of knowledge or learning. The medium of the first enquiry – asking figures of authority and learning to tell him about Do-wel – thus becomes the subject of the second. Perhaps the only way to keep the issues clear is to treat them one at a time.

Do-wel and the problem of salvation

The term 'Do-wel' derives from Truth's Pardon where it sums up Truth's and Piers' belief in the honest pursuit of worldly occupations as a means to salvation. The question left unanswered at the end of the second vision was not the nature of Do-wel, which had seemed to be adequately defined by the Pardon, but its value. We might have expected the third vision to develop the challenge to the Pardon, and to the whole concept of Do-wel as a means of salvation, which was so dramatically thrown down by Piers at the end of the second dream. In fact the various speakers reaffirm the importance of doing well and the primacy of human responsibility, and attempt a series of restatements of Do-wel which shift the emphasis somewhat away from society and secular work and towards a more specifically religious activity but do not seriously engage with the ideals of prayer and penance and the eremitic submission to God which had burst through at the end of the second vision. It is only with the narrator's outburst at the end of the vision that the challenge is taken up again.

The narrator's first meeting is with two learned friars who claim that Do-wel is to be found among them. The friars' way of life is, in theory, the life of 'preyour and penaunce' which Piers had chosen at the end of the second vision; the phrase is used of friars as well as monks and hermits at B xv 415ff, and 'penaunce' is used of friars in *Pierce the Ploughmans Crede* (see p. 54). In claiming to represent Do-wel the friars would seem to be renewing the challenge to the ideals of the second vision, which had sought to identify Do-wel with the active life of productive labour for the community and had found no place for the friars. But if Langland designed the meeting to explore further the value of the life of voluntary poverty and prayer it is a possibility which he fails to develop, at least explicitly. The argument centres instead on the distinction between deadly and venial sins, with only a passing identification of Do-wel with charity:

'Synnes the sad man sevene sithes in the day.
Ac dedly synne doth he nought, for Do-wel hym helpith,

62

That is charite the champioun, chief helpe agens synne.
For he strengtheth the to stonde and sterith thi soule
That, theigh thi body bowe as bot doth in the watir,
Ay is thi soule sauf but thou thi self wilt
Folewe thi flesshis will and the fendis aftir,
And don dedly synne and drenche thiselven.
God wile suffre the to deighe so for thi self hast the maistrie.'

(A ix 39–47)

The point of this analogy with a man in a boat is perhaps less the nature of Do-wel than its function in salvation: it is not identical with perfection, as the narrator assumes, and does not save man from sinning, but it does enable him to resist the full consequences of sin, unless he chooses to damn himself. This is a more subtle and complex argument than the claims of the Pardon that doing well could dispense man from Purgatory. It insists on man's own responsibility for his fate but does not make the same absolute distinction between doing well and doing ill as the Latin lines of the Pardon. Friars had a reputation in Langland's time for devising subtle ways of evading the rigorous demands of the Church, and that is perhaps what they are doing here, redefining Do-wel as 'Do fairly well' or 'Do as well as can reasonably be expected'. But the presentation here is not evidently hostile to the friars, and the more rigorous view of salvation does seem to have been challenged by the Pardon scene. In acknowledging the inevitability of sin and offering divine indulgence of it, the friars are – perhaps unwittingly – answering to the needs of the moment. It is a theme that is developed much more forcefully at the end of the vision.

The narrator moves on, falls asleep and dreams of Thought whom he questions about Do-wel. Thought defines it in terms that sum up the earlier ideals of Holy Church and Piers:

'Whoso is mek of his mouth, mylde of his speche,
Trewe of his tunge and of his two handis,
And thorugh his labour or his lond his liflode wynneth,
Trusty of his tailende, takith but his owene,
And is nought drunkelewe ne denyous, Do-wel hym
    folewith.' (A ix 71–5)

The emphasis on truth and on productive labour takes us back to the world before the tearing of the Pardon. The difference is that Thought goes on to invent two higher terms, Do-bet and Do-best, which go beyond the earlier idealisation of the working life; Do-bet seems here to represent the more positive acts of charity to others, while Do-best is the governing role of the bishop:

'Do-bet thus doth, ac he doth muche more.
He is as lough as a lomb, lovelich of speche;
Whiles he hath ought of his owene he helpith there nede is;
The bagges and the bigerdlis, he hath broken hem alle
That the erl Averous hadde, or his eires,
And with Mammones money he hath mad hym frendis,
And is ronne to religioun, and hath rendrit the bible,
And prechith the peple Seint Poulis wordis . . .
Do-best is above hem bothe and berith a bisshopis croce;
Is hokid at that on ende to holde men in good lif . . .'.

(A ix 76–87)

The thought is not fundamentally different from that of the second vision. The charity of the rich to the poor and the work of bishops had been part of Truth's Pardon, and the teaching role of the clergy had been included in Hunger's universal work ethic. Indeed, Hunger had earlier quoted the Scriptural text to which Thought alludes here:

'And alle maner of men that thou mighte aspien,
That nedy ben or nakid, and nought han to spende,
With mete or with mone let make hem fare the betere,
Or with werk or with word the while thou art here.
Make the frendis thermid and so Matheu us techith:
Facite vobis amicos.' (A vii 208–12)

There is, however, clearly a shift of emphasis: the honest toil of the peasant is no longer the central image for the good life, and its special sanctity has been forgotten; instead, the more specifically religious work of the clergy, and the charity of the rich, which were peripheral aspects of the earlier ideal, are here raised to a higher status. Plowmen and knights may still embody truth in their lives, but truth is no longer the central term for God; the third vision instead speaks of the Deity as Kynde, God and Christ. What Thought is proposing as a higher way of life is not, however, the 'preyour and penaunce' chosen by Piers; it is an active engagement with the lives and souls of others. Langland is still trying to articulate an ethic for society, albeit a more conventionally religious one than that explored earlier.

Wit's long account which follows is, like the friars', rather more concerned with the function of Do-wel than its nature. Where Holy Church and Piers had conceived of a Creator called Truth who provided the necessities of life for men to cultivate, and established the structure of society, Wit thinks rather of a God called Kynde who made a castle of the body for the safe-keeping of the soul against the devil. Do-wel, Do-bet and Do-best are for him spiritual qualities which protect the soul, not ways of life in the world. His concern is with the spiritual aspect of the individual. The image of the castle is essentially a psychological metaphor, designed to explain the relationship between God and man, between divine grace and human responsibility: God or Kynde has made the body and placed the soul in it for protection, but it is then up to the human qualities of Do-wel and Inwit (that is, both action and intellect) to defend the soul from the devil, he suggests. Wit is particularly emphatic on the question of human responsibility:

> 'Ac iche wight in this world that hath wys undirstonding
> Is chief sovereyn over hymself his soule to yeme,
> And chevisshen hym for any charge whan he childhod passith,
> Save hymself fro synne, for so hym behovith;
> For werche he wel other wrong, the wyt is his owene.' (A x 71–5)

This emphasis on individual responsibility for one's own fate is a view complained of by Archbishop Bradwardine in Langland's own time:

> I rarely heard anything of grace said in the lectures of the philosophers . . . but every day I heard them teach that we are masters of our own free acts, and that it stands in our own power to do either good or evil, to be either virtuous or vicious.[1]

Wit seems to be taking still further the rigour of the Pardon's Latin lines in his insistence that man is on his own. All this is a far cry from the philosophy of trust in God which Piers had adopted in the moment of tearing the Pardon. Wit goes on to justify the particular ranks of society, especially the laity, and to preach the virtue of remaining in one's station:

> 'Yif thou be man maried, monk, other chanoun,
> Hold the stable and stedefast and strengthe thiselven
> To be blissid for thi beryng, ye, beggere theigh thou were!'
> (A x 113–15)

As with the friars and Thought, there seems to be an acceptance of a rather unambitious notion of the good life, very different in spirit from the second vision. If your conscience tells you to do well, he says, do not strive to do better.

Wit's wife, Study, intervenes at this point to reproach him for wasting his pearls of learning on swine, to complain of the corruption and abuse of learning in her time, and to acknowledge her own role in fostering all knowledge, including the dangerous sciences designed to delude men, but she does eventually have the kindness to send the dreamer on to Clergie and his wife Scripture for further advice. The final definition of Do-wel thus comes from Scripture, who closely echoes the social theory of Thought. She reaffirms the value of honest secular work:

'It is wel lele lif', quath she, 'among the lewide people;
Actif it is hoten; husbondis it usen,
Trewe tilieries on erthe, taillours and souteris
And alle kyne crafty men that cunne here foode wynne,
With any trewe travaille toille for here foode,
Diken or delven, Do-wel it hatte.' (A xi 182–7)

Like Thought, however, she places a higher value on the pastoral and charitable work of the clergy and the governing role of the episcopacy:

'To breke beggeris bred and bakken hem with clothis,
Counforte the carful that in castel ben fetterid,
And seken out the seke and sende hem that hem nedith,
Obedient as bretheren and sustren to othere,
This beth Do-bet; so berith witnesse the Sauter . . .
Sire Do-best hath ben in office, so is he best worthi,
Be that God in the gospel grauntith and techith:
  Qui facit et docuerit magnus vocabitur in regno celorum.
Forthi is Do-best a bisshopis pere.' (A xi 188–97)

Again like Thought, she visualises the religious life in terms of active pastoral work, supported by estates and endowments, not as the contemplative life of poverty and prayer, trusting to God to provide, which was chosen by Piers. But the much more specifically religious cast of this social theory, compared with Truth's or even Thought's, is demonstrated by the exclusion of the secular lords, the kings and knights:

'I nile not scorne', quath Scripture, 'but scryveyns lighe,
Kinghod and knighthod, for aught I can aspie,
Helpith nought to heveneward at one yeris ende.' (A xi 225–7)

This is clearly very different from the earlier argument, embodied in the plowing of the half-acre and the Pardon of Truth, that the faithful performance of the duties of knighthood earns a safe passage to Heaven.

What Langland seems to be doing in this third vision, then, is to restate his earlier social theory in a way which still emphasises the concept of doing well, of a way of life in the world which carries moral value, but degrades productive labour and other secular occupations to the level of the merely acceptable and gradually elevates the explicitly religious and ecclesiastical aspects of life. It is as if he is trying to face the problem of the excessively secular and materialistic nature of Truth's ideal without going to the extreme of rejection expressed by Piers.

The poet's own lack of conviction in this sort of answer is already evident in the way his persona moves on each time to a fresh authority without any real attempt to explain what is inadequate about the answer already given or how the different answers relate. Now, suddenly, the dreamer begins to challenge the orthodoxies with which he has been fed. First he counters Scripture's exclusion of the secular lords with a claim that faith and baptism alone are sufficient for salvation:

> '*Contra*' quath I, 'be Crist! that can I the with-sigge,
> And proven it be the pistil that Petir is nempnid:
>   *Qui crediderit et baptizatus fuerit salvus erit.* (A xi 232–4)

The point behind this, presumably, is that it denies any significance to doing well in the sense of either honest toil or the work of charity. Scripture dismisses this view, arguing that the text only applies in extreme cases to eleventh-hour baptism, and that ordinary Christians need to live a life of charity to others. Langland then continues the discussion in a long, reflective and moving passage which seems slightly detached from the dream action, resembling in its tones neither the speeches of the dreamer within the dream action nor the direct addresses of the narrator to the reader.[2] He begins with an appeal to the idea of absolute predestination, which would deny all significance to doing well:

> Yet am I nevere the ner for nought I have walkid
> To wyte what is do-wel witterly in herte,
> For howso I werche in this world, wrong other ellis,
> I was markid withoute mercy, and myn name entrid
> In the legende of lif longe er I were,
> Or ellis unwriten for wykkid as witnessith the gospel.
>
>   (A xi 258–63)

The third line here is clearly designed to challenge Wit's earlier assertion of human responsibility and the importance of Do-wel:

> For werche he wel other wrong, the wyt is his owene. (A x 75)

The narrator illustrates the point that each individual is saved or damned according to a predestined scheme, regardless of his actions, by citing Solomon and Aristotle, who did well but went to Hell, and the thief on the Cross, Mary Magdalene, King David and St Paul, who all did ill but went to Heaven:

> And arn none, forsothe, sovereynes in hevene
> As thise that wroughte wykkidly in world whanne thei were.
>
> (A xi 291–2)

Finally he returns dramatically to the ideal of the plowman, who becomes, paradoxically, an argument *against* Do-wel; he and his fellow-workers are saved, according to the narrator, not by their honest toil and righteous living, as in Truth's Pardon, but by their poverty and ignorance:

> Arn none rathere yravisshid fro the righte beleve
> Thanne arn thise kete clerkis that conne many bokis,
> Ne none sonnere ysavid, ne saddere of consience,
> Thanne pore peple, as ploughmen, and pastours of bestis.
> Souteris and seweris; suche lewide jottis
> Percen with a *paternoster* the paleis of hevene
> Withoute penaunce at here partyng, into the heighe blisse.
>
> (A xi 307–13)

.The status of this whole section is remarkably difficult to pin down. It is not at all clear how seriously these objections are meant, or what kind of voice is being used. The appeal to faith and baptism rather than works has biblical sanction, justification by faith was an important tenet of some fourteenth-century theologians,[3] and there were well-known exemplars of salvation by faith, such as the thief on the Cross; but to claim, as the narrator does, that it does not need to be authenticated by one's subsequent way of life is a familiar absurdity. His use of scholastic jargon ('*contra!*') probably helps mark the claim as one of these delusions that the merely educated labour under, given the vein of anti-intellectualism which has developed by this stage. Still more provocatively extreme is the appeal to predestination. Augustine's notion that some were predestined from the beginning of time to be saved, and that those who were not so predestined would be damned, had become a central tenet of Christian doctrine, though more central for some thinkers than others. It was a doctrine which had clearly percolated down to the less-educated classes in Langland's time (Ockham tells of ordinary people stopping him to ask his views), and received new impetus from the arguments of Bradwardine and Wyclif. But the theory had always included the proviso that God also predestined the will of the elect so that they strove to do good, or that the predestination of the elect necessarily manifested itself in good works, and no serious thinker would accept that predestination made the quality of life irrelevant. To claim that 'how so I werche in this world, wrong other ellis' he is predestined to be saved or damned is to push Augustinian theology to an untenable extreme – though an extreme which, as it happens, could be read into some of Wyclif's arguments on this issue.[4] The narrator's view is perhaps again to be seen (or came later to be seen by Langland) as a piece of false learning: in the B version these ideas are blamed on Clergie (the personification of learning) while in the C version they are blamed on Theology and the whole speech is spoken by a character called Recklessness.

The examples which the narrator produces in support of his theory of predestination in the A version are equally perverse. The claim that Solomon was believed to be in Hell is one for which I can find no contemporary evidence and is later challenged in the B version by Imaginatif (B xii 268–74). The notorious sinners who are, according to the narrator, 'sovereynes in hevene' (King David, St Paul, Mary Magdalene and the thief on the Cross) are probably the four best-known examples of sinners who were saved by their whole-hearted repentance (and in the case of the first three at least, by their subsequent good works), but the narrator makes no reference to this important qualification to his argument. Again, Augustine's paradox that the simple seize Heaven while the wise go to Hell – 'Ecce ipsi ydioti rapiunt celum ubi nos sapientes in infernum mergemur' – has in its original context a degree of sense to it (it comes from the *Confessions* where Augustine describes his own attempts to escape from the trammels of pagan classical learning to the simple faith of Christianity), but the narrator's paraphrase takes it to an extreme form, suggesting that a mere *paternoster* carries the simple directly to Heaven.

On the surface, then, the narrator's objections to Scripture's emphasis on salvation through living a good life seem to be gross examples of misapplied knowledge. Yet possibly beneath them lurks something serious and important, a genuine yearning for a theology which places less reliance on doing well and knowing much, and more on God, grace and simplicity. The foolish narrator or dreamer is perhaps a stalking-horse for ideas, or at least feelings, of deep importance to the poet which he will develop later more seriously: the belief in the saving powers of faith is to recur with the later figure of Abraham, while the emphasis on divine rather than human will recurs with the Good Samaritan in B xvi. The return to the powerfully symbolic figure of the plowman under a different aspect is surely significant here. The plowman of the second vision had served Truth through secular work, but this one comes to him through prayer, 'a *paternoster*'. Where the earlier one had known Truth 'kyndely', through 'kynde wit' and conscience, this one's intuitive understanding is associated with the help of the Holy Ghost and grace, mentioned in Christ's words which are quoted a few lines earlier:

'Whanne ye ben aposid of princes or of prestis of the lawe,
For to answere hem have ye no doute,
For I shal graunte yow grace of God that ye serven,
The help of the holy gost to answere hem alle.' (A xi 298–301)

The plowman who in the second vision had come to stand as an image of man's productive labour which wins him Heaven now reappears to prove the irrelevance of striving, for 'such lewid jottes/percen with a *paternoster* the paleis of hevene/withoute penance at here partyng'. It is the simplicity and humility which Langland now invokes, not the honest toil which has faded away in the accumulation of definitions of Dowel, but the potency of the symbol remains. The divide which had opened up between plowman and hermit at the tearing of the Pardon now begins to close. As in the second vision, the restatements of social theory accumulate detail to a point of complexity where something in Langland rebels violently against them, in favour of something simpler and purer – like faith, or the divine will, or a mere *paternoster*.

The problem of knowledge

These dramatic lines on the plowmen are also the climax of a different though perhaps related argument which has been developing in the course of the third vision, on the function of learning and the intellect and the part they play in human salvation. This was an issue of some importance in Langland's time and it would perhaps be useful to pause here to consider the background to the argument.

The dilemma which he confronts goes back at least as far as St Augustine, who felt the need for Christianity to repudiate the pagan philosophers while at the same time drawing heavily himself on their traditions in thought and science. It was, however, particularly a problem of the later Middle Ages. From the twelfth century onwards there was a widening split between the *clerk* as man of learning and the *clerk* as cleric or man of religion.[5] The revival of knowledge of Aristotle and the development of scholasticism and the universities were part of a growing emphasis on the importance of knowledge for the Church's work, which drew in friars and often monks as well as secular clerics. It also had its effect on pastoral work, where the need for the laity to know certain things in order to be saved was increasingly stressed. A characteristic example is the widely circulated text of the mid-fourteenth century known as *The Lay Folks' Catechism* or (in a slightly different version) *John Gaytrygge's Sermon*,[6] which begins by explaining that the direct knowledge of God which men lost with the Fall has now to be replaced by the knowledge acquired from teaching and study, and then lists the essentials for men to know: the fourteen points of truth, the Ten Commandments, the seven sacraments, the seven works of mercy, the seven virtues, and the seven deadly sins. From the beginning there was hostility to this sophistication of religion, from those who preferred to emphasise the importance of faith and the enlightenment provided by the Holy Spirit. It was particularly hermits and mystics who expressed this view. Richard Rolle, the early-fourteenth-century Yorkshire hermit and mystic, fled from the university of Oxford because of its worldliness, and later defended his right to speak with authority despite his lack of learning because, he said, 'lovers of eternity are taught by an internal teacher, so that they may speak more eloquently than those who are taught by men'.[7] A similar point is made by an anonymous fourteenth-century mystic living on one of the Farne islands:

> Let the meek hear and rejoice, that there is a certain knowledge of holy scripture which is learnt from the Holy Ghost and manifested in good works, which often the layman knows and the clerk does not, the fisherman knows and not the rhetorician, the old woman has learnt and not the doctors of theology.[8]

As the word 'fisherman' hints, the apostles were often thought of as evidence for this anti-intellectual view. A Wyclifite text called *The Lanterne of Li3t* asserts in caustic vein 'the apostles of Crist and other seintis weren not graduat men in scolis but the Holi Goost sodenli enspirid hem'.[9] The idea is taken rather further (and less convincingly) by the Wyclifite adaptation of the *Ancrene Riwle* known as *The Recluse*:

> Where lerned Peter and Poule divinite, Jerome and Ambrose and Gregori? Of whom lerned thise men? Whether comen hi to her wytt thorough the holy gost, oither thorough stody of gret clergie?[10]

(The answer implied, presumably, is 'through the Holy Ghost'.)

In Langland's time anti-intellectual arguments often invoked the figure of the simple honest peasant whose ignorant faith is safer than the learning of the clerk or philosopher. Thus Gower in the Prologue to the *Confessio Amantis* (c. 1390):

> It were betre dike and delve
> And stande upon the ryhte feith,
> Than knowe al that the bible seith
> And erre as somme clerkes do.[11]

A similar sentiment appears in Thomas à Kempis's *Imitation of Christ*:

> Certeinly the meke ploweman that servith God is much bettere
> then the proude philosopher that, takyng noon hede of his owne
> lyvyng, considreth the course of heven.[12]

The closest parallel to Langland's phrasing is a Wyclifite aphorism,
though this is anticlerical rather than anti-intellectual in form:

> A simple paternoster of a ploughman that is in charite is betre
> than a thousand massis of covetous prelates and veyn religious.[13]

The Augustinian saying with which Langland closes the A version also
appears in *The Recluse*:

> Seint Austin seith that we clerkes lerne for to go to the pyne of
> helle and lewed folk lerne to go to the joye of hevene.[14]

In *Piers* the first two visions had been in general dismissive of the
clergy and emphasised the sufficiency of 'kind wit'. Holy Church was
necessary as a guide for the dreamer, but what she teaches him is, she
insists, merely the fundamentals of belief which he had absorbed in his
infancy. The one intervention by Theology, on behalf of Mede, is eventually discredited, and at the end of the second vision the priest's education is apparently contrasted unfavourably with the simple plowman's
wisdom. The action of the third vision testifies to a renewed concern
with the role of knowledge and study, as the dreamer questions in turn
the two learned friars, Thought, Wit, Study, Clergie (in the sense of *clergie* or learning) and Scripture, and the issue comes to the forefront in
the dialogue with Study. At first there seems to be a revival of confidence in learning. The definitions of Do-wel offered by these
authorities are practical and straightforward, not at all obviously examples of the abuse of knowledge. Whatever Langland may say of the
friars elsewhere, the two whom he meets here offer homely and sen-
sible arguments, refusing to take the opportunity offered them of
urging the pursuit of an impossible perfection. If there is any
anti-intellectual feeling at this stage, it is directed, oddly, at the
pseudo-intellectualism of the narrator, otherwise a simple man, in his
reply to the friars:

> '*Contra*', quath I as a clerk, and comside to dispute. (A ix 16)

His reply does seem to show the excesses of scholastic logic, though it
is far from clear how the narrator has come to be the representative of

scholasticism. In the persons of the friars, Thought, Wit and Scripture, learning seems to be working on behalf of a normative, acceptable (if rather mundane) social ethic which does give a high place to the clergy but does not especially emphasise the importance of knowledge. Their names point to Langland's concern with that issue but it plays little part in what they say. It does, however, play a central part in the speech of Study.

She begins with a strangely unwarranted attack on her husband Wit for casting intellectual pearls before swine in his explanations to the dreamer (his offerings had in fact been rather ordinary). Her complaints of the neglect of true learning gradually turn into a critique of the learned in contrast to the humble:

'God is muche in the gorge of this grete maistris,
Ac among mene men hise mercy and his werkis . . .
Clerkis and kete men carpen of God faste,
And han hym muchel in here mouth, ac mene men in herte.'

(A xi 53–7)

We seem to be returning here to the ideas of a 'kynde knowyng' of God springing from the heart which had been voiced earlier by Holy Church. Study goes on to direct her critique against learning itself. She admits responsibility for the dangerous sciences of astronomy, geometry, alchemy and sorcery, and contrasts them with the simple knowledge of Christ:

'Alle thise sciences, sikir, I myself
Foundit hem formest folk to desceyve.
I bekenne the Crist', quath she, 'I can teche the no betere.'

(A xi 163–5)

The best that can be said for theology, she says, is that it places love as the highest quality:

'It is no science forsothe for to sotile thereinne.
Ne were the love that lith therein a wel lewid thing it were.
Ac for it lat best be love I love it the betere.' (A xi 140–2)

But this – the priority of love – is precisely the kind of knowledge which least needs theology since, as Holy Church had explained earlier, it comes from the heart. Despite her name, Study has begun to voice an anti-intellectual position.

The dreamer then passes on to Clergie and hears Scripture's definition of Do-wel, and in his challenge to her the attack on intellectualism

resumes. His own role as pseudo-intellectual reappears in his first in-
terruption, with its '*contra*' and its Latin quotation. The appeal to predestination which soon follows from him may have been thought of by
Langland as a reflection of the same characteristic, as we have seen. But
then the dreamer or narrator takes up a strongly anti-intellectualist line
of his own. His comment that Solomon and Aristotle are both in Hell
is offered as proof of a predestination that takes no account of good
works, but it is impossible not to recognise that these two figures are the
greatest men of learning in the biblical and classical traditions respectively. There is a veiled implication that their learning has done nothing to save them, may indeed have condemned them. The point
becomes explicit in the narrator's final outburst:

> And yet have I forgete ferther of fyve wyttis teching
> That clergie of Cristis mouth comendite was it nevere
> For he seide it hymself to summe of his disciplis:
> *Dum steteritis ante reges et presides nolite cogitare,*
> And is as muche to mene, to men that ben lewid,
> 'Whanne ye ben aposid of princes or of prestis of the lawe
> For to answere hem have ye no doute,
> For I shal graunte yow grace of God that ye serven,
> The help of the holy gost to answere hem alle.'
> The doughtiest doctour or dyvynour of the trinite,
> That was Austyn the olde, and higheste of the foure,
> Seide this for a sarmoun, so me God helpe:
> *Ecce ipsi ydiote rapiunt celum ubi nos sapientes in infernum mergemur.*
> And is to mene in oure mouth, more ne lesse,
> Arn none rathere yravisshid fro the righte beleve
> Thanne arn thise kete clerkis that conne many bokis. . . .
>
> (A xi 293–309)

As we have already seen, the tone and status of this passage are difficult to decide; it is not even clear whether it is the poet's climactic
conclusion to his poem or a foolish intervention by the dreamer which
Langland had intended Scripture to counter, before he despairingly
abandoned the poem. The lack of clarity may well spring from his own
uncertainty as to how seriously he meant it. Casting the dreamer as an
intellectual, with his learned tags, and then allowing him to voice an attack on intellectuals suggests a deep-seated uncertainty of voice and
perhaps even identity (the sort of uncertainty which might well afflict
a poet of educated background seeking to speak for the common man).
But Langland's later revision of this section, and his creation of a further vision in which the attack on learning is much more explicitly conducted (B xiii), shows that the anti-intellectualism was a serious and

significant issue for him. In taking the plowman as representative of the simple ignorance that is saved when the intellectuals are damned, Langland was following a line pursued by the mystics and Wyclifites, as we have seen. He seems to be suggesting, however, not just the advantages of simple faith but also, like some of the mystics, a kind of understanding or knowledge which the man of learning does not possess but the simple plowman does. In the second vision this seems to be associated with the honesty of his labour and the austerity of his life, which bring Piers his knowledge of Truth; hence the line 'Abstinence the abbess myn a.b.c. me taught'. But what Langland is beginning to suggest at the end of the third vision is that this understanding is inspired by the Holy Spirit – an understanding, therefore, which can be shared by the hermit and the mystic.

The anti-intellectualism floats beneath the surface of the argument in the A version and is not easily connected with the question of Do-wel. It may indeed have had a sharply autobiographical point: as a clerk himself, Langland may well have seen the world of learning and study as his own proper form of Do-wel, though one that he resisted. But, judging from later developments, there seems also to have been a sense that the pursuit of higher knowledge was a deplorable sophistication of the original purity of the knowledge of Truth, just as the contemporary social world of merchants, lawyers and friars had complicated and therefore adulterated the simple hierarchy of the first created world. He was seeking to return to those qualities of simplicity and austerity which he had earlier associated with the plowman, while linking them with the more spiritual qualities associated with prayer and divine inspiration. The plowman is saved, but perhaps by his prayer rather than his work; he knows Truth, but perhaps by the light of the Holy Spirit rather than the knowledge that comes from human nature or experience.

Quite where the A version of the poem ended is far from clear. Of the twelve manuscripts of the A text which reach this point, four end with passus xi and the dramatic lines on piercing Heaven with a *paternoster*; five others go on from this point with material from the C version, presumably added by scribes faced with an A version which finished there; and three have, in part at least, a passus xii of which nothing appears in later versions. Passus xi ends with the third dream still apparently uncompleted,[15] but the fact that nine of the manuscripts have nothing of the A text after that point suggests that Langland did allow the poem to circulate in that form, and the fact that the continuation of the B version starts from the end of A xi suggests that Langland did think of that as the point where the A version came to an end, even though it was not completed. It was not uncommon for medieval poems to circulate in an unfinished state (one need only think of *The*

Romance of the Rose, Chaucer's *House of Fame* and both the *Canterbury Tales* as a whole and some constituent tales such as the Squire's, the Monk's and the tale of Sir Thopas), and that may have already happened with the Z version of *Piers Plowman*.

This does not mean that passus xii should be dismissed from consideration. It tells how Clergie and Scripture refuse to teach the dreamer any more of the hidden mysteries of religion, and send him on to meet Kynde Wit, in the company of a *clergeon* or schoolboy called *Omnia probate*, 'try all things', but the dreamer is then struck by a fever and dies. It ends with lines in which one John But claims responsibility for completing the poem after Langland's death:

> And so bad Johan But busily wel ofte
> When he saw thes sawes busyly alegged
> By James and by Jerom, by Jop and by othere,
> And for he medleth of makyng he made this ende. (A xii 106–9)

Yet he does not say that he wrote the whole of the final passus, and much of it has the authentic ring of Langland. It may be that, having left the poem incomplete and allowed it to circulate in that form, Langland subsequently attempted a continuation and then abandoned it again.[16] If passus xii is in part Langland's, it has some interesting indications of the direction of his thinking on the issue of learning and anti-intellectualism. What is being sketched is a journey through life acquiring experience and ending with the Kynde Wit who had guided Piers to Truth and who possibly represents the knowledge that comes from experience rather than from study.

Notes and references

1. Quoted by G. Leff, *Medieval Thought* (London, 1959), p. 297.
2. Skeat punctuates this as a further speech by the dreamer within the dream, to which no reply is given. Kane and Knott/Fowler punctuate it as a discourse by the narrator to the reader.
3. Cf. H. A. Oberman, 'Fourteenth-century religious thought: a premature profile', *Speculum* **53** (1978), 80–93, especially p. 87, citing Bradwardine.
4. G. Leff, 'John Wyclif: the path to dissent', *Proceedings of the British Academy*, **52** (1966), 159.
5. See A. R. Murray, *Reason and Society in the Middle Ages* (Oxford, 1978). On anti-intellectualism in the fourteenth century especially, see G. Pantin, *The English Church in the Fourteenth Century* (Cambridge, 1955), pp. 132–5.
6. *The Lay Folks' Catechism*, eds T. F. Simmons and H. E. Nolloth (Early English Text Society OS 118, London, 1901); *John Gaytrygge's Sermon* is in *Middle English Religious Prose*, ed. N. F. Blake (London, 1972).
7. Quoted in Pantin, *The English Church*, p. 251.

8. Quoted in Pantin, *The English Church*, p. 252.
9. *The Lanterne of Li3t*, ed. L.M. Swinburn (Early English Text Society OS 151, London, 1915), p. 5. Quoted E. Colledge, 'A Lollard interpolated version of the *Ancren Riwle*', *Review of English Studies*, **15** (1939), 131.
10. *The Recluse*, ed. J. Pahlsson (Lund, 1911), p. 98.
11. *Confessio Amantis (The English Works of John Gower*, ed. G. Macaulay (Early English Text Society OS 81, London, 1900)), Prologue, ll. 346ff.
12. From a Middle English version in *The Earliest English Translations of the De Imitatione Christ*, ed. J. K. Ingram (Early English Text Society ES 64, London, 1893), p. 5.
13. *The English Works of Wyclif hitherto unprinted*, ed. F. Matthew (Early English Text Society OS 74, London, 1880), p. 274.
14. Pahlsson, *The Recluse*, p. 97.
15. It is possible that the dream is supposed to end with Scripture's speech, leaving the final part to be spoken by the narrator outside the dream, as Knott and Fowler have argued (*The A-Text*, p. 169), but if so Langland left the text with no clear signal of the dream's end; in the B version he treats this final part as a speech by the dreamer within the dream.
16. See Kane, *The A-Version* pp. 51–2 and Anne Middleton, 'Making a good end: John But as a reader of *Piers Plowman*', in *Medieval English Studies presented to George Kane*, eds E. D. Kennedy, R. Waldron and J. S. Wittig (Wolfeboro and Woodbridge, 1988), pp. 243–63.

Chapter Five

Rewriting the poem: the revision of the A version and completion of the third vision (B xi–xii)

It was probably around 1380 that Langland completed a new version of the poem, the B text, embodying a substantial revision of the A text and a long continuation. The Prologue and passus i–xi of the A version become Prologue and passus i–x of the B version, and the continuation forms passus xi–xx. A new passage in the Prologue (ll. 112–208) referring to the problems of a realm where a boy is king presumably alludes to the situation in England after the death of Edward III's son and heir, the Black Prince, in 1376 and of Edward himself in the following year, leaving the throne to the nine-year-old Richard II. There are also passing references, at B xiii 173ff and xix 422–51, to the pope's involvement in conflict and warfare, which may indicate a date after 1378 when two rival popes emerged; there is no mention of any subsequent events.

Something of the process of revision is suggested by a passing comment made by Study in B x, near the end of the revised portion:

'Swiche motyves they meve, thise maistres in hir glorie,
And maken men in mysbileve that muse muche on hire wordes.
Ymaginatif herafterward shal answere to youre purpos.'

(B x 115–17)

Imaginatif is a character who enters the poem in the first passus of the continuation, B xi, where he does indeed attempt to deal with the dreamer's questions and complaints about the abuse of learning. Study's forward reference to him suggests that when Langland revised the existing section of the poem he had already begun the continuation. It may be that B xi and xii originated in another attempt by Langland to complete the A version, following the abortive effort which produced A xii, before he undertook the major revision of the A version and the long continuation. But since it is impossible now to uncover the no doubt complex processes of Langland's revision, which may have been carried out in several stages, I shall turn for convenience first to his revision of the A version.

The main structure of the three visions of the A version remains, together with much of the detail, but there are a number of substantial additions and substitutions, as well as some significant changes in details of argument. Some of the changes in the Visio are clearly a matter of filling gaps; thus for reasons which are now unclear, both of the lists of the deadly sins which appear in the A version, one in the story of Mede and the other in the confessions scene, lack a reference to Wrath, and Langland now adds it (B ii 83, v 134–87). But elsewhere we can watch the poet pondering his earlier work, shifting the emphasis where his thinking has changed, developing topics further, and overlaying his first account with further levels of drama and argument. One of the most striking qualities of Langland's poetic processes is his determination to preserve the essence of his original visions and formulations, while freely reinterpreting what they stand for.

Two main aspects of the revision are evident. Firstly, the critique of contemporary society is extended to focus more sharply on kingship and the Church. Secondly, there is a shift of emphasis in the discussion of salvation: there is less concern with an ethic of individual effort and human responsibility, and with the needs of society, and a new stress on the idea of trusting in divine indulgence for fallible humanity. Both can be seen as developing out of the two climactic moments of the A version, the end of the second vision and the end of the third. Both can also be seen to lead on to the major concerns of the continuation in the B version.

The revision of the first two visions

The most substantial addition to the Visio section in the B version is the discussion of kingship in the Prologue. The narrative line of the first vision in the A version had been very clear: the Prologue had presented all the occupations of ordinary society – plowmen, anchorites, merchants, minstrels, pardoners, priests, tradesmen, artisans; passus i and ii presented the universals by which society might be influenced and judged – Truth, Wrong, Holy Church, Mede, the deadly sins; and passus iii introduced the controlling figures which determined choices – the king, conscience, reason. In the B version, Langland introduces the idea of kingship and the king's power into the field full of folk and in the process forces the field to signify at three levels instead of one: social types, allegorical personifications and animal fable. It is a particularly fine example of the way in which Langland's rewriting simultaneously disrupts the original clarity of argument and creates the characteristic richness of his poetry. Though the king's power is not yet seen operating, its presence and its potential are strongly emphasised, to complete the picture of society. In the process, the king and kingship become part of the problem of contemporary society, and implicated in its decay, rather than part of the solution.

The opening lines of the passage present a brief allegory of the origins of kingship:

Thanne kam ther a Kyng: Knyghthod hym ladde;
Might of the communes made hym to regne.
And thanne cam Kynde Wit and clerkes he made,
For to counseillen the Kyng and the Commune save.
The Kyng and Knyghthod and Clergie bothe
Casten that the Commune sholde hem communes fynde.
The Commune contreved of Kynde Wit craftes,
And for profit of all the peple plowmen ordeyned
To tilie and to travaile as trewe lif asketh. (B Prol. 112–20)

This develops a concern, already present in the A version, with the original ordering of society in its natural or God-created state. If knighthood had begun with the orders of angels, and the work of the plowman had been part of the Creator's original dispensation, kings and clerks too had been in at the beginning, or nearly so. All three estates have their place in society, and a role in creating a king to rule them. The simple logic of the original dispensation contrasts with the complexity and disorder of contemporary society as it is described in the first vision.

This complexity is immediately taken up. The lines which follow are in part a symbolic re-enactment of the coronation of Richard II, which took place probably a few years before this passage was written. As the king processes through the field, the observers proclaim their expectations of the new monarch. A lunatic urges the king to rule well, the angel asks that mercy should temper justice, the *goliardeys* (vagabond clerk) emphasises the need for a king to keep the laws, while the commons proclaim their monarchist sentiments, that the word of the king has the force of law to them. Langland captures well the drama and conflict of the differing expectations of the new reign, as well as the varying theories of the fundamental nature of kingship.[1] Yet the sentiments are perhaps not as incompatible as they are made to appear on the surface: an energetic and active king insisting on the rule of law while exercising appropriate mercy and discretion was the essential safeguard for the common people against the encroachments of lesser powers – barons, Church, merchants and others. Such popular reliance on the monarch for support against the great lords and landowners found a tragic outcome in the peasant rebels' acceptance of Richard II as their leader in 1381 and his subsequent betrayal of them. Despite the nature of the speakers and the sense of conflict, the sentiments are compatible and need not be read ironically; they are complementary views of the role of the king, all insisting on its power and importance. (In the C version Langland clarifies the point for those who may have missed it by giving the lunatic's words to Kind Wit.) There is perhaps a topical and wry joke here, that in the circumstances of Richard II's coronation (he was nine at the time) it would take an angel or a lunatic or a learned pedant to assert the importance of the king's power.

The mock-coronation scene is then abruptly interrupted by an invasion of rats and mice. What emerges is another approach to the nature of kingship, expressed through animal fable, though it is characteristic of Langland's art to present it as another event on the field, working at the same level as the commons and the king. The rats seek to limit the powers of the cat from the court by attaching a bell to him, encouraged by a plausible spokesman, a rat 'most renable of tongue', but they lack the courage and fail, and are rebuked by the mouse 'that moche goode kouthe as me thought', who argues that a strong cat is needed to protect the citizens from the rats. The idea of strong and weak kingship is then developed in the references to the cat being a kitten and the king being a boy. Interpretation of the scene has been bedevilled by the coincidence that the fable was also used by Bishop Brinton in an address to the so-called Good Parliament of 1376 when it was seeking to limit the powers of the Crown. Langland's version presents a situation in which belling the cat would give power to the kitten, and this does not make sense in the context of 1376 when Edward III was still alive, even after the death of the Black Prince during the parliamentary session left the boy Richard as heir to the throne (limiting Edward's powers would not have transferred authority to the eight-year-old Richard). The story seems rather to apply to the situation a few years later, after the death of Edward, when the business of government was in the hands of the young king's uncles, particularly John of Gaunt.[2] These latter may in some respects be oppressive, the fable suggests, but to deprive them of their power (that is, to bell the cat) is to leave the country in the hands of the kitten, that is, the boy-king Richard. The strong government of the king's uncles, rather than the weak reign of a boy, is needed to protect the community from the depredations of the rats (the barons, presumably). Langland's perspective is very different from that of the Good Parliament, and indeed from the modern viewpoint which would call that Parliament good because it sought to limit the powers of the king. As in the coronation scene, and in the Visio generally, it is weak kingship which is the threat to the community, allowing Meed to flourish through the corruption of justice and wastrels to disrupt the work of the plowman. The authoritative voice is that of the humble mouse, accepting the need for the cat in all its power.

The concern of this whole passage is with the different aspects and views of kingship: the theory of its origins, the expectations of the coronation, the realities of power relationships in the England of 1380. In underlining the gap between the ideal and the reality of Richard's early years Langland is perhaps reflecting a growing sense of the limitations of a genuine secular authority and the need for something more like a Messiah figure. This is a note that creeps into the revision of the third vision, in a famous passage later seen as a prophecy of the Reformation but probably alluding to the second coming of Christ:

'Ac ther shal come a kyng and confesse yow religiouses,
And bete yow, as the Bible telleth, for brekynge of youre rule,
And amende monyals, monkes and chanons . . .
And thanne shal the Abbot of Abyngdon and al his issue for
  evere
Have a knok of a kyng, and incurable the wounde.' (B x 314–26)

The king is also one of the first additions that Langland makes to the second vision. In the A version the dreamer falls asleep for a second time and dreams again of the field full of folk where he had started. The two visions are in a sense complementary or parallel rather than consecutive, perhaps reflecting their origins as two distinct poetic experiences, almost two distinct poems. In the B version Langland revises this passage to make the action consecutive: Reason appears on the field, but to preach to the whole realm and in the presence of the king, reflecting the development of the field into a symbol of the kingdom, where in the A version it had been an area removed from king and court. But an increasing concern with the role of the king is clearly a factor too, for Langland also adds a brief couplet on the duties of the king to the sermon of Reason:

And sithen he counseiled the Kyng his commune to lovye:
'It is thi tresor, if treson ne were, and tryacle at thy nede.'

(B v 48–9)

Langland also adds to Reason's sermon a few lines of warning to the pope, and this reflects the other major aspect of his social criticism in the B version, the emphasis on the failings of the clergy. In the confession scene in the A version the representative sinners had all been laymen, but in the B version Langland extends the attack to the Church. The new figure Wrath speaks at length about his involvement with friars, nuns and monks (B v 135–79), while Sloth now tells of his thirty years as a priest (B v 416–22). A little later Langland adds the delightful brief vignette of the pardoner and prostitute who abandon the pilgrimage to Truth, doubtful of their chances of mercy:

> 'Bi Seint Poul!' quod a pardoner, 'paraventure I be noght
>   knowe there;.
> I wol go fecche my box with my brevettes and a bulle with
>   bisshopes lettres.'
> 'By Crist!' quod a commune womman, 'thi compaignie wol I
>   folwe.
> Thow shalt seye I am thi suster.' I ne woot where thei bicome.
>   (B v 639–42)

The pardoner thus joins those other men of religion whose concern with the forms of religion contrasts with the genuine knowledge of Truth shown by Piers: the palmer, the clerks who know books and the priest. There is a sharp irony in the notion of it being a pardoner, the professional peddler of pardon, who feels least confident of a welcome from Mercy.

What seems to lie behind these changes is a conviction that those who might have been seen as providing a solution to the corruption of society, kings and clerics, are themselves thoroughly implicated in the corruption. A sense of growing despair in Langland about the possibility of reforming contemporary society is perhaps evident in a substantial addition to Conscience's quarrel with Mede in passus iii (B iii 301–53). In the Z and A versions the new society which Reason had described still contained the main features of the fourteenth-century community; lawyers were to become labourers but others were to continue, though in purer form. Now, however, Conscience proposes a society much more radically different from the present world, one in which war will be no more and all swords will be beaten into plowshares. The earlier notion of knighthood as an institution going back to the angels now seems to be under challenge. Behind the revision one can recognise Scripture's claim, in the third vision in the A version, that neither knighthood nor kingship contributes anything to salvation.

This element of doubt about society and social duty is reflected in some further changes in the second vision. Hunger's confident assertion of the duty for all men to work, whether teaching or tilling, had been one of the more provocative and forthright expressions of the A version's emphasis on an ideal of social and co-operative labour. In the B version Langland changes this passage so as to acknowledge a place for the contemplative life of prayer, which had been adopted by Piers after the Pardon scene and was to play an important part in the story of Haukyn and Patience in B xiii and xiv:

'Kynde Wit wolde that ech a wight wroghte,
Or in dikynge or in deluynge or travaillynge in preieres –
Contemplatif lif or Actif lif, Crist wolde men wroghte.'

(B vi 247–9)[3]

Associated with this change is the addition of a brief passage on begging, at B vii 71–88, where the poet (or Truth?) urges that men should give alms to beggars without seeking to examine their individual worthiness. The non-working poor came increasingly to occupy Langland's mind as his poem developed, both because of the problems of distinguishing between genuine hermits dedicated to poverty through religious conviction and the indolent who merely claim a religious status, and, more particularly, because of the wedge they threatened to drive between a social ethic based on merit and reward and a religious ethic based on mercy and divine grace. The C version in particular shows an almost obsessive concern with the problem, and at that stage Langland was to add two further, quite lengthy, passages on this question to the Pardon (see p. 188). The brief passage added to the Pardon in the B version shows him already seeking to soften the Pardon's rigorous requirements and allow room for God in his mercy to judge men's hearts, a theme which recurs at the end of the revised third vision and again in the continuation.

This reflects in turn on the other major aspect of revision, the treatment of salvation. A variety of changes and additions show Langland's growing concern to represent the power of mercy alongside the stress on justice, and to explore the problems of their relationship, while drawing away from his earlier emphasis on human effort within society. Thus the Visio in the A version is strikingly devoid of references to Christ; its God is the Creator rather than the Redeemer. The one substantial reference to Christ and mercy in the A text was, significantly, an addition which Langland made at that stage to the Z text (see p. 57). But in B i Langland writes an extraordinarily moving passage about the Incarnation as an expression of God's love:

'For Truthe telleth that love is triacle of hevene:
May no synne be on hym seene that that spice useth.
And alle his werkes he wroughte with love as hym liste,

And lered it Moyses for the leveste thyng and moost lik to
　hevene,
And also the plante of pees, moost precious of vertues:
For hevene myghte nat holden it, so was it hevy of hymself,
Til it hadde of the erthe eten his fille.
And whan it hadde of this fold flessh and blood taken,
Was nevere leef upon lynde lighter therafter,
And portatif and persaunt as the point of a nedle,
That myghte noon armure it lette ne none heighe walles.'

(B i 148–58).

At the end of the confession of the sins, Repentance takes up the theme
with a similarly moving account of Christ's life and death, as part of a
plea for forgiveness (B v 478–506). One might note too the fuller part
played by Repentance in the dialogue with the sinners, and the introduction of the character Hope. The almost Old Testament emphasis
of the Visio on justice is being alleviated by a growing appreciation of
mercy. It finds its fulfilment in the great scenes of Christ's life and
Redemption of mankind in B xvi–xviii.

The revision of the third vision

The patterns of rethinking and revision evident in the first two dreams
are evident too in Langland's rewriting of the third vision. The attack
on the Church is renewed, with a new speech by Clergie complaining
of the inadequacy of priests and the corruption of monasticism (B x
271–327). Wit's powerful argument that every man has complete
responsibility for his own salvation (A x 71–5, 87–8), a view subsequently
countered by the narrator, is now dropped, along with his argument for
remaining in one's station in society, whether layman, monk or canon
(A x 109ff), and replaced by a shorter and rather digressive passage on
charity to the poor. Scripture's speech defining Do-wel as the active
life of manual labour followed by the laity, Do-bet as the life of the clergy and Do-best as the life of the bishops also disappears now. It is
replaced by a definition of Do-wel by Clergie, who speaks not of the
three levels of society but of three levels of religious behaviour; Do-wel
is to believe the basic teachings of the Church, Do-bet is to practise
them and Do-best is to rebuke others (B x 238–335). 'Doing' here has
become a much more specifically religious and moral activity than in
the earlier version. There is also an emphasis on the importance of
knowledge and teaching: where Scripture had thought of the clergy as
charity workers, Clergie naturally thinks of their role in teaching and
rebuking.

The most significant changes are those made to the final, confusing speech of the dreamer in A xi, which is remodelled in the B version both to concentrate its attack on the clergy as representatives of learning and to develop the idea of mercy and divine indulgence. The appeal to a theory of strict predestination is in the A version a blunt assertion by the dreamer, in terms calculated to make it unacceptable to the reader though the tone and stance of the speaker are difficult to define. Langland now makes the status of this doctrine clear; it is not a piece of blunt radicalism but the kind of idea that abstruse theology goes in for:

'This is a longe lesson,' quod I, 'and litel am I the wiser!
Where Dowel is or Dobet derkliche ye [Scripture] shewen.
Manye tales ye tellen that Theologie lerneth,
And that I man maad was, and my name yentred
In the legende of lif longe er I were,
Or ellis unwritten for som wikkednesse, as Holy Writ
    witnesseth.' (B x 369–74)

The phrasing now makes the doctrine a little more plausible, with the suggestion that predestination bears some relation to the quality of life ('for som wikkednesse'), but the point that primarily emerges is that the learned teach theories of salvation which render the pursuit of Do–Wel irrelevant; there is perhaps already a hint that their doing so reflects their own lack of concern with the quality of their lives. The conflict between learning and the quality of life is underlined in the story of the Ark which Langland adds a few lines later (B x 396–410): the knowledge-able builders of the vessel were drowned, while 'the blissid' Noah and his family were saved. The conflict becomes crucial too in the radical revision of the dreamer's comments on Aristotle, Solomon, David, the thief on the Cross, Mary Magdalene and St Paul. In the A version these had all functioned as rather perverse examples of arbitrary predestina-tion, the first two as men who did well but nevertheless went to Hell and the other four as those who did evil but went to Heaven. In the B version, Aristotle and Solomon become examples of men of learning who taught well but failed to live well and therefore were damned; they provide a lesson for the learned clergy of the present Church:

. . . As Salamon dide and swiche othere, that shewed grete wittes,
Ac hir werkes, as Holy Writ seith, was evere the contrarie.

(B x 392–3)

With the others, there are now references to the thief's repentance and simple faith (l. 413) and to God's awareness of the inner thoughts of men (ll. 428–32). The argument culminates naturally in an appeal to God's mercy, since no man is good:

> And he that may al amende, have mercy on us alle!
> For sothest word that ever God seide was tho he seide *Nemo bonus*. (B x 437–8)

This theme is taken up in the revision of the closing lines of the A version. There the dreamer or narrator had invoked Augustine's authority against the men of learning and proclaimed the superiority of the simple plowmen and other workers, who enter Paradise forthwith through their simplicity. That attack on the learned and the dangers of learning remains in the B version, but in describing the simple workers who are saved Langland emphasises now that their lives were imperfect and it was their pure faith that saved them:

> Arn none rather yravysshed from the righte bileve
> Than are thise konnynge clerkes that konne manye bokes,
> Ne none sonner saved, ne sadder of bileve
> Than plowmen and pastours and povere commune laborers,
> Souteres and shepherdes – swiche lewed juttes
> Percen with a Paternoster the paleys of hevene
> And passen purgatorie penauncelees at hir hennes partyng
> Into the blisse of paradis for hir pure bileve,
> That inparfitly here knewe and ek lyvede. (B x 454–62)

They now achieve a quality somewhat like that proclaimed by Piers *after* the tearing of the Pardon, when he takes his stand on submission to God rather than the quality of his work. The poet rests on an appeal to God's mercy which can save men for their simple faith and humility. The sense one had had with the A version, that the arguments against a scheme of merit and justice, however outrageously expressed, concealed a genuine concern on Langland's part, now prove justified.

The completion of the third vision

The issues evident in Langland's rewriting of the third vision – the role of the clergy, the problem of knowledge and the keys to salvation – come to the foreground in the two new passus with which Langland completed the third vision, B xi and xii. Scripture mocks the dreamer, who falls into an inner dream. He is led astray by Fortune and follows her for many years until old age and poverty overtake him. He argues with a friar, discusses the ethics of criticising others with Lewte (Justice), and renews the theological discussion with Scripture until the Emperor

Trajan interrupts with an account of his own salvation.[4] A long discussion of poverty and the problem of unlearned priests ensues. The dreamer is shown a vision of the wonders of the world by Kynde and argues with Reason about it until he awakes from the inner dream. He is then approached by Imaginatif, who rebukes the dreamer for criticising Reason and for wasting time with poetry, and attempts to resolve the problems of salvation and knowledge for him. The dreamer then wakes, at the end of the third vision.

The beginning of passus xi was an important moment for Langland, the successful crossing of a barrier which had frustrated him probably twice before. Surprisingly, he begins not by ending the dream but by creating an inner dream in which the narrator abandons the search for Do-wel for a long period – five and forty years, he claims, though in reality the interval between the A and B versions was probably only ten to fifteen years. There is clearly a recognition here that, despite the long break, the clash with which the A text ended cannot be left unresolved. The personal significance of this moment for Langland is evident from the degree of discussion of the poet's role and his relation to the poem. The opening account of the dreamer abandoning the search for Do-wel and pursuing Fortune and Lust of the Flesh is a kind of moral fable about life and temptation, but its placing, precisely at the point where Langland had abandoned the poem, suggests that it has a reference to reality, to the poet's own relapse from his poetic search for Do-wel. This self-concern on the part of Langland is evident eighty lines later with an argument between Scripture and Lewte about the justification of satirical poetry:

'It is licitum for lewed men to legge the sothe
If hem liketh and lest – ech a lawe it graunteth;
Except persons and preestes and prelates of Holy Chirche:
It falleth noght for that folk no tales to telle –
Though the tale were trewe – and it touched synne.
Thyng that al the world woot, wherfore sholdestow spare
To reden it in retorik to arate dedly synne?' (B xi 96–102)

Lewte is arguing that it is legitimate for the poet to tell the truth about the iniquities of others, though not for those who hold offices in the Church and not if the sins are otherwise hidden from the world (he is perhaps meaning to exclude truths learnt through confession). We are reminded of the poets of *Richard the Redeless* and *Mum and the Sothsegger*, who similarly pause to justify their role as speakers of truth. There is perhaps an implicit challenge to this view in the narrator's speech a hundred lines later, when he urges love and harmony and repudiates criticism of others:

Forthi love we as leve children shal, and ech man laughe of
    oother . . .
Forthi lakke no lif oother, though he moore Latyn knowe,
Ne undernyme noght foule, for is noon withoute defaute.

(B xi 208, 213–14)

The opposition between the role of satirist which Langland plays and
the ideal of charity which he preaches is one of the sources of tension
in the passus. There are too some reflections on his poetic activity in
the vision of Middle Earth, where Reason's and Imaginatif's criticism
of the dreamer for his intolerance seems to reflect back on the writing
of the Visio.

The debate about the value and nature of poetry is continued at the
beginning of the next passus, xii. Imaginatif criticises the dreamer for
spending his time uselessly in poetry when he ought to be dedicating
himself to prayer:

'And thow medlest thee with makynges – and myghtest go seye
    thi Sauter,
And bidde for hem that yyveth thee breed; for ther are bokes
    ynowe
To telle men what Dowel is, Dobet and Dobest bothe,
And prechours to preve what it is, of many a peire freres.'

(B xii 16–19)

The dreamer responds first by justifying poetry as an acceptable play
or relaxation to gather strength for more serious work, but then goes
on in a graver vein to defend and explain his poetry as a mode of
discovery:

I seigh wel he seide me sooth and, somwhat me to excuse,
Seide, 'Caton conforted his sone that, clerk though he were,
To solacen hym som tyme – also I do whan I make:
Interpone tuis interdum gaudia curis.
And of holy men I herde', quod I, 'how thei outherwhile
Pleyden, the parfiter to ben, in places manye.
Ac if ther were any wight that wolde me telle
What were Dowel and Dobet and Dobest at the laste,
Wolde I nevere do werk, but wende to holi chirche
And there bidde my bedes but whan ich ete or slepe.'

(B xii 20–8)

His work of poetry, he implies, must continue until he has discovered
the nature of Do-wel. It suggests, rather interestingly, that the debates

continually conducted within Langland's poetry are for him a genuine part of the process of discovering truth. Langland is here no longer presenting his poetry as primarily satiric, describing and deploring the iniquities of contemporary society, but suggesting a more positive role for it, seeking to discover and present the ideal.

The nature of the debate about poetry, and its placing at the beginning of the continuation, suggest that one of the things which Langland had to do in order to continue the poem was to come to terms with his own doubts about the purpose and function of his verse. The radical, critical voice with which he had ended the A version had troubled him, and he needed to discover for himself something like the more submissive spirit adopted by Piers after tearing the Pardon. It is an issue which he goes on to present dramatically in the next passus, with the character Patience seeking to restrain the dreamer from overt criticism of the doctor. Part of the difficulty for Langland is that he is himself in danger of being an example of the problem which he is confronting: he too is in some sense a clerk, as Imaginatif's words remind us, and like the clerks whom he criticises could be said to spend his life in studying and teaching when he might be living the better life of prayer and penance.

The poet's own role is, even so, really a side-issue in passus xi and xii, though it is difficult to say what the main issue is. The action and argument of these two passus, especially xi, are bewildering in the extreme. The disordered, apparently digressive character is amusingly acknowledged by Langland himself at one point, confessing that the problem of ignorant priests has made him wander off his real subject, poverty:

> This lokynge on lewed preestes hath doon me lepe from
> poverte. (B xi 317)

The previous pattern, of dialogues dominated by a single speaker, is replaced by one in which speakers appear abruptly from all sides; some begin speaking before the reader is aware of their presence, or even their existence in some cases:

> 'Ye? Recche thee nevere!' quod Rechelesnesse (B xi 34)
> '*Homo proponit*', quod a poete, and Plato he highte (B xi 37)
> 'He seith sooth', quod Scripture tho (B xi 107)
> 'Ye, baw for bokes!' quod oon was broken out of helle.
> (B xi 140)

Several issues are in play at the same time and it is far from easy to see which side the various speakers and their arguments are to be ranged on.

Passus xi of B begins with the suggestion that the anti-intellectualism with which the previous passus had ended was a piece of arrogance on the part of the dreamer:

Pride of parfit lyvynge . . .
. . .bad me for my contenaunce acounten Clergie lighte.

(B xi 15–16)

That is, it was a false confidence in the perfection of his own life that led the dreamer to disparage Clergie or learning. But the dreamer's anticlericalism soon reasserts itself, with an appearance of justification, as old age brings him into dispute with the clergy again, in the form of the mercenary friars. The argument with them leads the dreamer to revive the dispute about the means of salvation, as he reasserts the saving power of baptism, an issue on which he had quarrelled with Scripture in the previous passus:

'For a baptized man may, as maistres telleth,
Thorugh contricion come to the heighe hevene . . .
Ac a barn withouten bapteme may noght so be saved.'

(B xi 80–2)

In context there is perhaps an implication that the clergy would be better engaged in the simple task of baptising infants than in the dangerous pursuit of higher learning (a similar point is made in the attack on Clergie in passus xiii). The criticism of the learned and their theories of salvation becomes more explicit a few lines later, when Scripture suddenly interrupts with a severe and restrictive theory of salvation that is attributed to 'lettred men':

The matere that she meved, if lewed men it knewe,
The lasse, as I leve, lovyen thei wolde
The bileve of Oure Lord that lettred men techeth.
This was hir teme and hir text – I took ful good hede:
'*Multi* to a mangerie and to the mete were sompned;
And whan the peple was plener comen, the porter unpynned
    the yate
And plukked in *Pauci* pryveliche and leet the remenaunt go
    rome.'
Al for tene of hir text trembled myn herte,
And in a weer gan I wexe, and with myself to dispute
Wheither I were chose or noght chose. (B xi 108–17)

The last words suggest the dreamer may be seeing a doctrine of strict predestination in Scripture's speech, a doctrine attributed to Scripture and Clergie in passus x, thought it is perhaps merely the threat that only a few are eventually chosen. Again the dreamer responds, as he had to a similarly restrictive notion of salvation in passus x, by appealing to the more reassuring biblical text on salvation by baptism and faith, which seems to promise that all may at least be eligible for salvation; sin cannot take that possibility away, he argues, though it may send the sinner to Purgatory, and even then Mercy may play a part. Scripture now acknowledges the pre-eminence of divine mercy:

'That is sooth', seide Scripture; 'may no synne lette
Mercy al to amende, and mekenesse hir folwe;
For thei beth, as oure bokes telleth, above Goddes werkes.'

(B xi 137-9)

This had been the implicit theme of the revision of the A version and might seem to end the argument in the dreamer's favour, but at this point a new character, Trajan, abruptly intervenes to question the value of baptism as well as learning:

'Ye, baw for bokes!' quod oon was broken out of helle.
'I Troianus, a trewe knyght, take witnesse at a pope
How I was ded and dampned to dwellen in pyne
For an uncristen creature; clerkes wite the sothe –
That al the clergie under Crist ne myghte me cracche fro helle
But oonliche love and leautee and my laweful domes.
Gregorie wiste this wel, and wilned to my soule
Savacion for soothnesse that he seigh in my werkes.
And after that he wepte and wilned me were graunted grace,
Withouten any bede biddyying his boone was underfongen,
And I saved, as ye may see, withouten syngynge of masses,
By love and by lernyng of my lyvynge in truthe,
Broughte me fro bitter peyne ther no biddyng myghte.'

(B xi 140-52)

The Emperor Trajan, as every fourteenth-century schoolboy knew, was the most famous representative of the righteous heathen. His story is first recorded in a life of St Gregory composed by an anonymous monk of Whitby in the seventh or eighth century,[5] and became widely cited in medieval writings, notably Dante's *Divine Comedy* in the thirteenth century. His case raised crucial questions. Could a good heathen be saved? Were the elements of Christian faith and the sacraments of the Church essential to salvation? It was a question that vexed Langland's time as much as earlier periods. The earlier antagonisms of the

Crusades had given place, in some quarters, to a more sympathetic interest in Islam, voiced by Wyclif among others.[6] The issue is given a contemporary presentation in the late-fourteenth-century alliterative poem *St Erkenwald*.[7] Traditionally, Trajan had been the exception who proved the rule, that baptism was essential for salvation. He was an exceptionally righteous man but a pagan and therefore in Hell until Pope Gregory saw him in a vision and interceded with God for him; God agreed to save him, but instructed Gregory not to attempt such intercession again. According to some versions of the legend, Trajan was given salvation only after he had been brought back to life and baptised, or only after he had been baptised in death by Gregory's tears. (*St Erkenwald* tells a similar story.) Trajan was thus the great example of the heathen who was saved, but only through exceptional circumstances. Langland's figure will have none of this special pleading, insisting that he was saved by his own goodness and by God, not by baptism or the Church. Gregory had a role, but Trajan is insistent that neither prayer nor sacraments had any effect. The narrator too stresses this point:

> Lo! ye lordes, what leautee dide by an Emperour of Rome
> That was an uncristene creature, as clerkes fyndeth in bokes.
> Nought through preiere of a pope but for his pure truthe
> Was that Sarsen saved, as Seint Gregorie bereth witnesse.
>
> (B xi 153–6)

The implications are wide-ranging. The Trajan legend itself relates primarily to the necessity of baptism, but here it becomes a case against other aspects of the Church and clergy as well – their learning, and their provision of masses and prayers for the dead. The attack on learning in particular is reiterated by Trajan:

> 'Lawe withouten love,' quod Troianus, 'ley ther a bene –
> Or any science under sonne, the sevene arts and alle!
> – But thei ben lerned for Oure Lordes love, lost is al the tyme,
> For no cause to cacche silver therby, ne to be called a maister,
> But al for love of Oure Lord and the bet to love the peple.'
>
> (B xi 170–4)

Langland takes a traditional symbol of papal and clerical power and turns him into an argument against the external forms of religion. Trajan's intervention challenges the *clergie* or learning that Scripture stands for, but also the dreamer's reliance on faith and baptism; even that, Trajan's experience indicates, is too exclusive a theory of salvation.

The attack on clerks is continued, apparently by the narrator, at l.215, this time asserting the primacy of simple faith over knowledge:

For whatevere clerkes carpe of Cristendom or ellis,
Crist to a commune womman seide in commune at a feste
That *Fides sua* sholde saven hire and salven hire of synnes.
Thanne is bileve a lele help, above logyk or lawe.
Of logyk ne of lawe in *Legenda Sanctorum*
Is litel alowaunce maad, but if bileve hem helpe;
For it is overlonge er logyk any lesson assoille. (B xi 215–21)

The narrator is reasserting the argument of the end of the previous passus, that the simple faith of the plowman saves him when the learned
are damned. This theme of the ordinary laity who are saved by their
simple faith then leads Langland into a long, though perhaps digressive,
discussion of the poor. The point is at first the need to show love to the
poor, but it soon develops into an argument for poverty as the proper
way of life of the clergy:

'Why I meve this matere is moost for the povere;
For in hir liknesse Oure Lord ofte hath ben yknowe. . . .
And al was ensample, for sooth, to us synfulle here,
That we sholde be lowe and loveliche of speche,
And apparaille us noght over proudly – for pilgrymes are we
    alle.
And in the apparaille of a povere man and pilgrymes liknesse
Many tyme God hath ben met among nedy peple,
Ther nevere segge hym seigh in secte of the riche.
Seint Johan and others seintes were seyen in poore clothyng,
And as povere pilgrymes preyed mennes goodes.
Jesu Crist on a Jewes doghter lighte: gentil womman though
    she were,
Was a pure povere maide and to a povere man ywedded.'
                                        (B xi 230–1, 238–46)

Joseph the carpenter possibly serves as representative of the working poor, but the other examples (Christ himself, John the Baptist and
other saints) point to the voluntary poverty of ascetics and pilgrims.
The emphasis is confirmed by the citation of the Martha and Mary story,
where Martha's concern with providing the material things of life is
found wanting in contrast to the voluntary poverty of Mary. The point
is made explicit at B xi 270–6:

Wiser than Salomon was bereth witnesse and taughte
That parfit poverte was no possession to have,
And lif moost likynge to God, as Luc bereth witnesse:
Si vis perfectus esse, vade et vende &c

And is to mene to men that on this moolde lyven,
Whoso wole be pure parfit moot possession forsake,
Or selle it, as seith the Book, and the silver dele
To beggeris that begge and bidden good for Goddes love.'

Perfection of life is manifested in voluntary poverty. The ideal life of
the religious or the clerk is that which places him on a level with the
ordinary layman and sinner. The whole idea is developed more fully in
passus xiii (see pp. 102–9), but what Langland is evidently moving
towards here is the conclusion that, if the cleric cannot be justified for
his provision of learning or the sacraments, it is perhaps the sanctity of
a pure and humble life which must save him and others. Here at last
we return to the issues raised at the end of the second vision in the Pardon scene. Trajan's appeal to the quality of life rather than learning or
Church recalls the opposition between the good life symbolised by
Piers and the reliance on knowledge and the forms of religion symbolised by the priest. The appeal to voluntary poverty as an ideal of life
picks up the theme so dramatically announced by Piers when tearing
the Pardon. But what now becomes clearer is that voluntary poverty is
itself a form of the good life, far superior to either the pursuit of learning or the selling of sacraments as a mode of life for the clerk.

After this direct address by the narrator to the reader, the poem then
turns back to the experiences of the dreamer within the vision, in an attempt to resolve the uncertainties over salvation. The dreamer's experiences in this inner dream had begun with Fortune showing him a
vision of Middle Earth so that he might covet it, but now he is granted
a new vision of Middle Earth by Kynde himself, the Creator,[8] apparently to give the dreamer a clearer insight into the nature of God's ways:

And on a mountaigne that Myddelerthe highte, as me tho
    thoughte,
I was fet forth by ensaumples to knowe,
Through ech a creature, Kynde my creatour to lovye.
                                        (B xi 323–5)

The notion that through contemplating the world in all its variety one
could come to know of God and love him is a traditional one, often invoked to demonstrate the existence of God or to explain how the
heathen could believe in God without benefit of the Bible, but Langland
characteristically takes it further and discovers a problem. The dreamer
does recognise the goodness and wisdom of the Creator, but he is also
struck by the corruption of men and their failure to participate in the
order and harmony of the universe as the birds and animals do. The
vision relates in part to the question of learning, for the dreamer par-

ticularly remarks that the birds and beasts have a kind of knowledge that comes direct from Kynde, reminding us of the *kynde knowyng* appealed to by Holy Church in passus i. But the main point is a reflection on the question of human merit and divine mercy. The dreamer notes that Reason governs all creatures except man and remarks on this angrily to Reason:

> Man and his make I myghte se bothe;
> Poverte and plentee, bothe pees and werre,
> Blisse and bale – bothe I seigh at ones,
> And how men token Mede and Mercy refused. . . .
> Ac that moost meved me and my mood chaunged –
> That Reson rewarded and ruled alle beestes
> Save man and his make; many tyme and ofte
> No Reson hem folwede, neither riche ne povere.
> And thanne I rebukede Reson, and right til hymselven I seide,
> 'I have wonder of thee, that witty art holden,
> Why thow ne sewest man and his make, that no mysfeet hem
>   folwe.'
> And Reson arated me, and seide, 'Recche thee nevere
> Why I suffre or noght suffre – thiself has noght to doone.'
>   (B xi 330–3, 367–75)

There is an implicit challenge here to the ideals of the first two visions, which had assumed that man in his natural state served God (it was *kynde wit* that led Piers to Truth, and the reference to men following Mede strongly recalls the first vision) and that Reason could and would restore society to its primitive honest state. What Reason now says is that man's nature inevitably leads him to sin and no one can make himself good:

> 'For is no creature under Crist can formen hymselven,
> And if a man myghte make hymself good,
> Ech a lif wolde be laklees – leeve thow non other. . . .
> For man was maad of swich a matere he may noght wel asterte
> That som tyme hym bitit to folwen his kynde.' (B xi 387–9, 400–1)

The challenge here to the demands of the Pardon – 'Do good and you will enter into eternal life, do evil and you will enter eternal fire' – is clear enough. What Reason proposes instead is reliance on God's 'suffraunce' – his patience and tolerance with man's fallibility. Having created man's fallible nature, God will suffer it. The vision suggests a way of relating the Creator-God of the Visio with the Redeemer-God of the later parts of the poem. The dreamer's sense of shame on hearing this probably springs not only from his embarrassment at criticising Reason but also from the poet's own guilt at the rigour of his insistence on human merit in the Visio.

The dreamer now awakes from the inner dream and is confronted by a figure called Imaginatif who seeks to explain the vision to him. The name has caused considerable difficulties. Generally in medieval thought the *vis imaginativa* or imaginative power is conceived as a rather lowly faculty, acting as intermediary between the senses and the reason, but this does not seem particularly relevant here. Langland may alternatively have been thinking of the power of imagining things not experienced, or of forming similes to express ideas, and Imaginatif does indeed use a few images in his argument. But probably the best explanation is that Langland was drawing on a notion of the imagination as that power which, in the process of contemplation, surveys the whole range of the created world and draws from it conclusions about the nature of the Creator.[9] This indeed is what Langland and his persona have been endeavouring to do before Imaginatif appears. Langland perhaps conceived Imaginatif as an authority-figure who acquired his wisdom from the created world rather than the discredited books of Study and Scripture, and could therefore speak for *kynde wit* as well as *clergie*. What he offers does look like a final answer to the debate between those two powers:

> 'Forthi I counseille thee for Cristes sake, clergie that thow lovye,
> For kynde wit is of his kyn and neighe cosynes bothe
> To Oure Lord, leve me – forthi love hem, I rede.
> For bothe ben as mirours to amenden oure defautes,
> And lederes for lewed men and for lettred bothe.
> Forthi lakke thow nevere logik, lawe ne hise custumes,
> Ne countreplede clerkes – I counseille thee for evere!'
>
> (B xii 92–8)

The earlier conflict between *kynde wit*, the guiding spirit of the first two visions, and *clergie* seems here to be resolved, as is the opposition between *clergie* and Christ that had been suggested at B xi 215–16. Yet it is difficult to feel that Langland was at all confident about the defence of learning which Imaginatif now offers. It takes an extreme form, claiming that no one can be saved unless he is taught by clerks, who keep the keys of salvation and unlock it at their pleasure, giving mercy to the *lewed* if they ask politely (ll. 107–12). The homely image of two men thrown into the Thames, of whom the one with knowledge of swimming survives and the other drowns, is a somewhat unconvincing argument (the ability to swim is singularly unlike theological knowledge) and some of the other examples are nearly as dubious (for instance, that Christ stressed the importance of learning by choosing to reveal his nativity to the magi, or that by writing in the sand Christ used his learning to save the woman taken in adultery).

Eventually the dreamer raises the obvious objection to Imaginatif's claims, the case of the righteous heathen:

'Alle thise clerkes,' quod I tho, 'that on Crist leven
Seyen in hir sermons that neither Sarsens ne Jewes
Ne no creature of Cristes liknesse withouten Cristendom worth
    saved.'
'*Contra!*' quod Ymaginatif thoo, and comsed to loure,
And seide, '*Salvabitur vix iustus in die iudicii*;
Ergo – *salvabitur!*' quod he, and seide no moore Latyn.
'Troianus was a trew knyght and took nevere Cristendom,
And he is saaf, seith the book, and his soule in hevene.
Ac ther is fullynge of font and fullynge in blood shedyng,
And thorough fir is fullyng, and that is ferme bileve.' (B xii 275–4)

The dreamer's suggestion that it is clerks who deny the salvation of the righteous heathen revives the attack on the learned, with perhaps an implication that the denial is in protection of their own monopoly over learning and baptism. The association of intellectualism and the sacraments of the Church, implicit in the term clergy, comes out particularly strongly in Imaginatif's speech; compare, for instance, B xii 82ff where learning and the sacraments are linked. Imaginatif acknowledges that Trajan is saved but proposes an alternative kind of baptism to save his theory. What he is doing here is trying to reconcile the Scriptural texts about the necessity of baptism with the idea of God's fairness and mercy suggested by the vision of Middle Earth. But in the end he has to fall back on invoking the mysterious ways of God as the vision ends:

'Ne wolde nevere trewe God but trewe truthe were allowed.
And wheither it worth or noght worth, the bileve is gret of
    truthe,
And an hope hangynge therinne to have a mede for his truthe.'
                             (B xii 288–90)

It is surely significant that he goes on to quote the verse from the twenty-third psalm which Piers had quoted on tearing the Pardon: '*Si ambulavero in medio umbre mortis* etc' (though I walk through the middle of the shadow of death, I will fear no evil, for thou art with me). Despite the claims made for all that the clergy can do for salvation – learning, sacraments, prayers – and the biblical texts on baptism and faith and predestination, ultimately the poem returns to that idea of trusting in the mysteries of divine mercy.

In retrospect it is perhaps possible to glimpse an underlying structure in passus xi and xii: conflicting authorities present a variety of views on the issues of salvation but the battle is eventually resolved by God himself, through a vision which is then 'explained' by Imaginatif in passus xii, though in the event Imaginatif is more anxious to defend learning than to explain about divine mercy. The linking element for these issues is perhaps the question of the role of the clergy: purveyors of learning and the sacraments, teachers of dangerous doctrines such as predestination, but ideally exemplars of the life of poverty. There is a recurrent anticlericalism in the vision, and a tendency for speakers to use obtrusively learned tags as if to show their intellectual claims.

Looking back on Langland's revision and continuation of the A text, it becomes easier to see the kind of dilemma which had led him to abandon the poem. The great ideal of returning society to its first created form and rediscovering the values of work and the simple life, symbolised by Piers the plowman, had proved eventually to be almost more threatening than comforting. Yet the apparent alternative, of turning to the kind of values offered by institutionalised religion, especially the belief in higher learning, left him troubled and rebellious. The first two passus of the continuation show no great confidence on Langland's part that he had found a resolution of these problems, but as he explores his own role and weighs up the claims of Scripture and Trajan he can be seen moving gradually towards an ideal of simple poverty and trust in God which he at last manages to dramatise in the next vision.

Notes and references

1. See Anna Baldwin, *The Theme of Government in Piers Plowman* (Cambridge, 1981), pp. 5–23.
2. See the discussion by J. A. W. Bennett, *Medium Ævum*, **12**(1943), 55–64, and the notes to Prol. 146ff in his *Langland: Piers Plowman* (Oxford 1972).
3. This is the reading of all manuscripts of the B version. Schmidt amends the first half of l. 248 to match the A version, for metrical reasons, but leaves the crucial change, to 'travaillynge in preieres'. Kane and Donaldson make the same emendation but also substitute 'of hondes' for 'in preieres'.
4. The speaker of this section, B xi 153–318, is in doubt. It is attributed to Lewte by Skeat and to Trajan by Schmidt; Kane and Donaldson make no comment but the absence of speech marks around the passage in their edition presumably means that they attribute it to the narrator, addressing the reader directly (not, that is, to the dreamer speaking within his dream). The last solution seems the right one, given the tone of voice.

5. See *The Earliest Life of Gregory the Great*, ed. B. Colgrave (Lawrence, Kansas, 1968), pp. 126–8.

6. See R. W. Southern, *Western Views of Islam in the Middle Ages* (Cambridge, Mass., 1962).

7. See the discussion by Ruth Morse in her edition of *St Erkenwald* (Cambridge and Totowa, 1975), pp. 16–31.

8. Kynde means Nature, who is personified as a female figure elsewhere in medieval literature (cf. Chaucer's *Parlement of Foules*. l. 303), but Langland firmly makes Kynde male and apparently identical with God.

9. See H. R. B. White, 'Langland's Ymaginatif, Kynde and the *Benjamin Minor*', *Medium Ævum*, **55**(1986), 241–8.

Chapter Six

The fourth vision: Patience and Haukyn (B xiii and xiv)

The dreamer is invited to dine with Clergie, and meets there the hermit Patience. An argument develops between the two figures and Conscience decides to forsake Clergie and go on pilgrimage with Patience. They meet Haukyn the active man and discover his sinfulness; Conscience and Patience teach him the values of a new and purer way of life.

Passus xiii begins by announcing the end of a dream which had begun long before in passus viii, and in terms of Langland's life long before that, in passus ix of the A version written possibly some fifteen years earlier. It is full of signs of a fresh impetus in the poem. The debate structure continues, and with it some of the old issues, but the answers are now expressed in dramatic action and the figures involved are more than just voices. The sense of a break is marked by the retrospective summary with which Langland now proceeds, struggling to sum up the confusion of different themes in passus xi and xii. Twice in these opening lines Langland emphasises the passage of a long period of time after the third vision: 'forth gan I walke/In manere of a mendinaunt many yer after' (ll. 2–3): 'I lay down longe in this thought' (l. 21). The remarks suggest an actual break before the composition of the next vision, as Langland mused on what he had written and sought a way forward.

The Feast of Clergie

The vision begins by bringing before us yet again the representatives of learning, but this time they are opposed by a powerful new figure,

Patience, whose significance is then further defined and dramatised by the subsequent conflict with Haukyn. What the opening lines seem to promise as the theme of passus xiii is a reconciliation between the narrator and the representatives of learning:

> [Conscience] bad me come to his court – with Clergie sholde I
> dyne. (B xiii 23)

The imagery of eating together seems to suggest harmony. The dream thus offers to take up where Imaginatif had left off in passus xii, with a justification of *clergie*. The fact that the main action of this passus turns out to culminate in the rejection of learning suggests, once again, that Langland may have fully understood what he meant to say only by writing it.

Learning appears at the feast in double shape, both as the personification Clergie and as the *maister* or *doctour*, a learned friar who is possibly modelled on a fourteenth-century Dominican friar, William Jordan.[1] Opposed to Clergie and the doctor is Patience, who becomes the moral hero of both this episode and the next. (Those commentators on the poem who make Patience a *heroine* are being influenced by other traditions; for Langland he is firmly male.) Patience is identified as a hermit or pilgrim:

> Pacience in the paleis stood in pilgrymes clothes.
> And preyde mete *par charite* for a povere heremyte.
>
> (B xiii 29–30)

He thus personifies the ideal of voluntary poverty and asceticism which Piers had chosen at the tearing of the Pardon and which Langland had discussed at length in passus xi. His name reflects his identity. The word *pacience* originally meant suffering and it is used in this period, both in French and in English, as a term for the voluntary hardship of the ascetic or anchoretic life:

> And somme he lered to lyve in longynge to ben hennes,
> In poverte and in pacience to preye for alle cristene.
>
> (B xix 249–50)

Patience thus represents one of the great ideals of Langland's time, the cult of poverty. Poverty had since early Christian times been one of the three vows taken by monks but in monastic legend and polemic it seems never to have had quite the prominence of the other two, chastity and obedience, or of the seclusion from the world which was the great theme of the cloistered life. From the tenth century onwards especially, monasteries were places of conspicuous corporate wealth rather than privation, however poor the monks might technically be as individuals. But in the eleventh century what has been called the commercial revolution – a rapid rise in urban trade and wealth and the development of a cash economy – seems to have prompted a renewed enthusiasm for poverty as an ideal.[2] Its most prominent exemplars were the friars: St Francis was the son of a wealthy merchant and began his career by conspicuously giving away his paternal wealth to appear as a beggar. But it was also manifested by less well-known and more informal groups, such as the beguines, and by individual hermits, who seem increasingly to have defined their life by its poverty rather than its seclusion. All sought to express their religious idealism and distaste for material things by renouncing wealth and taking on the appearance of the urban or rustic poor. What particularly distinguished them from the monks was that they remained visibly within the world and supported themselves not by estates but by begging or manual labour or by the offerings of the faithful, in ways which made them conspicuous within society and similar to the secular, involuntary poor – the real beggars and the lowest levels of the working class. Voluntary poverty was perennially presented to everyone's gaze, as an ideal and an implicit rebuke: friars and hermits were conspicuous features of urban and domestic life.

Discussions of the nature of ideal poverty and the proper form of support for the religious poor became a prominent feature of the period, occurring in the most unlikely contexts. In *The Romance of the Rose* the allegorical character Faux Semblant (False Seeming) disguises himself as a hermit and friar, but also delivers a long critique of the mendicant orders, especially their dependence on begging.[3] In the *Canterbury Tales* the old hag who may be a queen of faery delivers a moving speech on the ideal of poverty[4]: in context it refers to involuntary poverty, but the arguments are drawn from debates about the religious ideal. One of the points which the hag makes is that Christ himself chose 'wilful' poverty, and the claim that Christ and the apostles exemplified absolute poverty, lacking either personal or communal possessions, became the centre of bitter debate between Franciscans and the rest of the Church. The condemnation of this claim by the pope in 1323 was followed by fierce persecution of its main supporters, the Spiritual Franciscans.[5] One of the arguments associated with the latter group was that absolute poverty was not merely an ideal to be followed by a particular sect but the proper way of life for all priests, and this was a view repeatedly voiced by the Lollards later.[6] The cult of voluntary poverty as a religious ideal also had some effect on views of the involuntary poverty of those among the laity who could not provide for themselves. Franciscans were urged to identify with the ordinary poor, and those of the latter who bore their hardships patiently were seen as sharing some of the virtue of the friars and hermits.[7]

Although hermits are mentioned favourably in the opening lines of *Piers Plowman* there is otherwise little reference to the ideal of poverty in the A version, though its importance is signalled in the tearing of the Pardon. But it is taken up for discussion in the first passus of the continuation in the B version and now comes to the centre of Langland's concerns, in the figure of Patience, who comes to embody not only poverty and asceticism but also the values of simplicity and love earlier associated with the plowman. Although, as I have indicated, his name primarily refers to poverty and austerity, the word also means patience in the modern sense, and some of his actions reflect that meaning, for instance when he restrains the dreamer from criticising the learned doctor:

> Pacience parceyved what I thoughte, and preynte on me to be
>   stille. (B xiii 85)

The restraint here recalls Langland's concern in passus xi and xii with satiric poetry and censure, and the contrasting idea of tolerance and acceptance – to see much and suffer more.

The doctor is a friar, and therefore notionally an exemplar of the life of voluntary poverty too, and this is indeed the theme of his preaching:

> Thanne seide I to myself so Pacience it herde,
> 'It is noght foure dayes that this freke, bifore the deen of Poules,
> Precched of penaunces that Paul the Apostle suffrede –
> *In fame et frigore* and flappes of scourges:
> *Ter cesus sum et a Iudeis quinquies quadragenas &c* . . .
> They prechen that penaunce is profitable to the soule,
> And what meschief and maleese Crist for man tholede.
> Ac this Goddes gloton', quod I, 'with hise grete chekes,
> Hath no pite on us povere; he parfourneth yvele.
> That he precheth, he preveth noght,' to Pacience I tolde.
>   (B xiii 63–6, 75–9)

But in reality it is his status as doctor that matters to him, rather than his role as friar: he is a representative of learning, for whom Do-wel is to do *as clerkes techeth*, and an enemy of asceticism, as his feasting reveals. The metaphorical feast rapidly turns into a real one, and while Clergie talks of learning, his *alter ego* the doctor enacts the reality of the life of the learned, preaching of the virtues of suffering but eating and living extravagantly. The interplay of allegorical and literal levels is brilliantly handled here: dining with Clergie is a metaphor for communion or reconciliation, and remains a metaphor for Patience, but it is a reality for the doctor, and the dreamer reflects on the difference between the two; it is the reality of the doctor's dining that frustrates its metaphorical function.

The doctor and Patience thus embody two extremes of the religious life. As A. R. Murray has shown, the twelfth century had developed a specialised sense of *clerk* meaning intellectual, or man of learning, in opposition to the traditional sense of one in holy orders, and the gulf between the two roles had rapidly widened.[8] Chaucer's portrait of the clerk of Oxenforde as a poor threadbare figure represents ideal rather than reality. The man of learning was often a man of wealth and privilege, and it was both common and meaningful to forsake the world of learning for the purity and poverty of the ascetic life, in the same way as a St Francis would forsake the world of urban commercial wealth for asceticism. The representation of the doctor as glutton and easy-liver is thus no idle piece of mud-slinging for Langland. It mirrors one of the essential differences between Clergie and Patience. The doctor's teaching does not stem from that living experience of *penaunce* which Patience can claim.

The identification of the doctor as a friar sharpens the point. As Langland later remarks, the first friars were ascetics, and charity could once be found in a friar's coat. But now the friars, especially the Dominicans, had turned to the universities and schools and come to identify themselves with the world of book-learning. The doctor is Clergie's real self, because *clergie* is a kind of knowledge that has broken free from holiness of life and fails for that reason.

The climax of the confrontation between learning and patience comes when Conscience invites those present to offer their definitions of Do-wel. The doctor predictably defines it in terms of learning and teaching:

'Dowel?' quod this doctour; 'do as clerkes techeth;
And Dobet is he that techeth and travailleth to teche othere;
And Dobest doth hymself so as he seith and precheth.'

(B xiii 115–17)

But Clergie separates himself from his literal representative and acknowledges the helplessness of learning:

'I have sevene sones', he seide, 'serven in a castel
Ther the lord of lif wonyeth, to leren hem what is Dowel
Til I se tho sevene and myself acorde
I am unhardy', quod he, 'to any wight to preven it.
For oon Piers the Plowman hath impugned us alle,

And set alle sciences at a sop save love one;
And no text ne taketh to maynetene his cause
But *Dilige Deum* and *Domine quis habitabit*;
And seith that Dowel and Dobet arn two infinites,
Which infinites with a feith fynden out Dobest,
Which shal save mannes soule – thus seith Piers the Plowman.'

(B xiii 119–29)

Well might Conscience respond to this cryptic utterance 'I kan noght heron'. The seven sons are the seven liberal arts of the university course, and they and Clergie cannot agree about Do-wel – a fact which the reader has perhaps already discovered from the multiple definitions offered in the previous vision. In contrast to the multiplicity of texts which such figures as Scripture, Clergie and Imaginatif have cited, Piers has just two simple texts, 'Love God' and 'Lord, who shall dwell in thy tabernacle? . . . He who walks without sin and does justice'. Earlier in the poem the only thing that had saved theology from total condemnation was that it acknowledged the primacy of love (A xi 140, B x 186). That anti-intellectual figure Trajan had similarly proclaimed that love was the only thing which redeemed the seven arts:

'Lawe withouten love', quod Troianus, 'ley ther a bene –
Or any science under sonne, the sevene arts and alle!
But thei ben lerned for Oure Lordes love, lost is al the tyme.'

(B xi 170–1)

What is now being suggested, by Clergie himself, is that love and learning may be hopelessly at odds. The riddling nature of Clergie's speech, with its reference to two infinites, is a reminder that the kind of knowledge affirmed by Piers is neither that of the intellectual nor that of the simple worker but something more like the inspired understanding of the mystic. (The two infinites are perhaps those implied by the biblical texts, love and justice.)

This is the first time that Piers has been mentioned since the end of the second vision six passus earlier, or, put another way, since the A version had been written some fifteen years before, and he is no longer quite the same figure. Clergie's words ascribe remarkable authority to Piers, and the reply of Conscience suggests something close to Messianic status:

'I kan noght heron', quod Conscience, 'ac I knowe wel Piers.
He wol noght ayein Holy Writ speken, I dar wel undertake.
Thanne passe we over til Piers come and preve this in dede.'

(B xiii 130–2)

Such language of a second coming to authenticate statements is to recur with reference to Christ in passus xvi and to Piers in the last lines of the poem. The identification of Piers with Christ or God, made explicit in passus xv, is already present in Langland's consciousness. What lies behind the words of Clergie and Conscience is a recognition, on Langland's part, that Piers' authority as agent of human salvation, the one who wins Truth's pardon for others, does not depend on his association with productive labour for the community. It is his association with simplicity and austerity and his opposition to learning that are now important, and the links with Patience suggest that these qualities are to be found as much in the eremitic life which Piers had apparently chosen on his last appearance, as in the working life which he had forsaken.

Patience now develops the argument attributed to Piers; Do-wel may be to learn, and Do-bet to teach, but Do-best of all is to love:

> '*Disce* and Dowel; *doce*, and Dobet;
> *Dilige*, and Dobest – thus taughte me ones
> A lemman that I lovede – Love was hir name.' (B xiii 137–9)

One is strongly reminded of A. R. Murray's formulation: 'Each, philosopher and monk, saw himself as a conduit by which intangible and invisible good flowed down into the everyday world. In the philosopher's case the good was truth, illuminating ignorance. In the monk's it was love, melting sin.'[9] Here, love is what the hermit offers.

An increasingly bitter argument ensues, as the doctor mocks Patience and urges Clergie and Conscience to dismiss him, while Clergie reasserts his own importance; but Conscience decides, nevertheless, to forsake Clergie and go with Patience:

> Ac Conscience carped loude and curteisliche seide,
> 'Frendes, fareth wel', and faire spak to Clergie,
> 'For I wol go with this gome, if God wol yeve me grace,
> And be pilgrym with Pacience til I have preved moore'. . . . .
> Thus curteisliche Conscience congeyed first the frere,
> And sithen softeliche he seide in Clergies ere,
> 'Me were levere, by Oure Lord, and I lyve sholde,
> Have pacience parfitliche than half thi pak of bokes!'
> (B xiii 179–82, 198–201)

Here as elsewhere in Langland Conscience seems to be used as the figure of the chooser, articulating the choices made by the poem. He had, crucially, rejected Mede and chosen Reason in the first vision (A iii

109–10). Here he similarly rejects Clergie in favour of Patience. (One might compare too the end of the poem, where Conscience abandons the barn of Unitee or Church to make a solitary search for Piers.)

Clergie is unwilling to accept the rejection, claiming that Conscience will regret it, and both he and Conscience seem then to look forward to a time of future reconciliation:

> Clergie of Conscience no congie wolde take,
> But seide ful sobreliche, 'Thow shalt se the tyme
> Whan thow art wery forwalked, wilne me to counseille.'
> 'That is sooth', seide Conscience, 'so me God helpe!
> If Pacience be oure partyng felawe and pryve with us bothe,
> Ther nys wo in this world that we ne sholde amende,
> And conformen kynges to pees, and alle kynnes londes –
> Sarsens and Surre, and so forth alle the Jewes –
> Turne into the trewe feith and intil oon bileve.'
> 'That is sooth', quod Clergie, 'I se what thow menest.
> I shal dwelle as I do, my devoir to shewe,
> And confermen fauntekyns oother folk ylered
> Til Pacience have preved thee and parfit thee maked.'
>
> (B xiii 202–14)

There is a suggestion from the poet here that in an ideal world learning and patient poverty might not be at odds with each other. Until then, however, Clergie's role is to be limited, apparently, to one of the most basic of priestly tasks, preparing children and others for confirmation. The high claims made for learning in the previous vision have shrunk to very little, and Langland never describes the moment when it resumes a distinguished position in the scheme for salvation; possibly it lies for him in a distant idealised future.

This moment of choice is the climax of the great debate on learning that had lasted since Langland began the third vision fifteen years earlier. Conscience is rejecting Clergie and the doctor for the purer and more spiritual values associated with Patience the hermit. It is a choice like that made by the dreamer at the end of the A version, when he rejected learning in favour of the simple faith of the plowman, but differs in important ways. Conscience is opting for an ideal of simplicity and reliance on God to provide and inspire, an ideal that is exemplified by the pilgrim-hermit rather than the honest plowman. One mark of that difference is the almost comic mixture of impatient indignation and courteous restraint in this scene. The dreamer repeatedly rises in anger against the doctor but is restrained by Patience. Conscience, on the other hand, is scrupulously polite when he makes his choices ('curteisly' l. iii, 'curteisliche' l. 179, 'faire spak' l. 180, 'curteisliche' l. 298, 'softeliche' l. 199), in striking contrast to the vigour of his attitudes at the end of the poem. There is a significant point here. Anti-intellectualism had earlier been expressed by impetuosity and anger (Piers at the tearing of the Pardon, the dreamer at the end of the A version, Trajan interrupting Scripture) and rebuked by sober authority figures. Here the impetuous anger is still evident, but is joined by the calmer, politer, more authoritative figures of Conscience and Patience, as if Langlands's emotional antipathy to the world of learning has now been reinforced by a more confident, reflective certainty.

The episode began with Conscience inviting the dreamer to dine with Clergie as a gesture of reconciliation, the reconciliation argued for by Imaginatif in passus xii. It culminates instead with Conscience himself repudiating Clergie, in order to follow the ideals of simplicity and faith represented by the hermit Patience.

What lifts this whole scene above the frustrations of the preceding dream is, first of all, the return to dramatic action and description, working both figuratively and literally, instead of mere debate. The personification Clergie has the doctor as his *alter ego*, a figure whose real identity and literal activity lend a fullness to the whole idea of *clergie*. Similarly, Conscience has his partner in the dreamer, enacting with passion and impatience the same choices as Conscience himself. Patience succeeds by being more than patience – hermit, pilgrim, *alter ego* for Piers. And the argument is partially enacted by the drama of eating and drinking – ' "Do-wel," quod this doctour, and drank after' (B iii 103) – or Conscience abruptly abandoning the feast to walk off into the wilderness with Patience. Secondly, however, the scene is superior because something happens in the argument – we reach a crisis in the thought and come to a critical decision, turning decisively away from the obsession with *clergie* and taking up energetically the themes proclaimed at the tearing of the Pardon. It seems to be at the moments of intellectual crisis and decision, rather than confusion and uncertainty, that the richest drama comes.

The meeting with Haukyn

In the closing scenes of the debate Clergie had appealed *in absentia* to Piers the Plowman, as an authority who set all sciences 'at a sop' save love alone. Langland is here reinterpreting the earlier Piers, building on the authority and anti-intellectualism he acquired in the Visio, but developing an association with love rather than work – an association perhaps heralded by his choice of *preyour and penaunce*. Patience, being a hermit, is what Piers chose to be. It is this emergence of Piers in a different form which frees Langland at last from the impasse of the tearing of the Pardon and enables him to develop it in the next scene.

Patience and Conscience set off talking together about Do-wel, and as if on cue, created by their discussion, the ultimate personification of Do-wel appears before them:

> And as thei wente by the weye, of Dowel thei carped;
> Thei mette with a mynstral, as me tho thoughte.
> Pacience apposed hym first and preyde he sholde telle
> To Conscience what craft he kouthe, and to what contree he
>   wolde.
> 'I am a mynstral', quod that man, 'my name is *Activa Vita*.
> Al ydel ich hatie, for of Actif is my name,
> A wafrer, wol ye wite, and serve manye lordes.' (B xiii 220–6)

Scripture, we recall, had earlier defined Do-wel as the active life or *activa vita*, and further explained it as the life of productive labour followed by plowmen, tailors, cobblers and others. This, in a way, is what the waferer claims to represent too, with his talk of providing food for the hungry masses. A waferer has usually been defined as a baker or confectioner but he seems rather to have been a kind of pedlar, a disreputable itinerant seller of not only the 'bake breed' (a kind of biscuit) that Haukyn mentions but also, it appears, fruit and nuts and other delicacies. A Wyclifite text satirically describes friars as pedlars and waferers:

> Yif thei becomen pedderis berynge knyves, pursis, pynys and girdlis
> and spices and sylk and precious pellure and forrouris for wym-
> men, and therto smale gentil hondis, to gete love of hem and to
> have many grete giftis for litil good or nought; thei coveiten evyle
> here neigheboris goodis. Yif thei ben made wafreris, gevynge lor-
> des, ladies and riche men a fewe peris, appelis or nottis to have huge
> giftis to the covent, evyl thei coveiten here negheboris goodis.[10]

Langland had earlier put a waferer in company with other disreputable street figures, a cutpurse and an apeward (A vi 640), and Chaucer includes the waferer in similarly disreputable company in 'The Pardoner's Tale':

> And right anon thanne come tombesteres
> Fetys and smale, and yonge frutesteres,
> Syngeres with harpes, baudes, wafereres,
> Whiche been the verray develes officeres
> To kyndle and blowe the fyr of lecherye,
> That is annexed unto glotonye.[11]

The name Haukyn, a diminutive form of Harry, must have been chosen as a pun on 'hawking' or 'hawker', an itinerant seller or pedlar.

The use of the disreputable figure of a waferer to represent the active life of working in the world is in sharp contrast with the poem's earlier representative of the active life, Piers the Plowman himself. Haukyn nevertheless associates himself with Piers:

'. . . the preest preieth the peple hir Paternoster to bidde
For Piers the Plowman and that hym profit waiten –
And that am I, Actif, that ydelnesse hatie;
For alle trewe travaillours and tiliers of the erthe,
Fro Mighelmesse to Mighelmesse I fynde hem with wafres.'

(B xiii 234–40)

Indeed, in the C version the equivalent figure is described as Piers' apprentice. Haukyn is, like Piers, a provider of food but at the opposite end of the spectrum of moral respectability, and thus functions as a kind of reversal of Piers' role in the Visio. The process of argument is similar. Piers the Plowman was introduced in the A version as the morally perfect exemplar of the active life, central to existence as ordained by God, so that through him that life can be justified; other modes of society – knights, bishops, merchants – are then gradually brought into association with Piers and with his sanctity, the sanctity of productive labour. Haukyn is introduced as the highly imperfect exemplar of the active life, wholly peripheral, as a waferer, to society's needs, despite his own claims (for though the world may need bread, it can easily get by without the biscuits and sweets sold by Haukyn), and he progressively swallows up in his imperfection all other occupations in the world, including that of plowman. As if the implications of characterising *activa vita* as a waferer were in any doubt, the dreamer discovers in the coat of Haukyn the marks of all the deadly sins and Haukyn goes on to reveal in himself the characteristic sins of labourers and merchants:

'If I yede to the plowgh, I pynched so narwe
That a foot lond or a forow fecchen I wolde
Of my nexte neghebore, nymen of his erthe . . .
And whoso cheped my chaffare, chiden I wolde
But he profrede to paie a peny or tweyne
Moore than it was worth, and yet wolde I swere
That it coste me muche moore – swoor manye othes . . .
And if I sente over see my servaunts to Brugges,
Or into Prucelond my prentis my profit to waiten,
To marchaunden with moneie and maken here eschaunges,

Mighte nevere me conforte in the mene tyme
Neither masse ne matynes, ne none maner sightes.'
(B xiii 370–2, 379–82, 391–5)

In representing the active life by the figure of the stained and sinful
Haukyn, Langland is at last giving full expression to that repudiation of
the ideal of labour so dramatically but cryptically signalled by Piers'
rejection of plowing at the end of the Visio. This, Langland seems to
be suggesting, is what *activa vita* is quintessentially like, however one may
strive to dignify it by appealing to idealised portraits of kings, knights,
or plowmen. It is fundamentally the pursuit of 'belly-joy', to use Piers'
term. Langland's awareness of his own belated recognition of the corruption of the active life seems to be suggested by his presentation of
the dreamer's gradual progress to perception of Haukyn's sin:

And he torned hym as tyd, and thanne took I hede;
It was fouler bi fele fold than it first semed. . . .
I waitede wisloker, and thanne was it soilled . . .
(B xiii 318–19, 342)

Once Haukyn's inherent sinfulness, as representative of the active life,
has been acknowledged, the poem raises the question of his possible
redemption. Haukyn explains that he has tried to cleanse his soiled coat
of sin many times through the penances proposed by the priest, but
without success. Conscience responds by offering a penance of his own
to cleanse it:

'And I shal kenne thee', quod Conscience, 'of contricion to make
That shal clawe thi cote of alle kynnes filthe –
Cordis contricio &c
Dowel shal wasshen it and wryngen it through a wis
    confessour –
Oris confessio &c
Dobet shal beten it and bouken it as bright as any scarlet,
And engreynen it with good wille and Goddes grace to amende
    thee,
And sithen sende thee to Satisfaccion for to sonnen it after:
    Satisfaccio.
And Dobest kepeth clene from unkynde werkes.
Shal nevere myte bymolen it, ne mothe after biten it,
Ne fend ne fals man defoulen it in thi lyve.
Shal noon heraud ne harpour have a fairer garnement
Than Haukyn the Actif man, and thow do by my techyng,
Ne no mynstrall be moore worth amonges povere and riche
Than Haukyn wil the wafrer, which is *Activa Vita*.' (B xiv 16–28)

What is radically different about Conscience's penance compared with the priest's is that it culminates in Do-best, a mode of living which will prevent Haukyn ever sinning again; just like Truth's Pardon, it goes beyond mechanical forms of temporary absolution, converting them by metaphor into a new way of life.

That way of life is not defined by Conscience himself, but the idea is then taken up by Patience the hermit, who, appropriately for his role, propounds the ideals of voluntary poverty:

'We sholde noght be to bisy abouten oure liflode:
Ne soliciti sitis &c; Volucres celi Deus pascit &c; Pacientes vincunt &c'
Thanne laughed Haukyn a litel, and lightly gan swerye,
'Whoso leveth yow, by Oure Lord, I leve noght he be blessed!'
'No?' quod Pacience paciently, and out of his poke hente
Vitailles of grete vertues for alle manere beestes
And seide, 'Lo! here liflode ynogh, if oure bileve be trewe . . .'
But I lokede what liflode it was that Pacience so preisede;
And thanne was it a pece of the Paternoster – *Fiat voluntas tua.*
'Have, Haukyn', quod Pacience, 'and et this whan the hungreth,
Or whan thow clomsest for cold or clyngest for drye . . .
By so that thow be sobre of sighte and of tonge,
In ondynge and in handlynge and in alle thi fyve wittes,
Darstow nevere care for corn ne lynnen cloth ne wollen.
Ne for drynke, ne deeth drede, but deye as God liketh,
Or through hunger or thorugh hete – at his wille be it.
For if thow lyvest after his loore, the shorter lif the bettre.'
(B xiv 33–9, 48–51, 54–9)

Patience is evidently recalling the ideal invoked by Piers as he tore up the Pardon, citing again the Gospel text on the birds of the air and again quoting *Ne soliciti sitis*, 'Do not be anxious' (about food and clothing). As we have noted earlier (see p. 54), this text was interpreted by some patristic and medieval commentators as a recommendation of moderation or detachment in the pursuit of worldly goods. In that sense it could offer some redemption for the active life. But as with Piers, it seems clear that Patience is primarily employing the text in the literal sense and arguing for the ideal of voluntary poverty – appropriately so, given his identity as hermit. The food which Patience offers Haukyn is purely spiritual, and his advice culminates in the assurance that he need never care about food, even if he were to die of hunger or thirst, since death should be welcome. A similar point is made in one of the Wyclifite sermons, which urges that priests should be supported by the willing offerings of the faithful, and if people are too greedy to offer help the priest has other alternatives, such as suffering voluntarily hunger and thirst:

for avarice of the peple mai be helpid on many maners, other to
turne to other peple, or to traveile as Poul dide, or to suffre wilful-
li hunger, and thrist if it falle.[12]

It is repeatedly beggars rather than honest workers that Patience invokes as exemplars of poverty, particularly those who choose for God's
love to leave wealth and live the life of a beggar:

> 'Forthi al poore that pacient is, may asken and cleymen,
> After hir endynge here, heveneriche blisse.
> Muche hardier may he asken, that here myghte have his wille
> In lond and in lordshipe and likynge of bodie,
> And for Goddes love leveth al and lyveth as a beggere.'
>
> (B xiv 259–63)

For all the earlier hints at the possibility of reforming Haukyn and the
active life, what essentially is proposed by Conscience and Patience is a
reformation which would change his very identity, as Haukyn's discon-
solate conclusion seems to acknowledge:

> 'Allas', quod Haukyn the Actif Man tho, 'that after my
>   cristendom
> I ne hadde be deed and dolven for Dowelis sake!
> So hard it is', quod Haukyn, 'to lyve and to do synne.
> Synne seweth us evere', quod he, and sory gan wexe.
>
> (B xiv 320–2)

The words recall Wyclif's insistence that it is impossible to follow the
active life without sinning.[13]

At the heart of the Haukyn episode is a rejection of the values associated with the active life in favour of those associated with *poverte*, in
the Langlandian sense of an eremitic life of voluntary hardship. Whereas the active life had proved to be irretrievably stained by the deadly
sins, Patience demonstrates that the life of poverty escapes unscathed
from all of them. The qualities of austerity, simplicity and dedication
which the Prologue had seen in both plowmen and hermits are now
firmly located in the latter. The confrontation thus re-enacts the tearing of the Pardon, developing and explaining the dramatic repudiation
of plowing in favour of prayer and penance. Working in the world and
for the world is after all essentially stained, and sanctity is to be found
not in labour but in the simple austerity of the hermit.

The fourth vision falls into two distinct episodes, as Patience confronts
first Clergie and the doctor, and then Haukyn. The seeds of the first

confrontation are in passus xi, where Trajan's attack on learning is followed by the moving account of poverty, while the seeds of the second are to be found in the end of the second vision, but it is only here that the issues are joined and dramatised. Clergie and the doctor assert the centrality of learning but Patience successfully opposes to this kind of striving the values of patient endurance and love. Previously the opposition to learning had been expressed in terms of the simple understanding of the layman, but Patience now goes on to define himself in opposition to that kind of striving too, in the form of Haukyn. In repudiating the clerk's privileging of knowledge and other clerical monopolies Langland does not after all need, he now discovers, to accept as an alternative ideal the worldliness of plowmen or emperors; he can choose a mode of living and an ideal of love which is different from both, and best represented by the hermit.

Notes and references

1. See M. E. Marcett, *Uhtred de Boldon, Friar William Jordan and Piers Plowman* (New York, 1938).
2. There is a vast literature on this movement. Particularly useful studies are L. K. Little, *Religious Poverty and the Profit Economy in Medieval Europe* (London, 1978); M. D. Lambert, *Franciscan Poverty* (London, 1961); and two recent volumes in the series *Studies in Church History*, vol. xxii (*Monks, Hermits and the Ascetic Tradition*, ed. W. J. Shiels, Oxford, 1985) and vol. xxiv (*The Church and Wealth*, ed. W. J. Shiels and D. Wood, Oxford, 1988).
3. *Le Roman de la Rose*, ed. E. Langton (Paris, 1914–24), ll. 11223– 2000.
4. *The Canterbury Tales* (*The Riverside Chaucer*, ed. L. D. Benson, Oxford, 1988), Fragment III, lines 1177–206.
5. See Lambert, *Franciscan Poverty*.
6. For Wyclif himself see T. Renna, 'Wyclif's attacks on the monks', in *From Ockham to Wyclif*, eds A. Hudson and M. Wilks (Oxford, 1987), pp. 275–80. For the vernacular Lollard writings, see, e.g., *The English Works of Wyclif hitherto unprinted*, ed. F. Matthew (Early English Text Society os 74, London, 1880), p. 98.
7. See B. Tierney, *The Medieval Poor Law* (Berkeley, 1959), p. 11.
8. See A. R. Murray, *Reason and Society in the Middle Ages* (Oxford, 1978). See also pp. 70–72.
9. Murray, *Reason and Society*, p. 385.
10. Matthew, *Wyclif*, pp. 12–13.
11. *The Canterbury Tales*, Fragment VI, lines 477–82.
12. *Select English Works of John Wyclif*, ed. T. Arnold, 3 vols (Oxford, 1869–71), I, 178.
13. *Iohannis Wyclif Sermones*, ed. J. Loserth (London, 1887), Sermo xx (l, 146–59).

Chapter Seven

The fifth vision: Charity and Redemption (B xv–xvii)

After a long interval, during which the narrator is scorned by others, he dreams again and sees the Soul or Anima, who explains his identity, talks of the failings of the clergy and reveals the nature of true charity. When describing the allegorical Tree of Charity he mentions Piers the Plowman, at whose name the dreamer swoons and passes into a dream within a dream. Piers now appears, shows him the Tree of Charity and as the fruit falls from the tree and is gathered by the devil, hurls a stick representing the son of God at the devil, thus initiating the Incarnation. The story of Christ's life up to the Crucifixion is briefly told, and the dreamer wakes into the 'outer' dream. He now meets in turn two characters identified variously as Abraham and Moses or Faith and Hope, who tell him of the beliefs which they represent. They pass by on the other side when a man is robbed and wounded by thieves but a Samaritan rescues and helps him. The Samaritan then tells the dreamer about the Trinity, and the dreamer wakes.

The fifth vision, even more than the fourth, deals in intense imaginative experiences and major crises of thought. Though it begins quietly enough with a lengthy retrospective discussion of the issues raised by the previous two visions, it suddenly takes off in passus xvi in a new direction, as Langland at last finds it possible to articulate the Messianic yearnings which had briefly surfaced on several occasions earlier in the poem.

The dialogue with Anima

After the dramatic action and debate of passus xiii and xiv, passus xv resumes the pattern of the earlier sections of the poem, with an authority-figure representing an aspect of the inner self, Anima, instructing the dreamer on the truths of salvation. It is a rambling speech covering a variety of issues, and Langland is clearly at times speaking in his own voice, forgetful of the nature of the supposed speaker:

'Gooth to the glose of the vers, ye grete clerkes;
If I lye on yow to my lewed wit, ledeth me to brennyng!'

(B xv 82–3)

Anima himself can, properly, neither describe his wit as *lewed* nor invite the clerks to lead him to the stake. Langland's primary concern here seems to be to develop the arguments raised in the previous two passus, with respect both to the problem of knowledge and to the proper life of the clergy.

A figure called Anima representing the human soul appears earlier in the poem, in Wit's account of the castle of Do-wel in B ix, but this is a quite different figure involving a very different conception of psychology. Wit had described a castle named Caro (the flesh), representing the human body, in which dwells the lady Anima (the soul), who is protected from the devil by Do-wel with the help of Inwit (conscience or the intelligence) and the five senses:

Kynde hath closed therinne craftili withalle
A lemman that he loveth lik to hymselve.
Anima she hatte; to hir hath envye
A proud prikere of Fraunce, *Princeps huius mundi*,
And wolde wynne hire awey with wiles and he myghte.
Ac Kynde knoweth this wel and kepeth hire the bettre,
And hath doon hire with Sire Dowel, Duc of thise marches . . .
Ac the Constable of that castel, that kepeth hem alle,
Is a wis knyght withalle – Sire Inwit he hatte.

(B ix 5–11, 17–18)

The active figures in this account are the male ones, Do-wel and Inwit, while Anima seems to be the prize. What Langland is presenting in B ix is a theory of the mind which was common in medieval vernacular writings and no doubt in popular thought. In this tradition, the soul is the immortal spirit while the intellectual faculties are associated with the mortal part of man. The soul is a passive victim or beneficiary, often represented in allegory therefore as a woman, as in B ix; its ultimate fate is decided not by its own act but by the vigilance of the (separate) intellectual powers in resisting sin. A familiar example from an earlier period is the early-thirteenth-century treatise *Sawles Warde*: there the soul, described as a precious treasure, resides in a house called man and is guarded by the constable Wit, with the help of four virtues.[1] A later example is the fifteenth-century morality play *Wisdom*, where the female character Anima is guarded by the male characters Mind, Will and Understanding; when they are corrupted by the devil she emerges stained and foul, but when they repent reappears thoroughly cleansed.[2]

There was, however, another very different psychological theory, derived from classical tradition and passing from Plato through St Augustine and Alcuin to the later Middle Ages. According to this theory, the soul and the mind are very closely identified, often indeed identical (a similarity reflected in the Latin terms *anima* and *animus*); the soul is the immortal part of man but it is also his rational spirit, embracing his memory, will and understanding. According to this theory the soul decides its own fate, by the exercise of its intellectual powers (while allowing for the operation of divine grace).[3] It is this very different tradition which Langland draws on in passus xv. The soul here is a male figure and he rapidly explains that he is not only the soul (*anima*) but also the mind (*animus, mens*), memory (*memoria*), reason (*racio*), wit (*sensus*), conscience, love (*amor*) and spirit (*spiritus*). (This list goes back to Isidore of Seville.[4])

Langland does not refer to the earlier and different account of Anima in B ix or explain his change of theory but, characteristically, prefers to develop the discussion obliquely through the apparently foolish responses of the dreamer rather than directly through his own authoritative voice. Superficially, Anima is yet one more in the line of authority-figures based on aspects of the human mind – Reason, Thought, Wit, Imaginatif, Conscience. But Anima's multiple identity suggests something new. Wit's account had implicitly emphasised the importance of the intellectual faculties in defending the soul. What this new account suggests is a closer identity of the intellect with the spirit and perhaps with God – for Anima here begins by proclaiming himself Christ's creature. If Thought, Wit, Clergie and Scripture had all in their various ways been found wanting, there is after all a possibility of an inner self which is in tune with the divine will. Anima's explanation that he embraces not only *mens*, the faculty of knowledge, but also conscience, the faculty of moral choices, and *amor*, the power by which man loves God and others, is potentially an answer to the great debate about *clergie* or learning, with its implied separation of knowledge from morality (a separation exemplified by the doctor and acknowledged by Clergie) and from love (a point claimed by Trajan).

Anima takes up the theme of knowledge immediately, and it rapidly becomes clear that the kind of understanding which he represents is very different from that espoused by Study and Clergie. The dreamer's absurd demand for universal knowledge is expressed in a language recalling their kind of skill, and it is firmly repudiated by Anima:

'Alle the sciences under sonne and alle the sotile craftes
I wolde I knewe and kouthe kyndely in myn herte!'
'Thanne artow inparfit', quod he, 'and oon of Prides knyghtes!
. . .
It were ayeins kynde,' quod he, 'and alle kynnes reson
That any creature sholde konne al, except Crist oone.'
(B xv 48–50, 52–3)

Anima then launches into a lengthy attack (ll. 50–148) on the learned, recalling the critique of *clergie* in passus xiii. The learned teach abstruse doctrine to the laity to enhance their own wealth and reputation, and neglect to teach the simple things that the people really need. This leads Anima into an attack on the mercenary nature of the clergy and thence into an imaginative account of the figure Charity himself. This account reminds us in many respects of the hermit Patience, both in his choice of poverty and his practice of love:

'Charite', quod he, 'ne chaffareth noght, ne chalangeth, ne
craveth;
As proud of a peny as of a pound of golde,
And is as glad of a gowne of a gray russet
As of a tynycle of Tarse or of trie scarlet.
He is glad with alle glade and good til alle wikkede,
And leneth and loveth alle that Oure Lord made. . . .
Of rentes ne of richesse rekketh he nevere,
For a frend that fyndeth hym, failed hym nevere at nede:
Fiat voluntas tua fynt hym everemoore,
And if he soupeth, eteth but a sop of *Spera in Deo*. . . .'
(B xv 165–70, 177–80)

Both the text *Fiat voluntas* and the eating imagery strongly recall Patience, and Anima goes on to quote the same aphorism, *Pacientes vincunt* (l. 267). He insists that the life of charity has been found in many vocations – among friars, kings, monks, priests, and in the king's court – but it is the desert saints and other representatives of the eremitic life who attract most of his attention (ll. 268–306). What Anima seems primarily to be describing here, and defining as charity, is the life of voluntary poverty exemplified by Patience the hermit, by the first friars (l. 230) and by the desert saints. That he is mainly concerned in both parts of his discourse with the way of life which should be followed by the clergy is confirmed by his return to direct criticism of their failings later in the passus (ll. 383–611). He concludes by arguing that since faith alone suffices for salvation and the Jews and Saracens are so close to Christianity in their beliefs already, the clergy should dedicate themselves and their lives to teaching them the remaining simple fundamentals, a belief in Christ.

What Langland seems to be doing here is to use the figure of Anima to articulate and develop the argument that began to emerge in passus xiii and xiv, that the ideal role of the religious was to be lovers rather than knowers, and that the life of love was particularly to be found in the eremitic state. But a new line of thought which is to become dominant in the next passus threatens to emerge at several points: the stress on the role of God as the true knower and lover.

The dreamer himself hints at an identification of Charity with Christ; having claimed that he has never seen such a man as Charity he goes on:

'Clerkes kenne me that Crist is in alle places;
Ac I seigh hym nevere soothly but as myself in a mirour:
Hic in enigmate, tunc facie ad faciem.
[Here in a dark manner, then face to face]' (B xv 161–2)

The hint is then taken up by Anima:

'By Crist! I wolde that I knewe hym', quod I, 'no creature
    levere!'
'Withouten help of Piers Plowman', quod he, 'his persone
    sestow nevere.'
'Wheither clerkes knowen hym', quod I, 'that kepen Holi Kirke?'
'Clerkes have no knowyng', quod he, 'but by werkes and by
    wordes.
Ac Piers the Plowman parceyveth moore depper
What is the wille, and wherfore that many wight suffreth:
Et vidit Deus cogitaciones eorum.
[And God sees their thoughts.] . . .
Therfore by colour ne by clergie knowe shaltow hym nevere,
Neither thorugh wordes ne werkes, but thorugh wil oone,
Ant that knoweth no clerk ne creature on erthe
But Piers the Plowman – *Petrus, id est, Christus.*'
(B xv 195–200, 208–12)

The initial point, that one cannot hope to see charity in person except through the help of Piers, who is then identified with God, seems to suggest the idea of Christ as Love personified. But the passage then quickly develops into a discussion of knowledge. It clearly alludes to, and rewrites, the lines with which Piers had introduced himself in the poem much earlier in A vi (B v):

'Petir!' quath a ploughman and putte forth his hed,
'I knowe hym as kyndely as clerk doth his bokis.' (A vi 25-6)

Piers had claimed to know Truth intimately while clerks only knew books; here, he knows charity and the human will intimately while clerks only know the outward, and deceptive, manifestations. But Piers is no longer the representative of the honest worker; he is now identified with Christ and God, and his kind of understanding is God's.

The lines develop something hinted at in passus xiii, where Piers is associated with the repudiation of clerical knowledge and acquires a Messianic tinge, but the explicit identification of Piers with God is new and tantalising. It is possible that Piers had always possessed some quality of the divine in Langland's mind and that Langland is doing no more here than reminding us in exaggerated language of that aspect of him, rather than really meaning to assert his identity with God. Yet Piers seemed to have been introduced in the second vision only as the ideal representative of the honest worker, and there is no hint there, or indeed in the whole of the A version, of his later divine aspect. A better way of understanding Piers is that proposed by Nevill Coghill, who argued that the 'meaning' of Piers develops in accordance with the poem's own development, so that he represents, or is identified with, the particular ideals which emerge from successive stages of the poem.[5] Coghill himself accepted Wells's theory that the structure of the poem was based on the three 'lives', active, contemplative and mixed (see p. 20), and consequently identified Piers with those three in succession. Although few critics would now accept Wells's interpretation, Coghill may well have been right in general terms about the way in which Langland uses and understands Piers. What seems to be involved for Langland himself is a rereading of Piers in the light of the arguments and ideals which have developed (both in the poem and in his own mind) since he first introduced the character. If Piers in the second vision had symbolised the kind of knowledge which best approached the ideal, Langland would now want to redefine that ideal while retaining Piers as its symbol; the knowledge required is a divine knowledge. The name Piers had been chosen as a type-name for a plowman, but the fact that it was also a form of Petrus which could be interpreted as Christ, with biblical authority, was for Langland one of those etymological coincidences which, like many other exegetes, he saw as a sign of a divine mystery.

Thus what Langland is doing in this passage is expressing his growing sense that the kind of knowledge which is so superior to that of the clerks, though earlier associated with the honest labourer and then with the hermit and mystic, is really to be associated with God himself. This has important implications for the idea of salvation and the poet's own kind of knowledge. The poem's agonising about *clergie* had always included an element of the poet's own agonising about the extent of his knowledge and authority as poet. Twice in this passus the dreamer speaks of his desire for knowledge and is frustrated. What Langland seems to be acknowledging to himself in this crucial passage is that questions of individual salvation and the route to Truth may be beyond any human mind, resting only in the mind of God. If Piers in the Visio had been able to speak for the poet as the authority on salvation, he is now, the passage suggests, beyond the poet's conception. It recalls the way in which Langland had revised the ending of the A version so as to suggest that the salvation of the thief on the Cross and other notorious sinners was evidence not of perverse predestination but of the mystery of the divine will. These implications are taken up with full commitment in the next passus.

The Tree of Charity

At the beginning of passus xvi Anima attempts once more to explain the nature of charity, this time using the image of the Tree of Charity. Initially the tree is a static, emblematic account of how Christian love develops in an individual and what it is composed of:

'Mercy is the more therof; the myddul stok is ruthe;
The leves ben lele wordes, the lawe of Holy Chirche;
The blosmes beth buxom speche and benigne lokynge;
Pacience hatte the pure tree, and pore symple of herte,
And so thorugh God and thorugh goode men groweth the
    fruyt Charite.' (B xvi 5–9)

The image develops the Visio's concern with the idea of the *kynde* or natural, and particularly the idea of a virtue, or impulse to virtue, which springs from natural inclinations in the heart. What transforms all this, both as poetry and as argument, is the mention of Piers:

'And Liberum Arbitrium hath the lond to ferme,
Under Piers the Plowman to piken it and to weden it.'
'Piers the Plowman!' quod I tho, and al for pure joye
That I herde nempne his name anoon I swowned after.
                                                (B xvi 16–19)

As we have seen, Anima had already associated Piers closely with God, and it eventually becomes clear that the invocation of Piers is an appeal to the divine, to a force outside man. Obsessively until this moment the poem has been concerned with what a man must do, whether Do-wel, Do-bet or Do-best, and love or charity looks at first like a continuation of that concern; indeed it *is* a continuation of that question as far as Anima is concerned. But what begins to emerge here, and is to become steadily stronger through these three passus until it submerges all else at the end of passus xviii, is the belief that what is urgently necessary for man is the divine, numinous, Messianic force from outside man (whether Redemption, grace or a second coming), and that the charity which saves is not man's but God's.

The mention of Piers causes the dreamer to faint and experience an inner dream which lasts until l. 166. Within that dream he sees the Tree of Charity described by Anima, and Piers himself. Piers' initial account of the tree to the dreamer is discursive and didactic; it continues the account of the moral nature of man but begins to develop hints of the role of God, represented by the three props which support the Tree of Charity and stand for the Trinity. But then the tree itself begins to change. In Anima's account, and Piers' at first, the fruit had been the charity produced or grown by the individual Christian. Now it becomes the different degrees of charitable or virtuous life enacted at different levels of society: the best life, and therefore the finest fruit, is the life of virginity lived by nuns, monks and others dedicated to God, the next is the life of chaste widowhood, and the last and lowest type of the good life is that of the married laity:

> 'Heer now bynethe,' quod he tho, 'if I nede hadde,
> Matrimoyne I may nyme, a moiste fruyt withalle.
> Thanne Continence is neer the crop as kaylewey bastard.
> Thanne bereth the crop kynde fruyt and clennest of alle –
> Maidenhode, aungeles peeris, and arest wole be ripe,
> And swete withouten swellyng – sour worth it nevere.'
>
> (B xvi 67–72)

It is one of Langland's wittier passages. Having introduced the image of fruit for the sake of an earlier argument, he now hints at matrimony's closeness to rotting with 'a moiste fruyt withalle'; identifies widowhood with a superior fruit, the 'kaylewey bastard' or pear from Cailloux, with 'bastard' (meaning 'grafted') perhaps hinting at the medial status of widowhood, having elements of both the other two orders; and develops that idea in order to pun on pears and peers (i.e. 'equals') in labelling virginity 'aungeles peeris'.

The threefold distinction and order of priorities is an ancient one, going back at least as far as St Augustine, whose use of it as an interpretation of the parable of the sower and the harvest of thirtyfold, sixtyfold and hundredfold corn may have influenced Langland here.[6] For both writers there is a perhaps deliberate paradox in the imagery: images of growth, fruit and fecundity are used in support of a doctrine which elevates virginity and sexual abstinence above marriage and sexual reproduction. The paradox underlines a shift in the moral argument. Anima had properly used the tree imagery to express the idea of man's charity 'growing' out of the exercise of various virtues – mercy, pity, following the laws of the Church, and so on; it is an appropriate image for what is conceived of as an organic process. But Piers uses it to express a kind of virtue which is 'preserved' rather than grown: a quality which the individual possesses at birth and struggles to keep free from corruption. (One is strongly reminded here of the contemporary poem *Pearl*, where a contrast is developed between ideas of moral growth and striving for righteousness, associated with images of growing gardens, and an ethic of stasis and innocence, linked with imagery of pearls and other precious stones.) This shift in the moral argument is something that has been developing in the poem as a whole. In the second vision Piers had offered an ideal based on human struggle and achievement, represented appropriately by the metaphor of the journey to Truth and by the image of labouring on the half-acre to grow the harvest and win the Pardon of Truth. As we have seen, Patience proposes an alternative ideal associated with the hermit, an ideal of simplicity, suffering and austerity, remaining free of the world's struggles. It is a development of the latter ideal that Piers now presents in his Tree of Charity: the highest way of life, virginity, is the 'cleanest' rather than the most useful. The latter had been seen to be spotted and stained in the account of Haukyn's coat; one might note the similar use of images of cleanliness in the later reference to hermits and anchorites in passus xix (ll. 253–4). In the elevation of virginity above matrimony there is some similarity to the earlier elevation of clergy above laity in passus viii onwards, but there are more important differences. The clergy had been preferred for their contribution to others, as teachers, guides, or givers of charity; virginity may be primarily a characteristic of the religious but it is here preferred for its own inner purity. The point is made more explicit in the C version, where the two higher fruits are identified with the contemplative life and the lowest with the active. If charity is still the issue, it has shifted its meaning from benevolence to others to become an inner quality, perhaps a benevolence to God.

Immediately, however, Langland subverts this argument in turn, by shaking the fruit from the tree. If the ideal of life is to preserve innocence unspotted by the world, this still will not save the fruit from corruption. It would probably be a mistake to read a moral significance into the dreamer's request to taste the fruit or Piers' acquiescence in shaking it down; the wit of this very witty scene lies in part in the space that lies between the surface drama of idle curiosity and the deeper significance of the event. For what is symbolised here is death itself:

> And Piers caste to the crop, and thanne comsed it to crye;
> And waggede widwehode, and it wepte after;
> And whan he meved matrimoyne, it made a foul noise
> That I hadde ruthe whan Piers rogged, it gradde so rufulliche.
>
> (B xvi 75–8)

In the face of death, even virginity is likely to call out in fear ('crye' – we should not read the modern sense of 'cry' here). But the lesser order, widowhood, weeps when confronted by death, knowing its greater danger, while matrimony, in greater danger still, makes 'a foul noise'. The flourishing fruit, image of man's achievement of charity, is nevertheless subject to death and the fear of damnation. As the fruit falls, Langland identifies it anew:

> For ever as thei dropped adoun the devel was redy,
> And gadrede hem alle togideres, bothe grete and smale –
> Adam and Abraham and Ysaye the prophete,
> Sampson and Samuel, and Seint Johan the Baptist;
> Bar hem forth boldely – no body hym letted –
> And made of holy men his hoord *in Limbo Inferni*,
> There is derknesse and drede and the devel maister.
>
> (B xvi 79–85)

These figures have nothing to do with the triad of virginity, widowhood and matrimony. The tree, which began as the individual heart and then became an emblem of the Christian community in the present, has now modulated into a symbol of world-history, producing as its fruit a succession of worthy individuals from the first man, Adam, to the last to go to Hell before the Redemption, John the Baptist. Just as, in the present, human worth quails before death and the threat of Hell, so in history it has proved inadequate to save men from Hell, even in the case of such virtuous figures as Abraham and Isaiah.

What is involved in these successive modulations of the tree is the use of the different levels of allegory deployed so often in patristic and medieval interpretations of the Bible. Here, the tree is originally conceived on a moral or tropological level as an allegory of the individual Christian producing his own life of charity. It is then reinterpreted, still on the tropological level, as an allegory of the Christian community, producing different kinds of virtuous lives – virginity, widowhood and matrimony. Now it is interpreted again, on the level of strict allegory or typology, as a figure for the world or perhaps humanity, producing numerous individuals through time who fall and are then redeemed. But characteristically, Langland uses the different levels to conduct an argument or dialectic: the initial idea of the achievement of charity through active virtues is overtaken by the concept of a kind of charity or virtue which is to be preserved from the world, and this in turn is overtaken by the recognition that neither kind of human virtue is sufficient in the face of death and the devil and that a divine intervention is needed. The immediate issue is a historical one, how the Fall of Man was reversed by the Son of God. But that itself is ultimately an image of a continuing relationship between God and man that asserts the power of God and the passive role of man. It is, among other things, a dramatic and more emphatic way of expressing the point which Piers had tried to make when he added to Anima's picture of the tree which grows in the heart of man a set of props representing the Trinity. When Piers converts the prop which represents the Son of God into a stick to hurl at the devil and launches the Incarnation, he elevates God from a subordinate to a central position in the salvation of man:

> And Piers, for pure tene, that a pil he laughte,
> And hitte after hym, happe how it myghte,
> *Filius* by the Fader wille and frenesse of *Spiritus Sancti*,
> To go robbe that rageman and reve the fruyt fro hym.
> And thanne spak *Spiritus Sanctus* in Gabrielis mouthe. . . .
>
> (B xvi 86–90)

With Piers' pursuit of the devil and Gabriel's annunciation to the Virgin a radical new time-scheme begins. We are now in the historical past at the time of the Incarnation, and the rest of the poem is to carry us steadily forward through the life of Christ, and the early history of the Church to the time of the poem's composition.

In his conscious mind Langland may not have planned fully the development of the tree image. He writes as if reacting to its existence and gradually discovering its potential for meaning, just as if he were an exegete pondering the meaning of a biblical image. Thus having punned on the notion of 'pears' he deftly redefines the fruit as an apple in order to pick up the associations of the Fall of Man:

> I preide Piers to pulle adoun an appul (B xvi 73)

(for medieval tradition identified the forbidden fruit of Eden as an apple). This leads neatly on to the identification of the individual fruits as Adam and his descendants, with perhaps a visual allusion to the medieval Jesse tree, pictorially representing the descendants of Jesse as roundels in a tree. Finally the props originally introduced to represent the power of the Trinity in supporting the Tree of Charity turn out to be handy weapons for striking the devil (ll. 50–1), and in his most dramatically witty coup Langland then 'sees' in Piers' use of the prop representing the Son of God against the devil who has taken the souls of the just not simply the individual invocation of divine aid against temptation but the historical intervention of the Son of God in the Redemption itself.

Like that earlier instance of Piers' anger in the tearing of the Pardon, where the same phrase 'pure tene' is used, an apparently unconsidered and impassioned act turns out to have major significance for the argument of the poem. Like that example too, earlier hints and later developments reveal that the sudden moment of passion does in fact spring from the deeper current of Langland's thought. The crucial movement of the vision, already hinted at in Anima's speech, is at last clear: from the charity of man to the charity, and eventually the power, of God.

The internal dream continues with an account of Christ's life, from the Annunciation to the Passion (ll. 90–166). The references to *lechecraft* and to Christ's miracles of healing perhaps invite us to see him as exemplar of charity,[7] possibly even as a model for the human charity initially announced as the subject of the passus. But if so this turns out only to be the minor theme. The dominant concern is divine power. The sequence is replete with language of conflict and battle: 'and thanne sholde Jesus juste [joust]' (l. 95), 'and of fightyng kouthe, To have yfoughte with the fend' (ll. 101–2), 'and manaced hem to bete, And knokked on hem with a corde' (ll. 127–8), 'justed in Jerusalem, a joye to us alle. On cros upon Calvarie Crist took the bataille Ayens deth and the devel, destruyyed hir botheres myghtes' (ll. 163–5). Even the *lechecraft* turns out to be primarily directed towards protecting Christ himself in his battle with his enemy (the devil) so that the healing miracles are merely incidental means to practise his skill:

> And Piers the Plowman parceyved plener tyme,
> And lered hym lechecraft, his lif for to save,
> That though he were wounded with his enemy, to warisshen
> hymselve;
> And dide hym assaie his surgenrie on hem that sike were,
> Til he was parfit praktisour, if any peril fille. (B xvi 103–7)

This witty subordination of healing to warfare is a key to the central nature of Langland's highly unusual presentation of the Redemption.

Ever since the twelfth century theologians had emphasised the human aspect of the Redeemer. The Son of God had become man in order to take upon himself the punishment due to man for his disobedience in Eden; his suffering all the pains that a man could endure had both shown his love for man and reconciled mankind to God the Father. Similarly, popular devotion and religious literature had emphasised the humanity of Christ and the suffering he had endured out of love for his fellow-man. The pathos of innocent suffering is the dominant feature. Langland will have none of this. His Redeemer is a powerful, energetic, essentially divine figure anxious to fight as soon as he is born, preparing through his life for the great battle to come and eventually triumphing in battle on the Cross. The healing miracles are less signs of his love than tokens of his power, like his promise to destroy and rebuild the temple (ll. 131–4). Redemption for Langland is an act of God not an act of man or man's representative. The emphasis reflects the argument already developed in the Tree of Charity, that the saving power is not human virtue but divine power.

Piers' role in this inner dream is obviously one of vital importance, and one inevitably asks what it is that he represents here. In passus xv Piers has been allusively identified with God and with Christ, but neither identification quite explains his actions here. His role in initiating the Incarnation suggests the action of God the Father, while his work in guiding Christ's life and preparing him for his conflict with the devil could be ascribed to the Father or the Holy Ghost. Yet Piers speaks of all three members of the Trinity in a way that distinguishes himself from them, and so does the narrator. At the same time the immensity of his role makes it difficult to identify him with either perfect humanity or the divine image in man. Langland himself would probably have been hard pressed to give an answer, and his solution in the C text, to replace Piers in this scene partly with the free will of God and partly with the free will of man, looks like a sign of desperation rather than explication. The answer seems rather to be that the question – 'what does Piers represent' – is itself at fault. Piers is a purely fictive and imaginary figure, not to be identified with anyone or anything outside the poem, and his role is to be explained by reference to the development of the poem itself. In the Visio Piers had entered as the representative of the honest worker and had thus acquired the role of the guide and authority-figure who organised the salvation of others through the co-operative labour of the half-acre. The opening section of passus xvi is in part a commentary on that episode. Piers is still a cultivator, though now of a symbolic garden rather than a real field, and he continues to organise the salvation of others, but because that salvation is now seen to depend on the divine act of redemption, Piers' fictive role is necessarily the supreme one of initiating divine action rather than organising human society.

Part of his significance is that he has ceased to be a model for man because what is needed is beyond man himself. What Piers performs in this episode, whether bringing the Trinity to the aid of man in the present or doing so in the past by initiating the Redemption, or teaching Christ the art of healing, is the work of neither God nor man; it is a dramatic and imaginative way of articulating what is needed for man's salvation, using the structures developed at an earlier stage of the argument in the Visio.

Abraham, Moses and the Samaritan

When the dreamer wakes from his dream within a dream he meets three characters in succession. As their identities, natures and actions are gradually revealed, a complex series of parallel threesomes begins to appear, and the parable of the Good Samaritan, enacted in the dream, is the climax of a process of choosing. The first figure is identified by the dreamer as Abraham, but promptly identifies himself as Faith:

> And thanne mette I with a man, a myd-Lenten Sonday,
> As hoor as an hawethorn, and Abraham he highte.
> I frayned hym first fram whennes he come,
> And of whennes he were, and whider that he thoughte.
> 'I am Feith', quod that freke, 'it falleth noght me to lye,
> And of Abrahames hous an heraud of armes.' (B xvi 172–7)

If his identity as Abraham seems to place us in the time of the patriarchs, two other time-schemes are rapidly superimposed. The reference to Mid-Lent Sunday alludes to the fact that the Book of Genesis, including the story of Abraham, was read in church services during Lent, so that the dreamer might be said to be 'meeting' him in present time; further references to liturgical time recur in the next passus. But Abraham goes on to tell the dreamer that he has recently heard John the Baptist telling the patriarchs in Hell of the coming of Christ, and the dreamer then sees in Abraham's bosom those patriarchs and prophets, along with Lazarus:

> I hadde wonder of hise wordes, and of his wide clothes;
> For in his bosom he bar a thyng, and that he blissed evere.
> And I loked in his lappe: a lazar lay therinne
> Amonges patriarkes and prophetes pleyinge togideres.
>
> (B xvi 253–6)

Abraham's bosom, mentioned as the resting place of Lazarus in Christ's parable of the rich man and the leper, was traditionally understood as a term for the domain of the just in Hell before the Redemption, and the message of John the Baptist to the patriarchs was addressed to the souls waiting there for the imminent arrival of Christ in traditional accounts of the Harrowing of Hell. The time, then, is within the lifetime of Christ and shortly before the Passion. Langland has imaginatively 'dreamed' Abraham out of Hell to look for the Redeemer promised to him centuries before and promised anew by John the Baptist.

Abraham is the historical figure, the patriarch, but like any other biblical figure in medieval tradition he could also be interpreted allegorically. He can appropriately stand for Faith because of the familiar story of his sacrifice of Isaac, mentioned at ll. 231–4. But he himself is much more concerned with his role as spokesman for a particular kind of belief in God, the doctrine of the Trinity. It seems a curious tenet for an Old Testament figure who lived before the full revelation of the Son of God, but there was a patristic tradition that the more favoured Old Testament figures knew of the Trinity, and Abraham's meeting with three angels in Genesis (mentioned at ll. 225–30) was generally understood as a revelation of the Trinity to him. The significance of this aspect of Abraham becomes clear when the dreamer is suddenly confronted by a second figure. This one identifies himself as *Spes* or Hope, but it soon transpires that he is also Moses, the receiver of the Ten Commandments:

> 'I am *Spes*, a spie,' quod he, 'and spire after a knyght
> That took me a maundement upon the mount of Synay
> To rule alle reames therewith – I bere the writ here.' (B xvii 1–3)

He too acts as spokesman for a doctrine of salvation, the principle of loving God and one's neighbour:

> He plukkede forth a patente, a pece of an hard roche,
> Whereon was writen two wordes on this wise yglosed:
> *Dilige Deum et proximum tuum* –
> This was the tixte trewely – I took full good yeme.
> The glose was gloriously writen with a gilt penne:
> *In hiis duobus mandatis tota lex pendet et prophete.*
> 'Is here alle thi lordes lawes?' quod I, 'Ye, leve me,' he seide.
> 'And whoso wercheth after this writ, I wol undertaken,
> Shal nevere devel hym dere, ne deeth in soule greve.
> For though I seye it myself, I have saved with this charme
> Of men and of wommen many score thousand.' (B xvii 10–20)

Again the association of the doctrine with Moses seems paradoxical if not provocative, since the law of love was traditionally considered to be the law of the New Testament and distinguished from the law of the Old. Yet Christ himself had identified loving God and thy neighbour as the essential teaching of the (Jewish) law and the prophets, and the idea is repeated in the preamble to the parable of the Good Samaritan in St Luke's Gospel. Indeed, the equation had already been made by Anima in passus xv:

> 'And Jewes lyven in lele lawe – Oure Lord wroot it hymselve
> In stoon, for it stedefast was, and stonde sholde evere –
> *Dilige Deum et proximum*, is parfit Jewen lawe –
> And took it Moyses to teche men, til Messie coome.'
>
> (B xv 580–3)

There is then a propriety in Moses or Hope carrying a stone tablet on which are carved not the Ten Commandments of the old law but the two commandments of love which belong to the new law. (The remaining peculiarity, that Hope should proclaim the law of love, which is really the third member of the triad, is one which turns out to be central to Langland's thought, as we shall see.)

Abraham supports Moses' claim to have saved 'many score thousand' through his special doctrine or 'charm', but the dreamer comically concludes that their two doctrines, belief in the Trinity and loving God and thy neighbour, are alternative modes of salvation. He weighs up their contrasting attractions and opts for Abraham because his rule is easier. For all the surface comedy of the dreamer's debate over the virtues of the two principles, the issue is an important one and the two principles have a long history in Langland's poem. Belief in the Trinity is what separates Christians from other believers, such as Jews and Saracens, and this point had been made at the end of passus xv by Anima. It is associated, therefore, with the earlier appeal to baptism as the one saving principle and, as Anima's remarks remind us, with the earlier importance attached to the clergy as teachers of the essential tenets of Christianity. Such views had been peremptorily denied by the righteous heathen Trajan, who claimed to have been saved despite his lack of baptism and ignorance of Christianity. What Trajan appeals to as the saving principle is love, the alternative principle proclaimed now by Moses, and it is this law of love which is taken up by Patience and Anima in passus xiii–xv. The dreamer's dilemma between Abraham and Moses re-enacts the earlier development in the poem's argument from faith to love.

At this point the argument is overtaken by events. In a re-enactment of the parable of the Good Samaritan, a Samaritan rides by on his way to Jerusalem and all three characters come across a man wounded and robbed by thieves. Abraham and Moses pass by on the other side, playing the roles of the priest and deacon of the parable, but the Samaritan stops and helps the wounded man, taking him to an inn and providing him with assistance to recover. The re-enactment acquires a multiplicity of meanings. The simplest is that suggested by the familiar saying of St Paul:

> And now abideth faith, hope, charity, these three; but the greatest of these is charity. (1 Corinthians 13: 13)

The parable of the Good Samaritan is introduced by Christ in the Gospel to illustrate the duty of loving one's neighbour, and the Samaritan is therefore a fitting emblem of charity. Faith (Abraham) and Hope (Moses) pass by but Charity (the Samaritan) has mercy on the wounded man. Both the parable itself and the allegorical aspects of the three figures assert the primacy of charity.

There was, however, a long-standing tradition of interpreting the parable not only in the literal fashion suggested by Christ's own words, as an example of charity between man and man, but also according to strict allegory or typology as a parable of the Redemption. On this level, the wounded man is mankind or Adam and Eve, who fell through the attack of the devils (the robbers) and were eventually redeemed by Christ (the Good Samaritan). The priest and deacon who pass by on the other side usually represent the upholders of the old law of Moses. The Wyclifite sermons give an orthodox statement of this interpretation:

> This man that cam doun fro Jerusalem to Jericho is oure firste eldris, Adam and Eve, for thei camen fro sight of pees to state of slydyng, as the moone. Thes theves that woundiden him ben the fendis that temptiden him, but thei lefte lyf in him. . . . This preest that passide first bi mankynde and sigh myscheffe that it was inne, weren patriarkes, bothe bifore the lawe, and in tyme that God gaf law. The dekene that passide bi this weye weren prophetis and othir seintis that weren binethe thes first seintis . . .; and bothe thei knewen that thei myghten not helpe neither other men ne hemsilf fro the synne that thei fellen ynne bi tempting of the fend. But the thridde Samaritan, that was Jesus, helpide mankynde, for he was an alien as anentis his godhede.[8]

Langland goes on to allude to this level of meaning in the Samaritan's speech:

> 'For he seigh me that am Samaritan suwen Feith and his felawe
> On my capul that highte *Caro* – of mankynde I took it –
> He was unhardy, that harlot, and hidde hym *in Inferno*.'
>
> (B xvii 108–10)

Several implications follow from this. Firstly, the historical one: the three figures form a triad of historical characters, Abraham, Moses and Christ, and the action of the parable reveals the historical truth, that the Old Testament representatives Abraham and Moses could not save mankind, Christ alone could. Langland is perhaps alluding here, in his choice of representatives, to the traditional division of world time into three ages: the time before the law, the time of the old law or law of Moses, and the time of the new law of Christ. Abraham is the supreme representative of the first age, Moses of the second, and Langland's version of the parable suggests that neither the virtues of the patriarchs nor those of Mosaic law were sufficient to save mankind.

The Samaritan's own words point to a further level of meaning, concerned with present time:

> May no medicyne under molde the man to heele brynge –
> Neither Feith ne fyn Hope, so festred be hise woundes,
> Withouten the blood of a barn born of a mayde.
> And be he bathed in that blood, baptised as it were,
> And thanne plastred with penaunce and passion of that baby,
> He sholde stonde and steppe – ac stalworthe worth he nevere
> Til he have eten al the barn and his blood ydronke. (B xvii 93–9)

Just as, historically, it needed the sacrifice of Christ to save mankind, so, the Samaritan is arguing, in the present it needs that sacrifice mediated through the sacraments of baptism and the mass to save the individual sinner, something which otherwise neither faith nor hope can do.

But yet another level of meaning, and perhaps the most important, is indicated by the lines of the narrative itself:

> Hope cam hippynge after, that hadde so ybosted
> How he with Moyses maundement hadde many men yholpe;
> Ac whan he hadde sighte of that segge, aside he gan hym drawe
> Dredfully, bi this day, as doke dooth fram the faucon!
>
> (B xvii 61–4)

As we have seen, Abraham stands not only for the time of the patriarchs and for Faith but also for the Christian tenet of belief in the Trinity, while Moses represents not only Mosaic law and hope but also the Christian tenet of love, specifically loving God and your neighbour. What the lines suggest is that neither Hope's 'maundement' of love nor, we may assume, Abraham's commandment of faith in the Trinity can do anything for fallen mankind. According to the other levels of interpretation, love is the greatest of the virtues, enacted by the Good Samaritan of the parable and completing the sequence of Faith, Hope and Charity. But this further level of interpretation deliberately subverts the others, identifying love with the second character, Moses/Hope/the deacon, who is found wanting when the wounded man needs help. The lines make explicit the failure of Hope's teaching, that is, of the saving principle of love. What is being enacted is not merely the inability of the Old Testament to save mankind in the past but also the inadequacy in the present of both belief in the Trinity and loving God and your neighbour.

At one level there is an argument that love is the supreme Christian virtue, with which man can save himself when neither the moral tenets of the Old Testament nor the virtues of faith and hope can help. This has been the argument, more or less, of Trajan, of Patience and of Anima. But the transfer of love to the second place in the triad, the position of failure or at least insufficiency, reflects Langland's deeper challenge to his own earlier (and partially continuing) position. What he is suggesting is that, if love or charity is what saves, it is not the love of man for God and his neighbour but the love of God for mankind. The Pauline doctrine, 'faith, hope and charity, but the greatest of these is charity', is asserted only to be challenged by a higher law, by which the faith and love achieved by men is overwhelmed by the divine love which is best expressed in the Redemption of mankind, though it has a continuing force. And as we have seen in the earlier episode, it is a love which can often be expressed in power and aggression as well as sacrifice and gentleness. The Samaritan talks of the need for the blood of a child to be shed, but is on his way to joust with the devil in Jerusalem.

To sum up this extraordinarily rich episode of the poem, at the heart is the parable of the wounded man who is abandoned by the priest and the deacon but rescued by the Good Samaritan. At a simple level the Gospel story illustrates human charity, and that theme is reinforced by using the three figures to stand for the Pauline triad of faith, hope and charity. But Langland subverts this by invoking the traditional interpretation of the parable as an allegory of redemption and identifying the three with Abraham, Moses and Christ. This in turn leads to a reinterpretation of the kind of charity which the Good Samaritan represents and a new identification of the three figures with belief in the Trinity, man's love of God and his neighbour, and God's love for man. The parable itself enacts the superiority of Christ and his love for man, and the dreamer's pursuit of the Samaritan, abandoning Abraham and Moses, similarly enacts the poem's choice of ideal. If the idea of the saving powers of man's love for others continues a much earlier line of argument about what qualities in man are necessary for salvation, the emphasis on the Redemption of man by Christ enforces a much newer kind of thinking, about the central importance of divine action and love.

If this analysis seems far more schematic than the poem itself, it is because the different levels are developed simultaneously and allusively, with ingenious linkings between the varying identities. At the same time, the whole story is given energetic direction by presenting the Samaritan not simply as a fictional emblem for Christ the Redeemer but as Christ himself riding on his way to Jerusalem to joust with the devil. Similarly, both Abraham and Moses turn out to be impatiently expecting the Redemption, and as they converse with the dreamer it begins to happen.

After the dramatic action and rich symbolism of these scenes, the Samaritan's long sermon (B xvii 133–351) is a bitter disappointment. Much of it is devoted to drawing complex analogies for the doctrine of the Trinity, which fascinated Langland more than one might wish. But one of the issues with which he seems to be grappling here is the difficult and highly relevant one of the relationship of divine power, divine mercy or grace and human merit. This seems to be behind the careful formulation of the roles played by divine redemption and the teachings of faith and hope:

> 'For the barn was born in Bethleem that with his blood shal
> save
> Alle that lyven in Feith and folwen his felawes techynge.'
>
> (B xvii 124–5)

That is, Christ's redemption will only save those who are qualified by their faith and love. Part of the point of the discussion of the Trinity seems to be that it is the Holy Ghost which converts the might of God the Father into a mercy which saves sinners if their merit is insufficient; thus the static and rather conventional image of the Trinity as a candle combining wax, wick and flame suddenly turns into something more unusual and more significant with the suggestion that the 'flame' of the Holy Ghost is what turns the Father's omnipotence into benevolence:

> 'So grace of the Holy Goost the greet myght of the Trinite
> Melteth to mercy – to merciable and to noon othere.'
>
> (B xvii 232–3)

As the last words indicate, Langland wants also to allow for a quality of sinfulness which will 'quench' the loving mercy of the Son and the Holy Ghost, and this is picked up more than once as the discussion develops:

> 'Thus is unkyndenesse the contrarie that quencheth, as it were,
> The grace of the Holy Goost, Goddes owene kynde.
> For that kynde dooth, unkynde fordooth.'
>
> (B xvii 272–4)

135

He seems to be struggling to explicate for himself the implications of the dramatic vision which he has just experienced, trying to reconcile the idea of divine power, seen in Christ's jousting, with the emphasis on his self-sacrificing love, seen in one aspect of the parable and the references to the blood of a child, and these in turn with the importance of human merit which had been such an essential concern of the poem hitherto and still played a part in the parable of the Good Samaritan. The idea of 'kyndenesse' in particular begins to gain importance as an attempt to suggest an element of reciprocity in the relationship of divine mercy and human merit, or divine charity and human charity, to use the terms of the vision's opening. But the poet's own impatience with the attempt to resolve such problems at the level of moral discourse is reflected in the abrupt closure:

'I may no lenger lette!' quod he, and lyard he prikede,
And wente awey as wynd – and therwith I awakede.

(B xvii 352–3)

The vision as a whole is one of the most complex in the poem, but it is also one of the richest in significance. The complexity stems in part from the very rapidity with which Langland shifts his ground and challenges his own arguments, but also from the multiple levels of symbolism and metaphor by which he develops his ideas. He starts rather deceptively rehearsing the issues and arguments which had dominated the poem for the previous three passus, concerning the role of knowledge and the ideal way of life, but then with increasing urgency draws into the poem his own dissatisfaction with this kind of man-centred debate and his intense, almost mystical, yearning for a Messianic authority-figure who will transfer the action to a higher plane. Both the Tree of Charity and the Good Samaritan parable become dramatic enactments of that shift, as Piers and the Good Samaritan, both of them figures for Christ, take over responsibility for the salvation of man and leave human virtues and struggles a merely supporting role. At times Langland expresses the argument sequentially, as we move from Anima's exposition of the duties of man to the account of Christ's battle to redeem mankind. But often he conducts it within the multiple levels of one scene. Thus he offers us the Tree of Charity at one level as an emblem of the human achievement of virtue, but then proposes a further level of meaning which qualifies this ideal and then subverts both by using the tree to reveal at a further level the weakness of man and the power of God and the devil. Similarly he offers the Good Samaritan parable as a metaphor for the triumph of love over faith and hope, but finds within it a further meaning which asserts the failure of love and the triumph of the Redeemer. It is difficult to imagine the mental and imaginative processes by which such extraordinarily rich scenes were conceived; they are perhaps the record of Langland's own successive rereadings of his imaginative creations. But there is no denying the excitement with which Langland responds to Piers and the Good Samaritan, nor the extraordinary energy they bring into the poem.

Notes and references

1. The most recent edition is in *Early Middle English Verse and Prose*, eds J. A. W. Bennett and G. V. Smithers, 2nd edn (Oxford, 1968), pp. 246–61. The distinction between mind and soul is introduced by the English author; the Latin source (printed in *Memorials of St Anselm*, eds. R. W. Southern and F. S. Schmitt (London, 1969), pp. 355–60) does not mention the soul specifically.
2. See *The Macro Plays*, ed. M. Eccles (Early English Text Society 262, London, 1969).
3. On the treatment of these two traditions in Anglo-Saxon and earlier writers, see my article 'Anglo-Saxons on the mind', in *Learning and Literature in Anglo-Saxon England*, eds M. Lapidge and H. Gneuss (Cambridge, 1985), pp. 271–98.
4. Isidore, *Etymologies*, XI i 13 (*Patrologia Latina* 82, col. 399).
5. N. Coghill, 'The Pardon of Piers Plowman', *Proceedings of the British Academy*, **30** (1944), 303–57.
6. See M. Bloomfield, '*Piers Plowman* and the three grades of chastity', *Anglia*, **76** (1958), 227–53.
7. Cf. J. A. Burrow, *Ricardian Poetry* (London, 1971), p. 89.
8. *Select English Works of John Wyclif*, ed. T. Arnold, 3 vols (Oxford, 1869–71), I, 32.

Chapter Eight

The sixth vision: the Passion
and Harrowing of Hell (B xviii)

The narrator dreams again and finds himself in Jerusalem on Palm Sunday. Christ's triumphant entry is followed by his trial and crucifixion, commented on by Faith. In the darkness before Hell there is a debate between Mercy, Truth, Righteousness and Peace. This is interrupted by the Harrowing of Hell itself, and a fierce argument between Christ and the devils. As Christ departs in triumph the four sisters sing and dance in celebration and the dreamer wakes to the sound of the bells of Easter Sunday.

Imaginatively and poetically, the sixth vision is the high point of Langland's work. Its subject, the Passion, is also one of the great themes of medieval religious literature, prompting much of the best work of the period. In drama it was the subject to which those two great but anonymous playwrights, the York Realist and the Wakefield Master, devoted their major efforts, and the autonomous two–part Passion play is the highlight of the N-town cycle.[1] It prompted the best of the Middle English lyrics, from 'Stond wel moder under rode' in the thirteenth century to 'Sodeynly afraid'in the fifteenth.[2] It also played a prominent part in major religious verse narratives such as the thirteenth–century *Cursor Mundi* and the fourteenth–century *Northern Passion*.[3] Much in Langland's account suggests the pleasure and the challenge he found in retelling this story in his own way: the passus contains more straight telling of stories already known than any other in the poem, perhaps more than the rest of the poem taken together, with the events of Palm Sunday and the Passion from the Bible and the stories of Longeus and the Harrowing of Hell from apocryphal legend. But it is also, like the work of the other artists of the period, a personal commentary on the significance of the events.[4] In the previous vision Langland had tried to articulate a growing sense that human faith, love and purity were as nothing compared to the redemptive power and love of God. Now he feels able to explore more fully, indeed to celebrate, that power, and to confront the challenges that might be made to it in the name of truth and justice.

As an account of the Passion Langland's vision is strikingly different from the treatment given in most Middle English writings. There is no long description of the trials and scourging such as we find in the mystery plays or *The Northern Passion*, and no emotional account of Christ's sufferings on the Cross and the lamentation of his followers, such as we find in the lyrics and art. Instead, Langland presents the Passion as a triumphant battle fought by God with death and the devil. The central debate is represented not by the familiar trial scenes, in which Pilate, Herod and the Jews condemn Christ, but by the Harrowing of Hell, in which Christ condemns the devils. The dominant character is the dramatic celebration of the power and divinity of Christ, not his suffering humanity. One of the first points that Langland makes is that Christ will not be harmed in his divinity:

> For no dynt shal hym dere as *in deitate Patris*. (B xviii 26)

Lying behind this difference of presentation may be an important difference of thinking about the Redemption. The image of Christ's suffering humanity seems to have been developed in close association with the doctrine of redemption by satisfaction: that is, that the Son of God became man in order to take upon himself the punishment that was due to man for his disobedience; the death of a wholly innocent man was necessary to redeem mankind, and since all men were guilty the Son of God had himself to become man and suffer for them. Such a doctrine naturally emphasised the extremity of Christ's pain and humiliation, not least because of the associated doctrine that this mode of redemption was chosen by Christ in order to demonstrate his love for man and win man's love. A good example of this theme is a lyric in the Harley collection, entitled by its editor 'The way of Christ's love', which captures both the theology and the associated pathos:

> He saw his fader so wonder wroth
>   with mon that wes yfalle,
> with herte sor he [i.e. the Father] seide his oth
>   we shulde abuggen alle.
> His swete sone to hym gon clepe ant calle,
>   ant preiede he moste deye for us alle . . . .

He brohte us alle from the deth
  ant dude us frendes dede.
Swete Jesu of Nazareth,
  thou do us hevene mede.
Upon the rode why nulle we taken hede?
His grene wounde so grimly conne blede.

His deope wounden bledeth fast;
  of hem we ohte munne.
He hath us out of helle ycast,
  ybroht us out of sunne.
  for love of us his wonges waxeth thinne;
  his herte blod he gef for al monkinne. [5]

The idea of a propitiatory sacrifice to be made by the Son of God to the Father on behalf of man seems entirely absent from Langland's account; indeed he makes little or nothing here of the distinction between Father and Son, and his Christ is throughout a powerful divine figure, the 'lord of life' (B xviii 59). His presentation of Christ and his imagery of warfare seem to relate to a rather different and older view of the Redemption, one which saw it as centring on the relationship between God and the devil rather than the relationship between God and man.[6] According to this theory, the Son of God became man in order to win mankind back from the devil and in some way destroy the devil's rights over mankind. A good example of this interpretation from an earlier English writer is this summary account by Ælfric:

> The justice of Christ is so great that he was not willing to take mankind by force from the devil unless he forfeited it. He did forfeit mankind when he incited the people to the killing of Christ, the Almighty God; and then through his innocent death we were redeemed from the eternal death, if we do not destroy ourselves. Then it befell the cruel devil as it does the greedy fish, which sees the bait and does not see the hook which sticks in the bait; then it is greedy for the bait and swallows the hook along with the bait. So it was with the devil; he saw the humanity in Christ, and not the divinity: he then incited the Jewish people to kill him, and felt the hook of Christ's divinity, through which he was choked to death, and deprived of all mankind who believe in God.[7]

This particular theory of the devil forfeiting mankind through his abuse of power had been firmly repudiated by Anselm at the beginning of the twelfth century:

As for that which we are accustomed to say – that by killing Him who was God and in whom no cause of death was to be found, the Devil justly lost the power which he had obtained over sinners; and that otherwise it would have been an unjust violence for God to make Man free, since Man had voluntarily and not through violence given himself over to the Devil: as for all this, I say, I cannot see what force it has.[8]

Although later theologians generally followed Anselm in abandoning the notion of the Redemption as an issue between God and the devil in favour of the theory of satisfaction, the older idea of the Redemption survived as a minority view. The thirteenth-century compendium of religious history, the *Cursor Mundi*, for example, takes over the earlier image of the baited hook and associates it with battle:

> Nu is the croice graven under greit,
>   and Jesus under stan,
> And hinges all hope of hali kirc
>   in maria mild allan.
> Ai till Jesus the thrid dai
>   had fughten gain sathan,
> And werid him on his aun bit,
>   als hund es on a ban,
> And als the fisch right wit the bait
>   apon the hok es tan,
> For thof he sagh him man als man,
>   his godd-hed sagh he nan. [9]

The thirteenth-century *Château d'Amour* of Grosseteste, which was translated into a number of Middle English versions, uses the idea of the devils' rights, associated now with the concept of ransom rather than forfeit: Christ takes on human life and offers the devil his life in exchange for all others.[10] The commonest way in which the later medieval writers preserved the old idea of the Redemption, however, was through the image of Christ the lover-knight, which combined the older idea with the new emphasis on loving self-sacrifice. The image is best known from the early-thirteenth-century English work the *Ancrene Riwle* but it appears quite widely in Latin and French texts.[11] The allegory describes how a king or king's son disguises himself as a knight in order to rescue his lady from enemies who had captured or besieged her; the king's son is Christ, the armour is his human nature, the lady is man's soul or mankind and the enemies are the devils.

It is this older, alternative tradition that Langland preferred to fol-

low. In passus xvi he had already employed the idea of redemption as
a battle with the devil, and the notion of ransom:

> 'Crist is his name
> That shal delivere us som day out of the develes power,
> And bettre wed for us wage than we ben alle worthi –
> That is, lif for lif.' (B xvi 265–8)

In the initial account of the events of the Passion in passus xviii, battle
images are the most striking. Christ enters as a knight coming to be
dubbed, and Faith plays the role of a herald proclaiming a joust. The
Crucifixion itself is represented as a tournament between Christ and
the devil, and between Life and Death, supervised by Pontius Pilate. The
theme of Christ's power and identity as God is underlined by the other
details which Langland uses here. As in the eighth-century poem *The
Dream of the Rood*, Christ's death is presented as an act of Almighty God
(l. 59). We are reminded of the ways in which creation acknowledged
the divine power even at that moment: the sun was eclipsed, walls shook
and split, the earth quaked and the men rose from the dead (ll. 60–3).
Men too testify to Christ's divinity: the officers dare not touch his body
on the Cross, and the blind knight who is eventually forced to pierce
his body is immediately healed by his blood (ll. 75–86). The final note
is Faith's proclamation of Christ's victory in the tournament over the
devil and death:

> 'For youre champion chivaler, chief knyght of yow alle,
> Yilt hym recreaunt rennyng, right at Jesus wille.
> For be this derknesse ydo, Deeth worth yvenquisshed;
> And ye, lurdaynes, han ylost – for Lif shal have the maistrye.'
> (B xviii 99–102)

The central figure whom the dreamer first sees resembles both Piers
and the Samaritan, but Faith explains that it is Christ who has taken on
the form of Piers in order to conceal his identity as God:

> 'This Jesus of his gentries wol juste in Piers armes,
> In his helm and in his habergeon – *humana natura*.
> That Crist be noght biknowe here for *consummatus Deus*,
> In Piers paltok the Plowman this prikiere shal ryde; . . .
> For no dynt shal hym dere as *in deitate Patris*.' (B xviiii 22–6)

Christ's disguise as man had been a feature of the older redemption
theory, as we have seen, but Langland's particular image of Christ as a
knight disguising himself in the armour that is human nature suggests

that he may have been influenced by the traditional allegory of Christ the lover-knight. If so, there are some important and significant differences. He clearly rejects the romantic love theme. This may partly reflect a distaste for that kind of culture, but it does indicate the character of his presentation. One of the characteristic emphases of late medieval redemption theory is that Christ chose the particular mode of redeeming mankind that he did in order to show his love for mankind and win man's love in return. This is reflected in the love theme of the allegory and the point is explicitly picked up by the author of the *Ancrene Riwle*:

> This king is Jesus, God's son, who . . . entered into a tournament and had, for his sweetheart's love, his shield pierced on every side in the battle like a brave knight. His shield which covered his Godhead was his beloved body that was spread on the cross. . . . 'But Lord', you say, 'What for? Could he not have rescued us with less pain?' Yes, truly, very easily, but he would not, Why? In order to deprive us of every excuse for not giving him our love which he so dearly bought.[12]

Similarly the version of the lover-knight allegory that is closest in detail to Langland, a thirteenth-century Anglo-Norman text by Nicholas Bozon which the poet may have known,[13] says that the king's son could have brought his army to fight but preferred to fight alone in order to win back the love of his lady as well as rescue her. This theme plays little part in Langland's account. For the idea of the lady he substitutes the image of Pier's fruit from the Tree of Charity:

> Lif seith that he lieth, and leieth his lif to wedde
> That, for al that Deeth kan do, withinne thre daies to walke
> And fecche fro the fend Piers fruyt the Plowman,
> And legge it ther hym liketh. (B xviii 31–4)

What is involved here is a view of mankind not primarily as a love object for the king's son, Christ, but as a possession or creation of God. As in the redemption doctrine of the earlier Middle Ages, Langland's picture places God in the centre and mankind on the periphery, with no part to play in the story except as the redeemed possession.

Langland now explores, in two dramatic scenes, the issues of justice and motive raised by the Passion. The dreamer finds himself in some undefined and unbounded space before the gates of Hell. Mercy appears from the west, Truth her sister from the east, then Righteousness from the north and Peace from the south. These characters come originally from Psalm 75:10: 'Mercy and truth have met together; Justice and Peace have kissed each other.' The personification of them as the four daughters of God had become a frequent feature of later medieval discussions of redemption, from Hugh of St Victor and St Bernard in the twelfth century through Grosseteste's *Château d'Amour* and the Middle English *Cursor Mundi* in the thirteenth to the morality play *The Castle of Perseverance* and the N-town cycle of mystery plays in the fifteenth century.[14] Its origins are thought to lie in earlier Jewish Midrashic texts. Given Langland's emphasis on the visual aspect and the approach of the daughters from four directions, it is possible that he was influenced by seeing this debate on the stage. It occurs in French plays as well as the English examples just noted, and although all the surviving examples of dramatic use post-date Langland there were mystery-play performances in London during the period when he was writing the B version[15] and it is possible that these included the debate of the four daughters (no text of the London cycle survives, though Chaucer's allusions to it in *The Miller's Tale* suggest it belonged to the same tradition as the more northerly cycles recorded later). But Hope Traver, who has investigated the topic most thoroughly, remarks, 'I have found it impossible to discover pronounced likeness to . . . any other version of the altercation of the sisters [in *Piers*]. . . . To me the work seems to stand apart, an example of the originality and power of its author.'[16]

The debate of the four daughters figured so prominently in theology and religious literature because it played an important part in explaining and dramatising the later medieval theory of the Redemption, as an allegory of what might be presumed to have taken place in God's mind. The concern of medieval scholasticism with the absolute qualities which define the Deity raised questions about whether God could be God if he was not identified with strict justice and truth to his word. According to the allegory of the four daughters, God's truth and righteousness required him to condemn man to Hell for his disobedience and leave him there for ever, while his mercy and concern for peace urged him on the other hand to pardon man and be reconciled to him. The impasse was resolved by the offer of God's Son to pay the penalty himself, satisfying the demands of strict justice and truth on the one hand and of mercy and peace on the other.

Langland's presentation is indebted to this tradition but strikingly different in its implications – as indeed one might expect, since the debate is normally associated with a theory of redemption which he does not share. He introduces it only to subvert its usual functions. Since the debate dramatises the decision to redeem mankind, it is normally placed in time immediately after the Fall or immediately before the Incarnation. (*The Castle of Perseverance*, being a morality play and therefore dealing with the fate of a representative individual, places it immediately after his death, which is the equivalent of the Fall.) Langland places it instead after the Incarnation and Crucifixion and while the climax of redemption is taking place, so that it becomes not a dramatic representation of God's decision but a commentary on the issues of redemption. It is in part an argument about whether God can break down the gates of Hell and rescue mankind, as he now is threatening to do; an argument, that is, about God's power rather than his will. Truth and Righteousness are undermined by the very certainty of Mercy and Peace that the Redemption not merely will take place but has taken place, so that while the first two produce the traditional arguments as to why man cannot be saved, the other two come to celebrate the fact of his salvation. They refuse to see God as being hampered by the demands of truth and justice, which are articulated in churlish language that contrasts strikingly with the measured harmonious language of Mercy and Peace:

'That thow tellest', quod Truthe, 'is but a tale of waltrot!'

(B xviii 142)

'What, ravestow?' quod Rightwisnesse; 'or thow art right
dronke!' (B xvii 187)

As is to become clear in the next scene, God's righteousness is of a very different kind from that espoused by Righteousness herself. God's personal whim is superior to the dictates of reason, and Mercy is able to applaud his guile and 'good sleighte'. The point is perhaps underlined for us by the choice of names. In the first two visions Truth had been the main name for God and had been used to emphasise the qualities of fidelity and duty associated with God; now Truth is only a subordinate and rather despised aspect of the divine will, if that, and God himself is obliquely referred to as Love. Mercy's argument that Christ's death will destroy the death introduced into Eden by the devil, and that his guile will overturn Lucifer's guile, implicitly deals with the problem of the devil's rights and the question of injustice to the devil, suggesting that Christ's death will provide a ransom or exchange and that the imprisonment of mankind in Hell is itself based on an earlier injustice. Peace then disposes of the problem of God's own justice in relation to man, offering a fresh explanation of the Fall and Redemption which denies all the usual notions of crime and punishment and presents the two events as part of the original dispensation; God intended that both he and man should have experience of pain as well as bliss, so as to appreciate bliss properly.

The theme of God's power is then asserted by Book, representing the Bible. What he recalls, on biblical authority, is that all creation acknowledged Christ's divine power: the sky, the sea, the earth, and Hell.

This argument was generally used to highlight by contrast the obduracy of the Jews in refusing to recognise Christ as God, but Langland is making a different point: simply that Christ has shown his power over all created things already, and will now reaffirm it in conquering Hell and releasing its inhabitants.

Traditionally at this point in the heavenly debate the Son of God intervenes to announce his willingness to save man through his own sacrifice and thus reconcile the four views. That, in a sense, is what happens here, but in a dramatically different form. The wrangling of the four sisters in the darkness above Hell is interrupted by an angelic voice at the gates of Hell demanding entrance for the King of glory. Instead of a debate in Heaven, Langland expresses Christ's determination to save mankind, and his justification for doing so, in a triumphant address to the devils in Hell at the very moment of redemption. The choice of the Harrowing of Hell as a major scene is itself significant. Christ's conquest of Hell, breaking down the gates and releasing the prisoners, perfectly epitomises the doctrine of the Redemption as a battle with death and the devil. Langland dramatises the scene in its full power, stressing the aggressive strength of Christ and the terror of the devils, because it fits so well with his own view of Redemption as an act of divine power. At the same time, in shifting the resolution of the debate of the four sisters from Heaven to Hell he underlines the fact that for him the resolution lies between God and the devil rather than between the Father and the Son.

In its general structure the narrative of the Harrowing of Hell in passus xviii owes much to the tradition which was established as early as the fourth century by the apocryphal narrative known as the *Gospel of Nicodemus* [17] and followed by the mystery plays and other medieval narratives of Christian history, such as the *Cursor Mundi*. The *Gospel* purports to be the narrative of two men who had died before the Crucifixion and thus been in Hell when the events occurred, though subsequently brought back in life. Thus the story is told from the perspective of Hell's inhabitants: biblical figures from Adam to John the Baptist rehearse their prophecies of redemption which they now see approaching, while the devils state their defiance, argue with Christ about his rights to mankind and are eventually defeated. Langland refers only briefly to the prophets and patriarchs (ll. 324–5) and concentrates his attention on the fears and defiance of the devils and on Christ's triumphant challenge to them. The structure emphasises the conflict between God and devil, but Langland uses it to articulate his own sense of the crucial images and themes of the Redemption. His central concern is the question of justification: how can the act of divine mercy which he sees in the Redemption be reconciled with a system of justice or righteousness? It is, one suspects, not merely a scholastic issue of 'saving' the concept that God is all justice and all truth; it is a matter of preserving the meaningfulness of existence from the threatening concept of an arbitrary, if benevolent, whim of an absolute God. Thus Lucifer insists on his rights over mankind, because of the Fall, and claims that God, being Truth, cannot go back on his promise that mankind should die and dwell in Hell:

> 'If he reve me of my right, he robbeth me by maistrie;
> For by right and by reson the renkes that ben here
> Body and soule beth myne, bothe goode and ille.' (B xviii 276–8)

Satan and Gobelyn, however, raise doubts that Lucifer's use of guile against Adam and Eve may invalidate their legal claim to man. The devil reiterates this fear, and claims that he had recognised Christ's divinity and the threat he posed and sought to prevent his death.

The angelic voice of power speaks and breaks down the gates of Hell, Christ enters in and takes his people into his protection. But not content with the mere act of power, he pauses to explore and expound, on the poet's behalf, the possible justifications for taking mankind from the devils. He acknowledges the claims already made by Truth and Righteousness, and again by Lucifer, that justice requires man to remain in Hell. His first words – 'lo here my soule to amendes for alle synfulle soules' (ll. 328–9) – seem to point to the doctrine of satisfaction. But the satisfaction which he proposes is of the devil rather than the Father, and it is one imposed on the devils by an act of divine power and will. In taking on man's mortality Christ takes on a life which he can offer in exchange for man's. The term he uses is ransom (l. 353), which seems to acknowledge the devil's rights of a sort, but it is an imposed ransom. The further justification for imposing this exchange or ransom is the guile used by Lucifer, a point already made by Mercy and by the other devils. Man only fell through the guile of the devil and Christ is therefore justified in guilefully using his disguise or personality as man both to lure the devil into conflict (the earlier joust or tournament) and to impose an exchange, his soul for man's. On the one hand, then, the deceit used by the devil in Eden affords justifications for undoing the effects of the Fall, on the other the symbols of exchange, of ransom, and of power in disguise suggest ways in which the Redemption itself might be enacted with fairness.

Christ now takes the problem of mercy and justice to a further stage by extrapolating it from the Harrowing of Hell to the Last Judgement in Heaven and extending it to cover not only those who have suffered in Hell before his coming because of original sin, but also those who sin individually in the future. According to orthodox doctrine the time for mercy will then be over and strict justice will be exacted on all, but with a series of analogies Christ now tries to circumvent even that kind of justice. At the Last Judgement, he suggests, the devils will be judged with strict justice, but Christ's nature will require him to show mercy to man (ll. 374–9). Equally (ll. 380–1), just as in earthly justice a man is not hanged twice, so God will not condemn man a second time.[18] Again (382–90), on earth a criminal is freed if the king chances to come into his presence; so too, by implication, God can be justified in saving, if he wishes, sinners who come into his presence at the Last Judgement. Finally Christ returns more emphatically to the notion that the human nature which he has acquired through the Incarnation will justify him in showing mercy at the end of time. The underlying theology seems to be that Christ disguised himself in human form to win the patriarchs back from the devils, but as an almost unforeseen corollary taking on human form gave him fellow-feeling for all mankind.

The intense pressure here to find some way of reconciling merciful acts of grace with an ideal of justice, or at least of fairness, can hardly be missed. Repeatedly the poet insists that love and mercy acquire their own kind of righteousness and legality:

'I may do mercy thorugh rightwisnesse, and alle my wordes
    trewe . . .
Thus by lawe', quod Oure Lord, 'lede I wole fro hennes
Tho that me lovede and levede in my comynge.'
                 (B xviii 390, 401–2; MS reading)

A point made by both Christ and Peace is that God can choose to exercise his grace if he pleases:

'And if lawe wol I loke on hem, it lith in my grace
Wheither thei deye or deye noght for that thei diden ille . . . .'
'Was nevere werre in this world, ne wikkednesse so kene,
That Love, and hym liste, to laughynge ne broughte.'
                 (B xviii 387–8, 415–16)

The final argument is that God cannot be constrained by notions of truth and justice:

'For inpossible is no thyng to Hym that is almyghty.'
                 (B xviii 421)

Truth and Righteousness cheerfully acknowledge their defeat and dance with Peace and Mercy in triumph. The note is picked up by the dreamer too as the vision ends:

'For swich is the myghte,
May no grisly goost glide there it shadweth!' (B xviii 433–4)

These final tensions are a key to the whole vision. The dominant
note is the celebration of the Redemption as an act of immense power
by God to regain possession of his creature, conquering death and the
devil and breaking through the constraints of truth and righteousness
as he breaks through the gates of Hell. The act is directed at the devil
rather than mankind, and notions of pleading with man for a response
which will validate the redeeming act (a feature of the *Ancrene Riwle*, the
lyrics and the mystery plays) play no part in his vision. Much of the
emotional excitement present in the vision, mirrored in the dreamer's
waking response, stems precisely from the picture of an all-powerful, all-
merciful God and the release which this gives from earlier concerns
with the duty of man. The denial that man's imprisonment in Hell was
part of a scheme of justice and punishment has major implications for
mankind in the present too. Yet Langland's introduction of the four
daughters debate and his presentation of the arguments in Hell show
that justification of the Redemption was an important part of his concerns. He is interested in how God reconciled salvation of man with
justice, both in terms of his relationship with the devil and in terms of
his own nature and principles, perhaps as much as a promise for the future as an explanation of the past. Justice and mercy have continually
been opposed in the poem, notably in the tearing of the Pardon where
the strict system of merit and reward symbolised by the plowing and
epitomised in the Pardon is contrasted with a simple trust in God. In
this passus Langland insists both on the power of God to save and his
ability to override the claims of justice. The claims of the devils are
rejected because of their use of guile and cancelled by the exchange of
Christ's life, while the troubling question of why God should wish to
save mankind without apparent regard to human merit is answered by
the appeal to Christ's natural feelings for his brothers. God's divinity
and power as Langland sees them dwarf questions of human merit, and
that is the dominant theme of the passus, powerfully symbolised in the
images of Christ in armour and the breaking of the gates of Hell. But
his continual return to the problem of justice and justification reflect
an underlying anxiety that the all-enveloping power of divine grace
may leave him with an irrational and meaningless world. The next two
passus are to show a more sustained attempt to relocate the idea of
redemption in the real world.

The end of the vision marks a crucial point in a long historical sequence. As the fruit falls from the tree in passus xvi we find ourselves
at the beginning of history with the allusions to the Garden of Eden

and the death of Adam. Old Testament time is continued with the figures of Abraham and Moses until we find ourselves in the time of Christ and watching the Crucifixion. But another time-scheme is suggested by the closing lines of passus xviii. The dreamer wakes to find the church bells ringing for Easter Day, celebrating the Resurrection. This is the culmination of a liturgical framework which began in passus xvi at the meeting with Abraham in mid-Lent. When the dreamer sleeps again it is Palm Sunday, commemorating the entry of Christ into Jerusalem, which is what, in a veiled form, he then dreams of. His vision takes him through the events of Good Friday and Easter Sunday to the Resurrection of Easter Sunday, when he awakes. What is being suggested, then, is that the events of the distant past seen in vision are being re-enacted in present time in the liturgy. The historical Redemption here finds a relevance to the continuing present. (The point is picked up at the beginning of the next passus where the Redemption is visibly re-enacted in the sacrifice of the mass.) Langland is perhaps offering an alternative here to the characteristic answers of his time about the continuing relevance of the Redemption. If one sees the Redemption as an act of loving sacrifice intended to win man's love in return, one must therefore respond by entering into the highly emotional and personal love relationship suggested by so much of medieval vernacular literature. But this is not Langland's view of the Redemption, and he has already captured in the Good Samaritan episode his conviction that love is not enough. The love he talks of there is in any case an extrapolation of Moses' law, not a response to the Crucifixion; it is the love of God not the love of the crucified Christ. The Redemption for Langland is an act of divine intervention which achieves what man cannot achieve, and its continuing significance for him lies in its subversion of earlier concerns with what man must do for salvation. One way in which that redeeming power is still manifested in the present is in the sacraments of the Church and the liturgy. Another, to be developed in passus xix, is in the emphasis on grace. But the last and perhaps most important is the idea of a second coming, hinted at in the closing lines of the poem.

Notes and references

1. For the York cycle see *The York Plays*, ed. R. Beadle (London, 1982). The Wakefield Master seems to have written or revised most of the plays on the Passion in *The Towneley Plays*, eds G. England and A.W. Pollard (Early English Text Society ES 71, London, 1897). The N-town passion play appears in *Ludus Coventriae*, ed. K.S. Block (Early English Text Society ES 120, London, 1922), pp. 225–349.

2. On lyrics on the Passion see R. Woolf, *The English Religious Lyric in the Middle Ages* (Oxford, 1968), pp. 19–66, 183–238. 'Stond wel' is in *The Harley Lyrics*,

ed. G.L. Brook (Manchester, 1948), no. 20; 'Sodeynly Afraid' is in *Religious Lyrics of the Fifteenth Century*, ed. C. Brown (Oxford, 1939), no. 9.

3. *Cursor Mundi*, ed. R. Morris (Early English Text Society OS 57, 59, 62, 66, 68, 99, 101, London, 1874–93); *The Northern Passion*, ed. F.A. Foster (Early English Text Society OS 145, 147, 183, London, 1913–30).

4. See the excellent accounts by N. Coghill, 'God's wenches and the light that spoke', in *English and Medieval Studies presented to J.R.R Tolkien*, eds. N. Davis and C.L. Wrenn (London, 1962), pp. 200–18, and R. A. Waldron, 'Langland's originality: the Christ-Knight and the Harrowing of Hell', in *Medieval English Religious and Ethical Literature: Essays in Honour of G.H. Russell*, eds G. Kratzmann and J. Simpson (Cambridge, 1986), pp. 66–81.

5. Brook, *Harley Lyrics*, p. 71.

6. See R. Woolf, 'The theme of Christ the lover-knight in medieval English literature', *Review of English Studies*, **13** (1962), 1–16.

7. *The Homilies of the Anglo-Saxon Church: the First Part, containing the Sermones Catholici or Homilies of Ælfric*, ed. B. Thorpe (London, 1844), 216.

8. Quoted and translated in R. W. Southern, *The Making of the Middle Ages* (London, 1953), p. 245.

9. Morris, *Cursor Mundi*, ll. 16923–34.

10. See *The Middle English Translations of Robert Grosseteste's Château d'Amour*, ed. K. Sajavaara (Helsinki, 1967).

11. See W. Gaffney, 'The allegory of the Christ-Knight in *Piers Plowman*', *Publications of the Modern Language Association of America*, **46** (1931), 155–68, and Woolf, 'The theme of Christ the lover-knight'; and for the *Ancrene Riwle* the convenient edition by Geoffrey Shepherd, *Ancrene Wisse* (London, 1959), pp. 21–3.

12. See Shepherd, *Ancrene Wisse*, p. 22 (the translation is mine).

13. See Gaffney, 'The allegory'.

14. See H. Traver, *The Four Daughters of God* (Bryn Mawr, 1907).

15. See Alan Nelson, *The English Medieval Stage* (Chicago, 1974), pp. 170–8.

16. Traver, *Four Daughters*, p. 150.

17. For the Latin text see *The Gospel of Nicodemus*, ed. H.C. Kim (Toronto, 1973); for the Middle English version, *The Middle English Harrowing of Hell and Gospel of Nicodemus*, ed. W.H. Hulme (Early English Text Society ES 100, London, 1908).

18. The first time, Schmidt suggests in his commentary, is death, but Langland may be thinking of the Fall and subsequent condemnation of mankind to Hell as the first occasion.

Chapter Nine

The seventh and eighth visions: Grace and Antichrist (B xix–xx)

The dreamer falls asleep in church and in his dream sees Christ in the form of Piers. Conscience tells him more about Christ's life, and the dreamer sees the coming of the Holy Spirit to the apostles. The Spirit, now called Grace, distributes talents to mankind and, with Piers, organises an allegorical plowing of the world and the building of a barn called Unitee. Pride with his army attacks, and Conscience with his followers retreats to the barn but individuals begin to rebel. The dreamer wakes and is lectured by Nede. He sleeps and dreams again, and sees Antichrist with his army devastate the crops and attack the barn. A battle ensues, Conscience is besieged in the barn and calls for help. The friars answer his call but work to undermine the followers of Conscience. Conscience swears to become a pilgrim and seek Piers' help. The dreamer wakes.

The note of confidence and celebration heard at the end of passus xviii was achieved by turning away from both society and the self to concentrate on the divine. This would have been the perfect note on which to end the poem, leaving it with a recognisable (if unpremeditated) structure: a search for perfection or salvation which moves from the reform of society to the purification of the individual and the inner self and then moves on again to the redeeming role of God. Instead, Langland turns back to the social concerns of the Visio. The decision to continue the poem perhaps reflects his determination to confront the major question left by the previous vision's triumphant account of the Redemption: how can the divine achievement be absorbed into human society? One of the major features of this last section, symbolised

by the central position of the character Nede, is the insistent concern
with the necessities of physical existence and the limitations posed by
human reality. Hence the return to the plowman role of Piers.

The framework of the narrative in the last two passus is the history
of Christendom from the time of Christ to the present. Langland is here
continuing a historical sequence that had begun in passus xvi. The Tree
of Charity had turned into a world-tree producing as its fruit figures
from the Old Testament period, from the beginning of time with Adam
down through Abraham, Isaiah, Samson and Samuel to John the Baptist. The subsequent narrative carried the story forward through the life
of Christ to culminate in the Resurrection at the end of passus xviii.
The same time sequence is dramatised in the intervening episode of
the Good Samaritan, with the dreamer meeting Abraham, Moses and
Christ in turn. The last two passus tell, symbolically, of subsequent history up to the present. Conscience narrates events up to the Ascension
and the dream then presents the first Pentecost and a symbolic account
of the development of the early Church: plowing with the four evangelists, cultivating with the four great Fathers of the Church, sowing the
seed of the cardinal virtues, growing the crop of truth and harvesting it
into the barn called Holy Church. The attacks by Pride and Antichrist
(associated particularly with the coming of the friars) represent the subsequent corruption of society and the Church. The historical sequence
thus culminates in the penetration and corruption of the Church by the
friars in the thirteenth and fourteenth centuries, taking us up to
Langland's own time. But on another level of meaning Langland uses
this historical sequence as the basis for a mythic account of human
society and its relation to the divine, describing the creation of a perfect
society and its gradual sophistication and collapse: the historical figures
of St Peter and the apostles are equated with the fictional characters
Piers and his fellows.

It is in a confident and positive mood that Langland resumes the
poem. Earlier points of transition had described the narrator wandering for some time and musing on his visions, but here there is a brisk
return to vision with no hint of a break in composition or mystification
about what has preceded:

Thus I awaked and wroot what I hadde ydremed,
And dighte me derely, and dide me to chirche,
To here holly the masse and to be housled after.
In myddes of the masse, tho men yede to offryng,
I fel eftsones aslepe – and sodeynly me mette
That Piers the Plowman was peynted al blody,
And com in with a cros bifore the comune peple
And right lik in alle lymes to Oure Lord Jesu. (B xix 1–8)

The poet initially develops the preceding vision's emphasis on divine power. The dual vision of Christ/Piers prompts Conscience to distinguish between Christ's appearance as suffering human and his divine reality as conqueror, and an innocent enquiry about Christ's two names, Jesus and Christ, allows Conscience to explain at length that the name Christ refers to the Saviour's identity as knight, king and conqueror:

> 'Thow knowest wel', quod Conscience, 'and thow konne reson,
> That knyght, kyng, conquerour may be o persone. . . .
>   for Jesus was yfulled
> And upon Calvarie on cros ycrouned kyng of Jewes.
> It bicometh to a kyng to kepe and to defende,
> And conqueror of his conquest hise lawes and his large . . .
> And tho conquered he on cros as conquerour noble;
> Might no deeth hym fordo, ne adoun brynge,
> That he n'aroos and regnede and ravysshed helle.
> And tho was he conquerour called of quyke and of dede . . .
> And sith he yeveth largely al his lele liges
> Places in Paradis at hir partynge hennes,
> He may well be called conquerour – and that is 'Crist' to mene.'
>   (B xix 26–7, 40–3, 50–3, 60–2)

Once again, as in passus xvi and xviii, Langland retells the story of Christ's life and death so as to reveal the underlying theme of divine power and conquest: the homage of the angels and the three kings at Christ's birth testified to his high status, and those aspects of his life which might point to a different view of him – patient suffering, concealment, flight – were, Langland ingeniously and perhaps half-jokingly suggests, but the necessary sleights of a leader and conqueror:

> 'As it bicometh a conquerour to konne manye sleightes,
> And manye wiles and wit, that wole ben a ledere;
> And so dide Jesu in hise dayes, whoso hadde tyme to telle it.
> Som tyme he suffrede, and som tyme he hidde hym,
> And som tyme he faught faste, and fleigh outherwhile,
> And som tyme he gaf good and grauntede heele bothe,
> Lif and lyme – as hym liste he wroghte.
> As kynde is of a conquerour, so comsede Jesu.' (B xix 99–106)

Conscience then develops this idea by adapting the earlier triad of Dowel, Do-bet and Do-best, a scheme lost sight of (except in the rubrics) since passus xiv. The way in which the scheme is now used shows how far Langland has travelled since then. Previously, the triad marked stages in the spiritual development of the individual or levels of moral worth within human society. Now, it marks stages in the redeeming role of Christ the conqueror. The difference reflects the new emphasis, evident since passus xvi, on the power of God to save rather than the merit of man. Thus, Conscience goes on to explain, Christ enacted Do-wel when he used his power and grace to turn water into wine, a miracle which testified to Christ's power not only literally but also figuratively, for it is interpreted by Conscience as an emblem of giving the new law of love in the manner of a conqueror imposing new laws (Langland is perhaps here drawing on a traditional exegesis which interprets the water vessels whose contents are turned to wine as the six ages of the world given new meaning by Christ).[1] Subsequently, he enacted Do-bet through his miracles of healing and feeding others, which caused him to be called by the royal title of Son of David, and through his resurrection, which led St Thomas to hail him as lord and king. The final stage, Do-best, is one resonant of the Visio's imagery: Christ granted pardon to mankind and gave Piers power to absolve them of their sins, provided that they observed the terms of the Pardon, that is, to pay what they owe:

> 'And whan this dede was doon, Dobest he taughte,[2]
> And yaf Piers power, and pardon he grauntede:
> To alle maner men, mercy and foryifnesse;
> To hym, myghte men to assoile of alle manere synnes,
> In covenaunt that thei come and kneweliche to paye
> To Piers pardon the Plowman – *Redde quod debes.*
> Thus hath Piers power, be his pardon paied,
> To bynde and unbynde bothe here and ellis,
> And assoille men of alle synnes save of dette one.' (B xix 183–91)

The passage may have been miscopied (l 186 is in fact heavily emended) and it is difficult to be sure of what precisely Langland wrote, but the straightforward point here is that the final and greatest act of divine power exercised by Christ was the Redemption of mankind. The specific terms are important, however. Langland was probably thinking of Christ's words to the disciples in St John's Gospel immediately preceding the episode of doubting Thomas: 'whose soever sins ye remit, they are remitted unto them; and whose soever sins ye retain, they are retained' (John 20: 23). But the specific reference to Piers, and the imagery of binding and unbinding (l. 190), while appropriately emphasising the idea of Christ as the conqueror, which is the main theme of Conscience's argument, draw on Christ's earlier words to St Peter:

> And I will give unto thee the keys of the kingdom of heaven: and whatsoever thou shalt bind on earth shall be bound in heaven; and whatsoever thou shalt loose on earth shall be loosed in heaven. (Matthew 16: 19)

Langland chooses to express the supremacy of Christ's redemption of man in language which points to the separation of that power from Christ himself. What interests Langland is the gradual devolution of redemptive power from the pure divinity of Christ through Piers/Peter to the complex and therefore corrupt humanity of the Church (cardinals, vicars, friars, priests). At the very moment of celebrating Christ's greatest act Langland is initiating what becomes a downward movement, the devolution of divine power from Christ himself to the Church. As a mark of that separation, the gradual identification of Piers with Christ in previous passus is now, equally gradually, being unravelled. Piers here is clearly St Peter rather than Christ. Appropriately, the next few lines describe the departure of Christ to Heaven, leaving mankind to carry on. But the mention of Piers and the Pardon also takes us back to the Visio and invites us to consider the relation of this scene to the earlier one, initiating a sustained reinterpretation of the imagery of plowing which is to carry us through the last two passus. An important further point is the emphasis on the reciprocity of salvation: through his redemption Christ grants pardon to all, but its effect depends on a response from mankind. Langland is here picking up again a dilemma prominent in passus xvii: the all-encompassing mercy of a powerful God dominates his thought, but an answering anxiety about the duty of man and the moral principles of selection continues to press. Indeed, one of the major concerns of these last two passus is the distinguishing of sheep from goats.

The building of the Church

The theme of devolving power is now taken further. The narrative passes from Conscience to the dreamer himself and he sees the coming of the Holy Spirit over the apostles at the first Pentecost being re-enacted over Piers 'and his felawes':

> and thanne cam, me thoughte,
> Oon *Spiritus Paraclitus* to Piers and to his felawes.
> In liknesse of a lightnynge he lighte on hem alle
> And made hem konne and knowe alle kynne langages.
>
> (B xix 201–4)

Conscience explains that the Holy Spirit is Grace, and the dreamer joins in the singing of a hymn to him. The lyrical moment suddenly lifts the vision to another plane and the poem moves from a literal account of New Testament events to an allegorical myth of the creation of Christendom. The Holy Spirit appears as Grace, Piers shifts in status from St Peter the apostle to a metaphorical plowman, and the coming of the

Spirit to the disciples is then re-enacted at another level as Grace sets off with Piers to distribute gifts to all mankind. In Acts (2:1–4) the Spirit brings to the apostles the gift of tongues, so that they are able to preach the word of God in words that are understood by all the nationalities present. In his first epistle to the Corinthians St Paul expands the topos:

> Now there are diversities of gifts, but the same Spirit. And there are differences of administrations, but the same Lord. And there are diversities of operations, but it is the same God which worketh all in all. But the manifestation of the Spirit is given to every man to profit withal. For to one is given by the Spirit the word of wisdom; to another the word of knowledge by the same Spirit; to another divers kinds of tongues; to another the interpretation of tongues: but all these worketh that one and the self-same Spirit, dividing to every man severally as he will. (Corinthians 12: 4–11)

Langland goes on to quote in Latin the opening words of this passage, but in his version the theme is totally transformed. The gifts which Grace now gives to men are not just the spiritual qualities mentioned by St Paul but all the talents which flourish in a 'modern' complex society:

> Some he yaf wit, with wordes to shewe –
> Wit to wynne hir liflode with, as the world asketh,
> As prechours and preestes, and prentices of lawe –
> They lelly to lyve by labour of tonge,
> And by wit to wissen othere as grace hem wolde teche.
> And some he kennede craft and konnynge of sighte,
> With sellynge and buggynge hir bilyve to wynne.
> And some he lered to laboure on lond and on watre,
> And lyve by that labour–a lele lif and a trewe.
> And some he taughte to tilie, to dyche and to thecche,
> To wynne with hir liflode bi loore of his techynge.
> And some to devyne and divide, noumbres to kenne;
> And some to compace craftily, and colours to make;
> And some to se and to seye what sholde bifalle,
> Bothe of wele and of wo, telle it er it felle –
> As astronomyens thorugh astronomye, and philosofres wise.
> And somme to ryde and to recovere that unrightfully was wonne;
> He wissed hem wynne it ayein through wightnesse of handes,
> And fecchen it fro false men with Folvyles lawes.
> And some he lered to lyve in longynge to ben hennes,
> In poverte and in pacience to preie for alle Cristene.
>
> (B xix 230–50)

Once again we see the devolution from spiritual simplicity to earthly complexity.

What is striking about the list of talents distributed by Grace is the very wide range of human activities to which it lends blessing, in comparison with the more limited list sanctioned by the Visio. It covers not only plowing and productive labour but art and science, trading and the law, and the eremitic life. A hierarchy of sorts is hinted at:

'Though some be clenner than some, ye se wel,' quod Grace,
'That he that useth the faireste craft, to the fouleste I kouthe
    have put hym.' (B xix 253–4)

but neither plowing nor the ascetic life is specified as the best, and the stress is on equality in the eyes of God. All this is highly important in the light of the earlier development of the poem's ideas. The high status and central position occupied by plowing in the Visio had been questioned by the tearing of the Pardon, and steadily challenged in succeeding passus until finally repudiated in passus xiii and xiv with the destruction of Haukyn and the elevation of the opposing ideal of patient poverty. Now both plowing and poverty have their place, alongside occupations that had barely passed for tolerable in the Visio, such as law and trade, all acceptable in the sight of God because they use the talents distributed by Grace. In turning back from the contemporary world to the Redemption and the idea of a redeemed humanity, Langland seems to have found it possible to achieve a satisfactory synthesis of the earlier conflict between social and spiritual ethics and to develop an image of society more tolerant of complexity.

The major difference between this vision of the ideal society and that of the first two visions is that the former one is based on Redemption while the latter was based on Creation. In the first two visions, Holy Church invokes the idea of God as Creator, and the conditions of creation are seen to define the duties of man. God is referred to as Truth, not as Christ (at least in the A version). Knighthood is justified by appealing to its existence since the beginning of time. The plowman is justified by his co-operation with God as Creator, tending God's cattle and sowing his seed. The emphasis on *kynde* in the Visio similarly reflects the attempt to develop an ideal of man and society which takes its terms from the fact and nature of God's creation of man and the world. The same sort of appeal to the origins of society is made in the B text addition on kingship: this is how society was first formed and how it should be. But the social myth of the last two passus is quite different. Its source and starting-point is the Redemption, and its parameters are Christ and the Church. It is a society designed to produce the crop of Christendom, not to plow the half-acre. Crucially,

the occupations of the working world are now seen to stem not from
the creation of earth, man and animals, but from inner gifts or talents
given to individuals by divine grace. To work is thus defined as a fulfilment of the divine gift in man rather than a pursuit of material things,
which had become increasingly ambivalent in the Visio. Work is also
presented, following a monastic tradition, as a weapon against sloth
rather than as a contribution to others.

Langland's own awareness that he is rewriting or reinterpreting the
poem's past is evident from his next move: he recalls the other aspect
of Piers, the plowman, and draws on the imagery of agriculture to create
an allegory of the development of Christendom:

'For I make Piers the Plowman my procurator and my reve,
And registrer to receyve *redde quod debes*.
My prowor and my plowman Piers shal ben on erthe,
And for to tilie truthe a teeme shal he have.'
Grace gaf Piers a teeme – foure grete oxen. (B xix 260–4)

The imagery seems to suggest, in optimistic vein, the naturalness of truth
in man, but the details of the allegory also strongly emphasise the role
of divine grace and its agents: Grace and Piers sow the cardinal virtues
in man's soul, cultivate them with the help of the four evangelists and
the four doctors, and harvest them with the help of priesthood. Grace
and Piers together cultivate truth in man (l. 335). It is a myth which emphasises the role of divine grace and the church in salvation rather than
the efforts of the individual Christian.

The limitation implicit in this is acknowledged in the scenes which
follow. Grace and Piers depart from the scene and Langland imagines
in their place a society of workers led by Conscience, who here seems a
representative of human efforts. Grace had already warned of the future assaults of Antichrist and Pride and spoken of his own departure
(ll. 219 ff); Piers presumably must disappear too, as the agent of Grace.
Their departure is part of the gradual devolution of redemptive power
from God to humanity. Conscience goes on to acknowledge the helplessness of Church and society in the absence of God:

'we beth noght of strengthe
To goon agayn Pride, but Grace weere with us.' (B xix 361–2)

Both the subsequent weakness of Conscience and his final departure
to seek Grace make it clear that Grace is not 'with us' any more.

Langland sees the attack of Pride as in part a growing sophistication
of society which complicates moral issues; thus Pride's emissaries tell
Conscience that

> 'youre carte the Bileeve
> Shal be coloured so queyntely and covered under oure
>   sophistrie,
> That Conscience shal noght knowe by Contricion
> Ne by confession who is Cristene or hethene;
> Ne no manere marchaunt that with moneye deleth
> Wheither he wynne with right, with wrong or with usure.'
>   (348–53)

The response is a defensive one. Prompted by Kynde Wit, Conscience retreats from the field with its optimistic, positive imagery of cultivating and reaping, into Holy Church, which is transformed from a barn to a fortress – 'as it a pyl weere' (l. 366). Though Grace had talked earlier of the crafts and talents as weapons with which to fight Pride, it is now the more purely religious gestures of prayer, pilgrimage, penance and almsgiving which are used for defence. The initial optimism about the world's work gives way, as in the earlier Pardon scene, to a reliance on prayer and penance and retreat from the world. Yet the tone is at first hopeful. All but a few of mankind – prostitutes and other sinners – retreat with Conscience and play their part in defending the barn by their penance, and Conscience expresses confidence about the outcome. But almost immediately there is rebellion, and this seems from the start, as Pride's emissaries had threatened, to be closely related to the complexities of a modern economic world:

> 'How?' quod al the comune. 'Thow conseillest us to yelde
> Al that we owen any wight er we go to housel?' (B xix 394–5)

The commons are perhaps right to exclaim: in the sophisticated world of fourteenth-century trade, debts are more complicated than that.[3] What Langland seems to be describing here is the confrontation between the simple spiritual verities of divinity and the complex earthy actualities of humanity. Thus the brewer insists on the contrast between the abstract spirit of justice and his *kynde* or nature as brewer:

> 'Ye? Baw!' quod a brewere, 'I wol noght be ruled,
> By Jesu! for al youre janglynge, with *Spiritus Iusticie*,
> Ne after Conscience, by Crist! while I kan selle
> Bothe dregges and draf, and drawe at oon hole
> Thikke ale and thynne ale; that is my kynde,
> And noght hakke after holynesse – hold thi tonge, Conscience!'
>   (B xix 399–404)

He is implicitly challenging the earlier attempt to present the cardinal virtues as something natural to man.

The latter point is then taken up by the landowning lord who laugh-ingly acknowledges that the virtues of understanding and fortitude have been converted in his case into qualities necessary for collecting rents, and by the king who claims that the virtue of justice allows him, as head of the law, to seize what he needs. What Langland is playing with here is a kind of parody of his earlier microcosmic picture of society. In the Prologue to the B version he had presented a brief fable showing the interrelationship of king, knights, clergy and commons. Here the brewer represents the commons, the lord stands for knighthood, the king for kingship and the vicar for the clergy. There is even an echo of the Prologue's 'Thanne kam there a kyng' in the 'And thanne cam ther a kyng' of B xix 469. But if the Prologue gives us the ideal, this passage presents the reality, a competitive society in which each order appeals to its *kynde* or nature to justify exploiting the others.

The 'lewed vicory' (that is, an unlearned parish priest, perhaps to be thought of as lowly in status, lower than a parson or rector) seems to be one of those morally ambivalent, blunt speakers of realism already seen in the Prologue with the lunatic and the mouse. He is perhaps a figure for Langland himself, whose persona is often presented in the poem as an ignorant character too; when the dream abruptly ends, the lord, the king and Conscience have all spoken since the vicar was last mentioned but it is the latter who is specified, in close association with the dreamer:

> The viker hadde fer hoom, and faire took his leeve –
> And I awakned therwith, and wroot as me mette. (B xix 484–5)

Despite his 'lewedness' the vicar is an authoritative commentator on the transformation in society, drawing out the implications of the claims made by brewer, lord and king. What he particularly tries to capture is the corruption of the original vision of spiritual idealism: the cardinal virtues have been replaced by grasping cardinals, the pope has lost the all-encompassing mercy of God and Piers, and the spirit of prudence has turned into guile among the laity. Yet one of the important virtues articulated by the vicar is toleration for the sinner. He criticises the pope for organising war against his enemies, and contrasts this with his image of a God who sends rain and sunshine to the just and the unjust alike, and is patient with the sinner – 'And suffreth that synfulle be til som tyme that thei repente' (l. 444). Rather confusingly he refers to Piers both in his allegorical sense, as ruler of Christendom, and in his literal sense as a plowman:

> 'And Piers with his newe plough, and ek with his olde
> Emperour of al the world – that alle men were Cristene.
> Imparfit is that Pope, that al peple sholde helpe,

And soudeth hem that sleeth swiche as he sholde save.
Ac wel worthe Piers the Plowman, that pursueth God in
  doynge . . .
Right so Piers the Plowman peyneth hym to tilye
As wel for a wastour and wenches of the stewes
As for hymself and hise servaunts.' (B xix 429–33, 437–9)

But the ideal which he is trying to capture is the fusion of these two images: an authority-figure who will have both the power to guide and protect mankind and the generosity to spare them.

The dialogue with Nede

The dream described in passus xix ends very suddenly without an acceptable conclusion. The break between visions is perhaps intended to mark a passage of dream-time or world-history, covering the span from the assault of Pride to the later attack of Antichrist, but its main function seems to be to move into a different mode that will allow the meeting of the dreamer himself with Nede in waking time. Nede is the arch-realist, intensely aware, as his name implies, of the necessities of existence.[4] He is the culmination of the series of commons, brewer, lord and king. Just as they have converted the cardinal virtues to their own earthly needs so Nede now urges the dreamer to appeal to the virtue of temperance to justify taking the necessities of life from others. Taking as his authority human nature as well as a corrupt view of temperance, Nede is able to justify deceit and theft:

'And he cacche in that caas and come therto by sleighte,
He synneth noght, soothliche, that so wynneth his foode.
And though he come so to a clooth, and kan no bettre
  chevyssaunce,
Nede anoon righte nymeth hym under maynprise.
And if hym list for to lape, the lawe of kynde wolde
That he dronke at ech dych er he for thurst deide.' (B xx 14–19)

The implication seems to be that the ideal of temperance can be interpreted as a justification for each man having enough to live on, and therefore for those in need to take from others. Nede is perhaps drawing on the kind of argument voiced by Aquinas: 'he who suffers from extreme need can take what he needs from another's goods if no one will give them to him'.[5] But his language seems to suggest more than merely theft: *wynneth* implies gain or acquisition and *cacche* is used in B xi 170 of clerics obtaining money in fees for ecclesiastical services. Unlike the other speakers, Nede is not explicitly associated with a particular social group, but he seems to be primarily the spokesman of the religious mendicant. Nede is perhaps here calling on the double meaning of his name, not merely necessity but also neediness. The climax of his speech is an appeal to the ideals of voluntary poverty, which he claims to have been practised by God himself:

'Philosophres forsoke welthe for thei wolde be nedy,
And woneden wel elengely and wolde noght be riche.
And God al his grete joye goostliche he lefte,
And cam and took mankynde and bicam nedy. . . .
Forthi be noght abasshed to bide (*or* bidde⁶) and to be nedy,
Sith he that wroghte al the world was wilfulliche nedy,
Ne nevere noon so nedy ne poverer deide.' (B xx 38–41, 48–50)

His elevation of temperance over the other virtues is at bottom a claim for the qualities of the simple life, and his dismissal of prudence, originally said to be a virtue sown by Grace, as merely human wisdom and therefore inferior to divine knowledge, is a perverse echo of the earlier arguments voiced by the hermit Patience and Anima, more genuine spokesmen for the ascetic life. The association of Nede with voluntary poverty and the suggestion of its dangers are made more explicit later in the passus when Nede, standing outside his character for a moment, warns Conscience not to trust the friars, whose neediness will lead them to flatter and lie:

Nede neghede tho neer, and Conscience he tolde
That thei come for coveitise to have cure of soules.
'And for thei are povere, paraventure, for patrymoyne hem
   failleth,
Thei wol flatere, to fare wel, folk that ben riche.' (B xx 232–5)

The authoritative status of this warning is confirmed by Conscience, who ends the poem with the wish 'that freres hadde a fyndyng, that for nede flateren'. The point is perhaps that while there had once been a time when holy men had chosen voluntary poverty, like Christ himself, the modern exemplars (particularly the friars) use specious arguments to justify begging and deceit to gain their material needs. Neediness, a static, chosen, holy state, has become necessity, a restless, violent, disruptive condition.[7]

The primary point of Nede's speech, then is to suggest how temperance, like the other cardinal virtues, has become corrupted to suit the material needs of contemporary society. In that respect it resembles the speeches by the brewer, the lord and the king, with the commentary by the vicar. Yet it has a rather special status, between the two visions, as well as a special complexity, because it concerns what for Langland was the crucial case: a reduction of the divine spark to earthly needs by the Church itself, and more particularly the corruption of an ideal which had meant a great deal to Langland within and outside his poem, the eremitic values and life exemplified by Patience.

The fall of the Church

The corruption of the Church itself, and especially of those vowed to poverty, is the point which Langland immediately takes up when the vision resumes. Antichrist now attacks the crops, overturning truth and substituting a concern for material needs, and he is welcomed by friars and monks:

> Antecrist cam thanne, and al the crop of truthe
> Torned it tid up-so-doun, and overtilte the roote,
> And made fals sprynge and sprede and spede mennes nedes.
> In ech a contree ther he cam he kutte awey truthe,
> And gerte gile growe there as he a god weere.
> Freres folwede that fend, for he gaf hem copes,
> And religious reverenced hym and rongen hir belles. (B xx 53–9)

In early Christian tradition the coming of Antichrist was associated with the end of the world, but in Wyclifite writings it is presented as an event that has already happened, causing the corruption of the Church, and Langland seems to be using the same idea. For the Wyclifites, the friars were the prime followers of Antichrist,[8] an idea which Langland articulates too (B xx 58).

Once again Conscience retreats for safety to the barn, this time accompanied by the few representatives of the religious orders, ironically termed fools, who have not fallen to Antichrist. With the rebellion of the laity at the end of passus xix and the corruption of the religious voiced by Nede at the beginning of passus xx, the mood turns dark and despairing. The scenes of battle and siege possibly owe something to French allegorical poetry[9] but the nearest contemporary parallel is once again in English drama, with *The Castle of Perseverance*.[10] There the powerful, energetic forces of the World, the Flesh and the Devil force the weak and helpless figure of Mankind to retreat into the castle where he undergoes a long siege and is eventually undermined by the temptations of Coveitise (Avarice). It is only the intervention of God himself, in an act of mercy and grace to undeserving man, that saves Mankind from Hell.

In *Piers* too there is a retreat to an enclosed shelter, and it is divine intervention that Conscience now despairingly summons, in the form of Kynde:

> Kynde Conscience tho herde, and cam out of the planetes,
> And sente forth his forreyours – feveres and fluxes,
> Coughes and cardiacles, crampes and toothaches. (B xx 80–2)

Kynde had earlier been the name used of God as the Creator: it is Kynde who makes the castle of the body for Anima in passus x and the beautiful world of Middle Earth in passus xi. It is a mark of the shift in the mood of the poem that Kynde is now the agent of death and disease. Similarly, and perhaps even more poignantly, in passus xviii Christ had been called the lord of life, indeed was life (B xviii 31), and engaged in a conflict with death and the devil (l. 65). Now Kynde, who is an aspect of God and fights for Conscience, has Death and Elde in his army, while Life is in the army of Pride on the other side. It is of course a different concept of life, earthly and transient rather than heavenly and eternal, but the shift is nevertheless significant: the initial elevation of life, nature and secular labours now gives way to a grimmer picture in which Life is left whistling in the dark.

Kynde now attacks mankind with his diseases, in a manner that perhaps draws on Langland's memories of the Black Death. When Conscience begs him to pause, the forces of Antichrist immediately resume their attack on Conscience and the barn of Unitee, led by Lechery, Coveitise and Life himself. The moral values here are all on the side of death and disease: it is only under their threat that mankind will turn to Conscience and Unitee. But there is a kind of brittle joyfulness on the opposing side, marked by the colloquial zest of the writing:

> Thus relyede Lif for a litel fortune.
> And prikked forth with Pride – preiseth he no vertue
> Ne careth noght how Kynde slow, and shal come at the laste
> And kille alle erthely crature save Conscience oone.
> Lyf lepte aside and laughte hym a lemman. (B xx 148–52)

The tone culminates in the comic account of Elde's attack on the dreamer himself, robbing him first of his hair and then of his sexual powers:

> And Elde anon after hym, and over myn heed yede,
> And made me balled bifore and bare on the croune . . .
> And of the wo that I was inne my wif hadde ruthe,
> And wisshed wel witterly that I were in hevene.
> For the lyme that she loved me fore, and leef was to feele –
> On nyghtes, namely whan we naked weere –
> I ne myghte in no manere maken it at hir wille,
> So Elde and heo hadden it forbeten. (B xx 183–4, 193–8)

Despite the comedy, there is a sharp point to be made; the vigour of life is over, man and the world are at the end of their time and the last moment has come for the retreat into the barn or church, which increasingly comes to resemble both the cloister and the sick-house. There is a pessimistic recognition that Christendom is not after all a thing of life and the world.

The point is made explicit in Kynde's advice to the dreamer to forsake both the world and its work:

'Counseille me, Kynde,' quod I, 'what craft be best to lerne?'
'Lerne to love,' quod Kynde, 'and leef alle othere.'
'How shal I come to catel so, to clothe me and to feede?'
'And thow love lelly, lakke shal thee nevere
Weede ne worldly mete, while thi lif lasteth.' (B xx 207–11)

The advice not to care for the necessities of human life seems strikingly unsuited to Kynde in his usual sense of Nature or in his earlier role as the Creator, but it is wholly appropriate to his new role as the destroyer of life. The sentiments are ones we have heard before, voiced by Patience in passus xiii and xiv, but the argument of the poem had appeared subsequently to move into a more optimistic vein of thought about the material aspects of life. Grace had given mankind a variety of crafts with which to win their livelihood and fight Antichrist; there had seemed to be an assurance there that the use of human talents, the pursuit of the material needs of life and the spiritual resistance against sin and Antichrist were all aspects of the same actions. What Kynde seems now to be insisting is that the dreamer, and perhaps therefore man in general, must abandon all such 'crafts' and devote himself to love alone. It is another sign of how far the world of Grace has fallen. Kynde's advice is perhaps appropriate to a dreamer with whom Elde has dealt so harshly, but the dreamer is representative of man himself.

The dreamer takes Kynde's advice and enters Unitee, but finds it a place of little security. Sloth attacks with his army of priests (a priest had also exemplified Sloth in the Visio) and despite Nede's warning Conscience accepts the help of the friars who rapidly undermine the community of the barn. The central position of the friars in the fall of Unitee and the climactic last section of the poem is hard to explain. Something is no doubt due to contemporary disputes and the strong vein of anti-fraternal feeling evident in such literary contexts as *The Romance of the Rose* and the poetry of Chaucer as well as in polemical tracts.[11] There is a strong feeling too in the poem that the friars cannot be fitted into a scheme of society – hence Conscience's use of the technical argument that the numbers of friars are limitless. They are late additions to the social order and have no place in the list of talents and occupations distributed by Grace, but usurp the duties and rights of others, such as the beneficed priests. But perhaps the crucial point for Langland is that they represent a betrayal of an ideal to which he himself was deeply committed. St Francis and St Dominic, as he remarked earlier, had forsaken everything for a life of poverty and simplicity; their successors had turned to the world of learning and the pursuit of wealth, introducing complexity and moral uncertainty:

> Envye herde this and heet freres go to scole
> And lerne logyk and lawe – and ek contemplacion –
> And preche men of Plato, and preve it by Seneca
> That alle thynges under hevene oughte to ben in comune.
>
> (B xx 273–6)

As we shall see, the issues of voluntary poverty and begging come to dominate Langland's subsequent revision of the poem to form the C text.

The role of Conscience in the fall of Unitee is an unexpected one. Hitherto Conscience had played the part of Langland's 'chooser', directing the poem along the right path. In these last two passus he plays the major role in guiding and defending the Christian community once Piers and Grace have departed, but his judgement seems curiously soft-hearted. He lends partial support to the king in his claims to be above the law, he persuades Kynde to withdraw from the battle with Antichrist, he rejects Nede's warning and allows the friars into the barn, and he invites Friar Flatterer to enter. As Pride's emissaries had prophesied, Conscience's function as moral arbiter has become clouded. The role of Conscience here seems to reflect Langland's despair over the problem of moral choices, and especially the conflict of justice and mercy. The rigorous lines pursued by Kynde and eventually Nede are evidently severe, but sympathy with human limitations produces the soft-speaking friars who undermine the Church.

This despair lies behind the impassioned closing lines of the poem. The final sequence of the poem, covering the last two visions, had begun in confidence and celebration of divine power and success. Langland had seen a community redeemed from its natural sinfulness and inspired with God-given talents, setting up a new society which successfully combined the material and the spiritual. The attacks of Pride are at first successfully resisted but the laity begin to rebel and adapt the cardinal virtues to their own needs. Then the Church itself begins to fall into complexity and corruption, the attack of Antichrist is reinforced by the clergy and the barn of Unitee is penetrated. Conscience's response is a radical one:

'By Crist!' quod Conscience tho, 'I wole bicome a pilgrym,
And walken as wide as the world lasteth,
To seken Piers the Plowman, that Pryde myghte destruye,
And that freres hadde a fyndyng, that for nede flateren
And countrepledeth me, Conscience. Now Kynde me avenge,
And sende me hap and heele, til I have Piers the Plowman!'
And siththe he gradde after Grace, til I gan awake. (B xx 381–7)

He abandons the barn or castle, an image of the embattled Christian community gathered together for protection and shelter, to become a pilgrim on a solitary journey through the wide world, an act of individual daring and faith. In doing so, he throws himself anew on the mercy and grace of God, calling on Kynde, Piers and Grace.

Piers' role in the last two passus is a remarkably varied one. He had been a manifestation of Christ at the beginning of passus xix. He had modulated into a figure for St Peter and then become an idealised head of the Church, organising the Christian community on behalf of Grace, as passus xix progressed. But the references at B xx 77 and 321 seem to hint at an identity with Christ again. As we have seen before, Piers' essential role in the poem is as the organiser of man's salvation and a nexus of the current ideals and aspirations of the visions in which he appears. His oscillation in these two visions reflects the poem's own fluctuation between an optimistic belief in human possibilities and a commitment to God. But the common ground is the idea of an authority-figure, or a figure of power, who offers both mercy and kingship, who will organise the Christian community without the terrifying and impersonal effects of Kynde or Hunger but with the power to prevent the threatening anarchy of a purely human world. That seems to be what Conscience is calling for when he names Piers, and the narrator is naming the same sort of power when he refers to Grace. Like some contemporary popular movements on the Continent,[12] Langland ends the poem looking for the Messiah and a second coming.

The action of Conscience, and the feeling behind it, strongly recall the end of the second vision. The tearing of the Pardon, and the words of Piers as he does it, involve the same kind of rejection of the social order for individual commitment to a merciful and all-powerful God. Langland's imagination oscillated between the reformer's desire to conceive of a redeemed social order and the mystic's thankful commitment of everything into the hands of God. Comparable movements are Conscience's earlier decision to forsake the world of learning to wander the world with Patience, and the dreamer's pursuit of the Samaritan as the only one who can save. Yet even in the midst of this final appeal to Grace there is something from the social reformer – 'And that freres hadde a fyndyng, that for nede flateren' (l. 384). When Piers is found, he will create a new social order in which economic provision will be made for the friars, somehow reconciling the sanctity of poverty with material stability.

This final appeal to Piers and Grace is in some ways implicit throughout the last two visions. The sequence begins with an emphasis on the role of Christ as conqueror. The dominant figures are Grace, Piers, Conscience, Pride, Antichrist, Kynde, Elde. As in the morality plays, man is by turns the protégé and victim of powers greater than himself. When he departs the scene Grace recognises that Antichrist will replace him and Pride will become pope. In that recognition of human vulnerability there is perhaps an explanation for the amused sympathy with which human nature is often regarded in the last part of the poem.

The chronological sequence ends with the present. The narrative of the last passus has brought us through the coming of the friars in the thirteenth century to their corruption in the fourteenth. The fall of Unitee brings us to the time of Langland himself, and the fallen world which he had already described in the beginning of the Visio. In that sense the poem ends with no answers, only an enrichment of experience and understanding.

Notes and references

1. See Bede, *Homiliae*, ed. D. Hurst (Corpus Christianorum Latinorum 122, Turnhout, 1955), I, 14.
2. Most MSS of the B text have *taughte*; the editors emend to *thoughte* on the basis of the C text.
3. L. K. Little, *Religious Poverty and the Profit Economy in Medieval Europe* (London, 1978), gives an excellent study of the development of arguments, especially by the friars, to take account of the complexity of the late medieval money economy.
4. There is a good discussion by R. Adams, 'The nature of Need in *Piers Plowman* XX', *Traditio*, **34** (1978), 273–301.
5. *Summa Theologiae*, 2a 2ae, q. 77, art. 4.
6. Some manuscripts read *bide* 'endure', others *bidde* 'beg', leaving it unclear whether Nede sees the dreamer as a mendicant or merely one who should patiently endure poverty.
7. Similar criticisms of the dangers of voluntary poverty are made in *Le Roman de la Rose* (ed. E. Langton, Paris, 1914–24) by the hypocrite-figure called Faux Semblant, who takes on the role of a friar and a hermit and was perhaps an influence on Langland's presentation here.
8. See, for example, *Select English Works of John Wyclif*, ed. T. Arnold, 3 vols (Oxford, 1869–71), I, 202.
9. See D. Owen, *Piers Plowman: a Comparison with some earlier and contemporary French Allegories* (London, 1912).

10. Edited by M. Eccles, *The Macro Plays* (Early English Text Society 262, London, 1969).

11. See P. Szittya, *The Anti-Fraternal Tradition in Medieval Literature* (Princeton, 1986).

12. See N. Cohn, *The Pursuit of the Millennium* (London, 1977), esp. pp. 214–17.

Chapter Ten

The C version

Some years after completing the B version Langland turned his attention to the poem again and undertook an extensive rewriting. Quite how long after is a matter of some dispute. The dating of the C version has generally depended on parallels with a long prose work called *The Testament of Love* by Thomas Usk, a contemporary of Langland's.[1] In his edition of this work W. W. Skeat noted some apparent borrowings from *Piers Plowman*[2] and although he himself drew no conclusions for the date of the poem from them, a thesis produced in 1928 by M. A. Devlin argued that the borrowings could be shown to be from the C version.[3] On this basis the C version could not be any later than 1387, since Usk was executed in the following year for political reasons, and independent evidence that the *Testament* was actually written in 1384–85[4] would make the C version still earlier than that, and very close in time to the B version. Devlin herself argued that the C version was written before 1381, since it fails to mention the Peasants' Revolt of that year, but most recent discussions seem to have settled for the view that it was at least composed before the death of Usk in 1388.[5] If one takes a fresh look at Usk, however, the argument soon collapses. Most of the supposed borrowings are in fact similarities in individual phrases of a rather general kind; there is no reason to suppose that they originated with Langland and they look on the whole like medieval commonplaces or proverbs. The one substantial parallel which Skeat notes is a similarity between Langland's Tree of Charity and an allegorical tree in Usk. But tree imagery is common in medieval writing, and the parallels of detail are neither close nor numerous. Indeed, the parallel only looks at all significant because Skeat himself had rearranged two chapters of Usk's text at this point[6]: as a result, the allegory of the tree begins very abruptly in a way that might suggest borrowing from another work, but if the text is restored to its proper order the image can be seen to arise naturally and gradually out of Usk's argument.

Without the illusory evidence of Usk we are left only with internal evidence from the poem.[7] The precise topical allusions of the earlier versions largely disappear at this stage: the reference to the south-west wind of 1360 remains but the account of Richard's coronation is rewritten in more general terms and the passages discussing the Normandy campaigns and peace of 1362 and the dearth of 1370 are dropped. Instead we have two new passages which seem to point to a time quite late in Richard's reign (he was deposed in 1399). Thus at C iii 134 the king tells Mede that she has often behaved misguidedly and that he has forgiven her many crimes and granted his favour to her and her followers in hope that she would amend. One can perhaps hear a satiric reference to Richard's lenience towards corrupt followers. More convincing are ll. 207–9, where Conscience tells the king that Mede and her sister 'Unsittyng soffraunce', that is, 'improper indulgence', have almost brought it about that no land loves him, least of all his own. This suggests a time when Richard was no longer the boy-king of the B version but had taken on personal responsibility for government and begun to acquire a bad reputation of his own. It was not until 1389 that Richard officially declared himself of age and determined to rule independently, though it is true that attacks on the mismanagement of the country were already being levelled at Richard himself by 1386. Mede herself, in another new passage, remarks that the king has led campaigns in other countries but been hindered by Conscience from felling his foes (C ii 238–9). This could be a reference back to the wars of Edward III, the king originally alluded to in the first dream, but being a new passage it is more likely to refer to Richard, and if so would suggest a date fairly late in his reign, after the Scottish campaign of 1385 or even the Irish one of 1394–95, the only ones which Richard appears to have led in person. The evidence is not strong, but what there is would suggest a date for the C version in the late 1380s or the 1390s, perhaps ten years after the completion of the B version.

The revision at this stage was of a quite different kind from the revision of the A version. That had been primarily a matter of extending the poem from the unfinished ending, together with occasional additions to the existing part. In his revision this time Langland left the overall shape unchanged, and the total length is only a little more, about 7,340 lines as against about 7,280 in the B version. The only alterations to the sequence of dreams are that the fourth and fifth visions are merged into one by deleting the waking gap, the inner dream in the third vision begins at an earlier point (see p. 192) and there is no longer an inner dream in what was the fifth vision. Yet behind this general appearance of similarity is an extensive recasting of the poem. Langland added substantial new passages in nearly every vision, while deleting others, including such major episodes as the tearing of the Pardon. In places he transferred passages from one part of the poem to another: an attack on the clergy in B x becomes part of Reason's sermon in C v, while the account of Haukyn's sins in B xiii is adapted to form part of the account of the sinners in the second vision, in C vi–viii. He substantially recast a number of episodes, such as the account of the Tree of Charity. And virtually all through the poem there is rewriting in matters of detail even where the general substance is unchanged.

The revision does not extend to the last two passus of the poem. Up to that point there is extensive revision, with B xvi, xvii and xviii all showing signs of careful consideration and improvement by the author. In B xix and xx there appear to be no revisions at all; the few differences from the manuscripts of the B version that look authorial are thought by the editors to be readings that were in fact present originally in the B text but miscopied by the scribes of the surviving manuscripts of the B version.[8] One possible explanation is that Langland found himself entirely satisfied with the last two passus and saw no need for change, since they presumably were the latest work in that B version. But this would hardly explain the abrupt change from frequent revision in passus xviii to none at all in passus xix, and the nature of the changes elsewhere in the poem suggests that Langland would in fact have found plenty of grounds for rewriting in passus xix and xx; Piers himself plays a major part in this last section, and his appearances elsewhere in the B version are heavily revised for the C version.[9] It seem probable that Langland failed to complete his revision, and this is confirmed by the signs that the poem lacks the final polish needed to fit additions to their context or to adjust other parts of the text to match revisions elsewhere. An extreme case occurs in B xiv/C xviii, where Langland rewrote the passage which had described the inception of a dream within a dream but failed to delete the end of that dream (C xviii 179). But there are many lesser examples. The role of Piers in the Tree of Charity scene is eliminated, but there are still references to the fruit of Piers the Plowman in passus xx (ll. 18 and 32). In C xii the cancellation or accidental omission of seven lines (B xi 176–82) leaves an extraordinarily abrupt transition in the argument at l. 98.

The general view has been that it was death that prevented Langland from completing the revision, with the implication that someone else put the C text together and had it circulated.[10] It is perhaps also possible that it was pressure of time: if the impetus behind the revision was demand from a reader or patron wanting an up-to-date version, time perhaps ran out before the work was completed. Given that Langland allowed an unfinished A version to circulate, and perhaps an unfinished Z version as well, there is no reason to suppose that he could not have allowed the C version to leave his hands in an unpolished state.

Two rather different accounts have been offered of the process of revision, both by editors of the poem. E.T. Donaldson suggested in 1949 that Langland undertook a line-by-line revision of the poem from the beginning, and then, as he neared the end, turned back to add to the earlier sections some further passages taken from the later part of the poem or at least inspired by it.[11] This second stage of revision would thus explain some of the awkward transitions. The current editor of the C text, George Russell, argues that the rewriting was in large part a 'repair-job': that Langland was confronted with an extremely corrupt copy of the B version and, being unable to locate a better copy, attempted to make something coherent and acceptable out of passages which had been miscopied by scribes but for which he could no longer recall the original.[12] He suggests that such repair work then prompted the poet to examine the surrounding lines and rewrite those, while leaving untouched passages that were free of corruption. He goes on to cast doubt on Donaldson's views:

> We should be careful not to assume that the reviser necessarily sat down to revise his poem by means of an orderly and thorough-going review which began with the opening lines of the prologue and was designed to continue through to the end of the final passus. The evidence of the text does not seem to me to indicate that the process of revision was of this orderly and systematic kind. One might even suggest that it was sporadic; that it had certain points of departure which were, presumably, points of dissatisfaction and that, while the revising activity might be intense at these points and might continue through relatively long passages, quite large stretches of the poem were left to stand and may, indeed, never have received close scrutiny since the need for revision did not represent itself to the reviser. This is to say that it seems to me at best doubtful if the C revision was undertaken – as I believe the B revision was undertaken – to offer a radical and large-scale rewriting of the whole poem: rather it was designed to be a limited operation to meet specific problems.[13]

One's readiness to accept this picture of Langland as a writer who so neglected his poem that when he looked for it again he could neither recover an accurate copy nor recall what he had written perhaps depends in part on whether one sees Langland as primarily a cleric engaged in other duties, who might therefore have forgotten his poem for ten years at a time, or primarily a poet who might expect to be called on to recite his work repeatedly. Even so, the degree of rewriting and the evidence of new thinking suggest much more than an attempt to repair scribal errors.

The revision at this stage was varied in its nature and perhaps therefore in its motives. Some of the changes, especially in details of expression, suggest the work of a poet who would simply wish to say things in a different way ten years on, and takes this opportunity to do so; they may in part have arisen casually and gradually in his recitations of the poem, and then have been incorporated from memory in a new text. Some additions suggest that Langland was taking the opportunity to air views that were on his mind but not essential to the argument, especially in parts of the poem which already had something of that general sermonising character (the early parts of the third vision, the speeches of Anima and the Good Samaritan in the fifth, for example); Langland does indeed acknowledge that he is digressing in one of these additions, a brief passage which complains of lying and urges clerics and lawyers not to deceive the laity:

> A litel I over-leep for lesynges sake,
> That I ne sygge nat as I sihe, suynde my teme! (C xx 357–8)

Much of the revision, however, suggests the work of a poet still thinking hard about the poem, still vitally concerned with the issues and trying both to clarify the arguments and to perfect his vision of truth in all its complexity. Perhaps the keynote of the spirit behind the revision is to be found in two parenthetic remarks in the third vision by the character Recklessness, who is closely identified with the dreamer. Recklessness develops the radical attack on learning already seen in the B text but then pauses to explain that he does not mean to dismiss the value of learning altogether:

> 'Ac I countresegge the nat, Clergie; ne thy connyng, Scripture;
> That who-so doth by youre doctrine doth wel, I leve.
> Ac me were levere, by oure lord, a lyppe of Goddes grace
> Thenne al the kynde wyt that ye can bothe and kunnyng of
>   youre bokes.' (C xi 225–8)

Similarly in passus xiii Recklessness delivers a long and impassioned speech on the ideals of poverty and the dangers of wealth, but again pauses to say that he does not mean to criticise wealth:

> 'Ac leveth nat, lewede men, that I lacke rychesse
> Thogh I preyse poverte thus and preve hit by ensaunples
> Worthiore as by holy writ and wyse fylosofres.

175

Bothe thei ben gode, be ye ful certeyn,
And lyves that oure lord loveth and large weyes to hevene.
Ac the pore pacient purgatorye passeth
Rather then the ryche thogh they renne at ones.' (C xiii 25–31)

There is an anxiety to get the balance right, to assert the primacy of
great ideals without wholly disparaging lesser but acceptable ways of
life, which is observable in much of the revision that Langland undertook at this stage and may reflect the balance of ideals which he briefly achieved in B xix. But there is also a consistent series of changes in
the conception of Piers himself, whose role is sharply reduced and
whose numinous, Messianic quality is replaced by a more human identity as plowman and pilgrim. There is a pervasive extension and up-
dating of the social satire and complaint in the first two visions, and a
corresponding reduction in the rest of the poem. Above all, there is a
whole series of changes and additions related to an issue which had ob-
sessed Langland from the beginning: the problems of work, poverty,
begging and the eremitic ideal.

The first vision

Something of the character of the C version is suggested by the opening lines. In the B version Langland left them exactly as they were in the
A text, but for the C vision he partially rewrote them:

In a somer seson, whan softe was the sonne,
I shoop me into shroudes as I a sheep were,
In habite as an heremite unholy of werkes,
Wente wide in this world wondres to here.
Ac on a May morwenynge on Malverne hilles,
Me bifel a ferly, of Fairye me thoghte.
I was wery forwandred and wente me to reste
Under a brood bank by a bourne syde;
And as I lay and lenede and loked on the watres,
I slombred into a slepyng, it sweyed so muyrye.
Thanne gan I meten a merveillous swevene—
That I was in a wildernesse, wiste I nevere where. (B Prol. 1–12)

In a somur sesoun whan softe was the sonne
I shope me into shroudes as I a shep were;
In abite as an heremite, unholy of werkes,
Wente forth in the world wondres to here,
And say many sellies and selkouthe thynges.
Ac on a May mornyng on Malverne hulles
Me biful for to slepe, for werynesse of-walked;

176

And in a launde as I lay, lened I and slepte,
And merveylousliche me mette, as I may telle.
Al the welthe of the world and the wo bothe
Wynkyng, as hit were, witterliche I sigh hit;
Of treuthe and tricherye, tresoun and gyle,
Al I say slepynge, as I shal telle. (C Prol. 1–13)

The substance is much the same and one might wonder why Langland
bothered to revise, but the mood is clearly different: the hint of fairyland,
the sweet sound of the brook and the sense of excitement in the vision
with which Langland had begun the poem many years before are
replaced by a note of weariness and a sober account of the whole
panorama of good and evil which appear in this poem.

When revising the first two visions for the B version Langland had
strengthened the criticism of contemporary society, especially of the
king and the Church, and he extended it still further in the C version.
The difference is evident almost as soon as he begins his account of the
field full of folk: the original cheerful acceptance of minstrels (A Prol. 33–
4) is now dropped and they share in the criticism directed at the japers
and janglers. A little later in the Prologue (ll. 95–124) Conscience now
intervenes in the dreamer's account of the field to deliver an attack on
bishops for allowing the laity to be deceived by churchmen, especially
by pardoners.[14] In passus ii (ll. 243–8) Langland adds lines attacking the
practice of taking appeals against the king's decisions to the pope, again
using the voice of Conscience. In passus iii (ll. 85–107) he expands a
passage on the malpractices of merchants and traders, in his own voice,
warning that God often punishes them by sending fire and floods upon
the cities to the harm of the innocent as well as the corrupt. Later in
the same passus (ll. 202–9) he extends Conscience's account of the corruption caused by Mede, telling how she has undermined the religious
orders, fomented war in many cities and realms and caused the king
himself to be hated. A few lines later (ll. 235–57) Mede's brief and somewhat puzzling account of how she supported the king's wars in Normandy and how Conscience undermined them, by now perhaps
out of date, is replaced by a longer and more general account of how
she fosters success in war while Conscience encourages peace. The
vision ends with another new passage (passus iv, ll. 187–94) in which
Reason warns the king against indulgence of criminals and the corruption of justice and urges him to depend on love rather than merchants,
bishops and Lombard money-lenders for financial support.

Perhaps the most striking point about these additions is Langland's
willingness to carry his attack further against those in high authority –
city officers, bishops, the king, the pope. The original account, in the A
version and extended in the B version, of a king who has been unaware

of the corruptions of his country but, having acquired the knight Conscience, has only to listen to him to institute reform, has given way to a picture of a king whose own practices have been corrupted and made him unpopular.

In the A and B versions two contrasting views of Mede had been presented and it was not until the trial of Wrong that the more hostile view expressed by Holy Church had prevailed. Holy Church had identified Mede as the daughter of Fals and the source of all evil but Theology had later intervened to insist that she was in fact the child of Amendes (that is, Restitution) and so essentially good; the king had accepted this view of her and sought reconciliation but Conscience and Reason had eventually convinced him of the essential evil of Mede. In the C version Langland instils that recognition into the debate from the beginning, sharpening the criticism of Mede as a force in society. The king himself now acknowledges in detail her past crimes (C iii 133–44) and the description of the threats which she poses is expanded at several points, as we have seen (C iii 85–107, 202–9, 235–57). Theology too seems to accept her evil nature, acknowledging that Mede's father was indeed Fals, as Holy Church had claimed, and her grandfather Fikeltonge, though he insists that her mother was Amendes, and still argues that she is essentially good and should be married to no one but Truth (an odd conclusion about the daughter of Fals; Theology's penchant for bad judgements has become clearer since the A version). In the A and B versions the ambivalence of meed as a concept had been implicitly acknowledged by Conscience, who had drawn a distinction between the meed which takes the form of heavenly reward and the unacceptable meed which takes the form of payments here on earth, though he paused to make an acknowledgement of the propriety of due payments for work done, 'mesurable hire'. In the C version Langland seems to lose confidence in this argument, allowing the distinction to be preempted by Theology who insists that the two kinds of meed are analogous and both acceptable (C ii 129–36). What Conscience offers instead in the C version is a detailed distinction between meed, which is generally corrupt and unacceptable, and *mercedem*, due payment for work and goods, which is fair and right (C iii 290–405). He then goes on to draw an elaborate analogy between this distinction and the difference between direct and indirect relationship in grammar. This is quite the most difficult and abstruse passage in the whole poem, and as elsewhere in his work Langland seems to be using analogies less to clarify than to draw together a variety of different concepts. What he aims at here is the notion of an ideally co-operative, cohesive society, with all parts in direct and hierarchic relation to each other, in contrast to the independent, unrelated, anarchic and free-floating role that money seems to confer on many people in his own world, though he wants also to use the imagery of direct relationship to include the religious relationship to God. If the dramatic poetry of the A and B versions had reflected a tension between two conflicting but cogent views, a realistic acceptance of Mede's place in modern society and an idealistic, other-worldly repudiation of all that she stands for, this gives place in the C version to a single view which sees Mede as wholly destructive but accepts *mercedem* as a basis for contemporary society.

The second vision

The sharpening of social criticism seen in the first vision is still more evident in the second vision. In the A version the vision had begun with a sermon by Conscience addressing the various orders of society on their proper duties. In the B version Langland makes the speaker Reason and adds the king, the pope and those responsible for the law to the ranks and orders addressed. In the C version he expands further, adding to the two lines on monks in the original sermon a further thirty-three lines drawn from B x, on the duties and corruptions of the monastic life in his time, and ending with the dire prophecy that a king will come and impose reform on the religious orders:

> For the abbot of Engelonde and the abbesse his nese
> Shal have a knok uppon here crounes and incurable the wounde.
>
> (C v 176–7)

(This is altered from the possibly too pointed 'Abbot of Abingdon' in B x.) The confession scenes too show a steady expansion from the earliest version: from 72 lines in Z they grew to 226 in A, 413 lines in B and now about 560 lines in C, with much of the earlier text deleted. Pride, Wrath, Coveiytise, Lechery and Sloth are all substantially expanded, while the portrait of Envy is entirely rewritten in shorter compass and only Glutton remains unaffected. Much of the additional material is taken from the account of Haukyn's sins in B xiii, but there is new material as well in all but the account of Sloth. The main concern seems to have been to broaden the account of sin, if necessary at the cost of drama and realism. Thus for pride the B version had only nine lines on Peronelle Proud-heart, and Langland now adds some thirty lines from B xiii and a further sixteen new lines on intellectual pride; the additional material is not at all in character for Peronelle, but does extend the social range of the picture. For Envy the B version's colourful account of an envious character, primarily a layman, in his relations with society is replaced by a shorter and more general picture. The account of Wrath in the B version concentrates almost entirely on his involvement with the religious orders; in the C version Langland deletes the first part and substitutes new material which is more wide-ranging, including descriptions of Wrath's inner nature and his presence among the laity.

The other, and more extensive, set of changes which Langland made to the second vision are those which in various ways involve the issues of poverty, labour and begging. These issues had been important at all stages of Langland's poetry but they acquire a particular prominence in the C text revision and it would be convenient here to review the background to his discussion.

Poverty had long been a prominent feature of medieval European society: current estimates suggest that those who were unable to support themselves and had to rely on alms or begging amounted to between 10 and 20 per cent of the population in the later Middle Ages.[15] In England the problem of 'sturdy beggars' became particularly prominent in the second half of the fourteenth century, and legislation was enacted to compel the able-bodied poor to work and to discourage others from giving them alms:

> Because a great part of the people, and especially of workmen and servants, late died of the pestilence, many seeing the necessity of masters, and great scarcity of servants, will not serve unless they may receive excessive wages, and some rather willing to beg in idleness, than by labour to get their living; we, considering the grievous incommodities, which of the lack especially of ploughmen and such labourers may hereafter come, have . . . ordained:
>
> That every man and women of our realm of England, of what condition he be, free or bond, able in body, and within the age of threescore years, not living in merchandize, nor exercising any craft, nor having of his own whereof he may live, nor proper land, about whose tillage he may himself occupy, and not serving any other, if he in convenient service, his estate considered, be required to serve, he shall be bound to serve him which so shall him require. . . . And because that many valiant beggars, as long as they may live of begging, do refuse to labour, giving themselves to idleness and vice, and sometime to theft and other abominations; none upon the said pain of imprisonment shall, under the colour of pity or alms, give anything to such, which may labour, or presume to favour them toward their desires, idleness, so that thereby they may be compelled to labour for their necessary living.
>
> (Proclamation concerning labourers, 1349)[16]

The long-term cause of this problem was probably the gradual shift from a feudal economy, in which labourers were tied to the land as serfs, to a money economy in which they were paid in wages and free to sell

their labour to any employer, but the difficulty had no doubt been ex-
acerbated by the effects of the Black Death, as the proclamation suggests, and perhaps also by the return of disbanded soldiers from the wars
in France. It was largely an economc and social problem but did contain a moral issue, as the proclamation implies: whether the non-working poor should be treated with indulgence and charity, or with rigorous
severity so as to compel them to work. The Church in particular had a
long tradition of treating alms-giving to the poor as a central feature
of pastoral work and private virtue, and it could not easily adjust to a
more rigorous attitude, though the need to discriminate had been acknowledged by churchmen for some centuries.[17]

The issue was complicated by the fact that voluntary poverty was
one of the great religious ideals of the period (see p. 102). The problems
and doubts associated with the material aspects of voluntary poverty
became increasingly prominent in Langland's time. Criticism of the
friars' reliance on begging is prominent from the thirteenth century onwards; thus Faux Semblant in *The Romance of the Rose* fiercely objects to it, arguing that everyone had an obligation to provide for
himself.[18] The thirteenth-century Bishop of Lincoln, Robert Grosseteste, an early supporter of the friars, had nevertheless told them that
their way of life, though apparently perfect, was inferior to the life of the
beguines, an informal religious community who supported themselves
by their labour.[19] Lollard texts argued that priests should live in a state
of poverty, but repeatedly insisted that they should be supported by the
voluntary offerings of the faithful, not by begging. One of the grounds
given for accusing Wyclif of heresy was his assertion that friars should
support themselves by manual labour, and a later Lollard was similarly
charged with heresy for arguing that parish priests should support
themselves by labour.[20] There were also anxieties about 'false' hermits.
The problem of distinguishing between genuine hermits living a life of
voluntary poverty from religious motives and sturdy beggars who
pretended to have a religious vocation to cover their idleness seems to
have been particularly evident in the later Middle Ages. Cases of idle
laymen masquerading as hermits appear in court records of the time,
and the 1388 Statute of Vagrancy attempted to deal with the problem
by exempting from its provisions only 'approved' hermits carrying letters from their bishop.[21] Malory somewhat later mentions the problem
of 'lower-class' hermits in an amusing aside on the different situation
in Arthurian times:

> For in tho dayes hit was nat the gyse as ys nowadayes; for there
> were none ermytis in tho dayes but that they had bene men of
> worship and of prowesse, and tho ermytes hylde grete househol-
> dis, and refreysshed people that were in distresse.[22]

The problem of able-bodied men refusing to work and of fraudulent begging is raised by Langland in the plowing scene in all four versions, while the moral problem of discrimination in alms-giving to the poor is dealt with summarily in the Pardon scene in the A version but discussed more fully in B and much more extensively in C. The issues associated with religious poverty find a very frequent and increasing echo in Langland's poetry. There is the discussion of the ideal of poverty in B xi, the arguments of Patience for voluntary poverty in B xiii and xiv, the arguments of Anima against begging in B xv, the anxieties about material provision for friars in B xx, and further discussions in the C version. But what particularly marks Langland's approach to the issue is the close relationship he sees between the secular and religious aspects of work and poverty. This is evident from the beginning in his coupling of shepherd and hermit in the opening lines, and of plowmen and hermits in his description of the field. The active and contemplative lives are repeatedly defined not as two states of religious life but as the lay and religious lives respectively (so Hunger in the second vision, Study in A x, Haukyn). In the plowing scene hermits take up spades under the pressure of Hunger and become workers, while Piers at the tearing of the Pardon forsakes plowing for the life of prayer and voluntary poverty. In B xi a speech about the needs of the poor gradually turns into an argument for the clerical ideal of voluntary poverty. In B xiii and xiv the secular work of Haukyn is contrasted with the eremitic poverty of Patience. The boundary between the physical work and involuntary poverty of the secular life and the spiritual work and voluntary poverty of the religious life is one repeatedly crossed in Langland's world, both by his characters and by his argument.

In its original form, in the Z version, the second vision had presented an ideal of labour, symbolised by Piers the Plowman and ultimately enacted in the corporate plowing of the half-acre. In the A and B versions that picture had been retained and strengthened but was then challenged at the very end of the vision with the tearing of the Pardon. In the C version Langland retains much of the old account but introduces a series of critiques and qualifications which set up a critical dialogue with the vision as first conceived, radically shifting the emphasis from labour to poverty.

The challenge begins with a new and lengthy prologue to the vision which dramatises the conflict between the ideal of labour for the community and the religious ideal of poverty and prayer. The dreamer presents himself as an idler, living in a cottage in Cornhill with his wife Kitte, capable of manual work but preferring a life of ease, drinking and sleeping. Reason rebukes him, urging that he should labour for the community at some useful task; the first occupation he suggests is that of a priest or at least a cleric, but the others are all manual tasks such as

hedging or ditching. Reason thus becomes the spokesman for the work
ethic. The dreamer claims in self-defence that he is not strong enough
for manual work:

> 'Sertes,' I sayde, 'and so me God helpe,
> I am to wayke to worche with sykel or with sythe
> And to long, lef me, lowe to stoupe,
> To wurche as a werkeman eny while to duyren.' (C v 22–5)

The language here, with its repeated protestations of truth ('Sertes', 'so
me God helpe', 'lef me'), suggests a hollowness and insincerity which
recall the false excuses of the beggars in the plowing scene of the A and
B versions (B vi 121–44), and of course the claim is in direct contradic-
tion with the narrator's opening acknowledgement that he was in full
health and able to work. But when Reason challenges him again about
his means of support and accuses him of being an idler and beggar, he
produces a very different account of himself, apparently contradicting
the initial picture and offering a spirited defence of his life as a kind of
beggar doing no useful work. He claims that he is a cleric who should
not be expected to do secular work, that he does do work of a kind, by
praying, and that those who support him by their charity when he visits
them seem content to do so.

His defence looks at first like the weak excuses of an idle layman
pretending to a religious vocation, the sort of figure Langland describes
later in the Pardon scene, and initially the tone is still self-indulgent:

> 'And fond I nere, in fayth, seth my frendes deyede,
> Lyf that me lykede but in this longe clothes.' (C v 40–1)

But as he continues, the realistic details begin to lend conviction to the
picture and a more authoritative tone appears, as if the narrator is speaking for the poet himself. The argument culminates in a powerful
repudiation of Reason's concern with food and material needs and a
claim that this life of prayer and penance is the highest kind of life:

> 'Forthy rebuke me ryhte nauhte, Resoun, I you praye,
> For in my consience I knowe what Crist wolde I wrouhte.
> Preyeres of a parfit man and penaunce discret
> Is the levest labour that oure lord pleseth.
> *Non de solo,*' I sayde, 'for sothe *vivit homo,*
> *Nec in pane et in pabulo,* the *pater- noster* wittenesseth;
> *Fiat voluntas dei* – that fynt us alle thynges.' (C v 82–8)

The narrator thus allies himself with Piers, who in the A and B
versions had chosen the life of prayer and penance, and with

Patience, who also took *Fiat voluntas dei* as his creed. Though the narrator may not actually be living the ideal life, he has effectively undermined Reason's enthusiastic call for productive labour. Conscience accepts the truth of this argument, though questioning the perfection of the narrator's actual practice of the ideal:

> Quod Consience, 'By Crist, I can nat se this lyeth[23];
> Ac it semeth no sad parfitnesse in citees to begge,
> Bot he be obediencer to prior or to mynistre.' (C v 89–91)

The Prologue is thus a kind of parable, re-enacting in brief compass the structural movement of the action of the second vision as it appears in the A and B versions. That is, the vision had gradually established an ideal of co-operative labour through the plowing of the half-acre, in opposition to the religious pretences of idlers, only to subvert that, with the tearing of the Pardon, in favour of the life of prayer and penance which Piers then adopted. So here, the initial picture in C v of an idle sensualist is designed to provoke Reason into what appears at first a perfectly justified and rational argument for the duty of labouring for the community's material needs; but the revelation of the narrator's true status, as a cleric and exemplar of religious poverty, is used to undermine that ethic in favour of the higher ideal of prayer and penance.

There are, however, some qualifications to be noted in that idealisation of prayer and penance. The rejection of the work ethic in the Prologue is a personal one based on the dreamer's status as a clerk, and he half-accepts that the criteria proposed by Reason might be right and perhaps ought to apply to him as well; his prayer is a kind of labour, he says, with which he earns a living, and although he is indeed a kind of beggar it is one of the more acceptable kinds of begging and avoids the worst of the evils to which Reason objects. Whereas Piers had presented his ideal of prayer and penance as in part a repudiation of labour, the narrator couches it in the language of work, as if acknowledging the appeal of Reason's arguments. (One might note too the contrast with the language used in the debate with Imaginatif at B xii 27–8, where the dreamer refers to a life of prayer as something different from work.) At the same time, the arguments for the ascetic life in the new passage are somewhat undermined by the questionable moral status of the narrator himself. The debate ends in a recognition that the life which the narrator claims to lead is not perfection, though its ideal form may be. While the main line of argument sets up Reason's apologia for the active life only to overturn it with the dreamer's defence of the contemplative, the use of the imperfect figure of the dreamer as exemplar of the contemplative, as well as the doubts cast by the Cornhill story, foster strong reservations about the nature of asceticism in practice, reservations that are developed later in the C version. The closing note of the episode is, appropriately, the narrator's moving acknowledgement of his failure to achieve perfection:

> 'That is soth,' I saide, 'and so I beknowe
> That I have ytynt tyme and tyme myspened;
> Ac yut, I hope, as he that ofte hath ychaffared
> And ay loste and loste, and at the laste hym happed
> A bouhte suche a bargayn he was the bet evere,
> And sette al his los at a leef at the last ende,
> Such a wynnyng hym warth thorw wordes of grace . . .
> So hope I to have of hym that is almyghty
> A gobet of his grace, and bigynnne a tyme
> That alle tymes of my tyme to profit shal turne.' (C v 92–101)

Though the episode undermines the status of work and society, the final point is not the narrator's achievement of perfection through penance and prayer but the reliance on divine grace to save him.

Thus the new Prologue acts as a kind of critique and commentary on the vision which is to follow, challenging at the outset the idealisation of productive labour which is its hallmark and inviting us to question the perspective offered by Piers. A similar function is served by an additional passage just before the plowing scene. In the A version Piers' account of the route that must be followed to Truth is greeted with dismay by three disreputable street-figures, a cutpurse (pickpocket), apeward (presumably a man with a monkey performing tricks) and a waferer, but Piers tells them of the hope of mercy. In the B version Langland then adds a further brief passage in which two more recalcitrants, a pardoner and a prostitute, drop out from the pilgrimage. In the C version he deletes this passage and substitutes a new and longer one in which three other figures draw back from the pilgrimage:

> 'Ye, *villam emi*,' quod oon, 'and now I moste thedre
> To loke how me liketh hit'; and took his leve at Peres.
> Another anoon riht nede he sayde he hadde
> To falewe with five yokes, 'Forthy me bihoveth
> To goo with a good wil and graytheliche hem dryve.
> Forthy I pray yow, Peres, parauntur yif ye meten
> Treuth, telleth hym this, that I be excused.'
> Thenne was oon hihte Actif, an hosbande he semede:
> 'I have wedded a wyf, wel wantowen of maneres;
> Were I seven nyhte fro here syhte, sighen she wolde
> And loure on me and lightly chyde and sygge I lovede another.
> Forthy, Peres the plouhman, I preye the telle hit Treuthe

I may nat come for a Kitte so a cleveth on me.
Uxorem duxi et ideo non possum venire.'
Quod Contemplacioun, 'By Crist, thogh I care soffre,
Famyne and defaute, folwen I wol Peres.' (C vii 292–306)

These are obviously taken from the parable of the marriage feast in
Luke 14:

> And they all with one consent began to make excuse. The first
> said unto him, I have bought a piece of ground [but the Latin Vul-
> gate has *villa*], and I must needs go and see it: I pray thee have me
> excused. And another said, I have bought five yoke of oxen, and I
> go to prove them: I pray thee have me excused. And another said,
> I have married a wife, and therefore I cannot come.

The earlier recalcitrants were parasites on society and appropriately contrasted with Piers, the honest worker who knew the way to Truth,
and with the other penitents who were prepared to work on his half-
acre. The pardoner as supposedly a man of religion and servant of the
Church joined the palmer who did not know the way to Truth, the
clerks who only knew books and the priest who mocked the Pardon, all
of them superficially engaged in the service of God but not knowing
him as Piers the Plowman did or willing to seek him as the knight was.
These new figures, however, are more like ordinary working laymen,
challengingly close in status and occupation to Piers himself. The first
is perhaps a man of wealth; *villa* seems to mean at this period a village
or town rather than a piece of ground (the Wyclifite sermons render
the word *toun* and the contemporary poem *Cleanness* gives *toun* and *borh*,
implying a town).[24] But the second man is a plowman like Piers, too busy
with his team to go on pilgrimage, while for the third it is simply marriage that apparently holds him back. One might expect Piers, a plowman and married man himself, to sympathise; he too eventually forsakes
the pilgrimage in order to follow his team, and does so on the instruc-
tions of Truth himself. But these three in context are clearly back-
sliders, penitents who have set off to find Truth but now abandon the
search. According to patristic commentary, the three men are to be interpreted allegorically, as sinners too committed to worldly pleasures;
the villa stands for material possessions, the oxen for the five senses
which are misused, and the wife represents bodily pleasures.[25] The
Wyclifite sermons offer a similar interpretation, by which the villa represents worldly status, the oxen worldly goods and the wife fleshly sins
such as gluttony and lechery.[26] Langland may be influenced by that
tradition but his identification of the third recalcitrant as Actif invites
us to make a more general association of the three men with the active

life. The same Latin verse, *Uxorem duxi*, is in fact quoted by Haukyn/Actif in B (xiv 3), and later in the C version Langland identifies the active life with the life of matrimony in a firmly literal sense (xviii 78–80). In the A version Langland had presented the active life as the worthy life of the honest worker, but already in the B version he had begun to associate the term, in the shape of Haukyn, with worldliness and materialism, and this is taken further in this scene, where Actif and his friends cannot or will not follow Truth. The essence of the plowing and Pardon scenes had been that the honest workers for society could find Truth and receive his pardon through their work when the specialists in religion – the palmer, the clerk, the pardoner, the priest – could not. But what Langland now invites us to consider in this new passage is the possibility that the representatives of the active life cannot pursue Truth, being too committed to their worldly life and labours. To follow that road they must apparently renounce family and occupations.

While Actif and his companions make excuses, it is Contemplation who is willing to pursue Truth. The last time Langland had used the term contemplation it was with a pejorative connotation, referring to the way of life entered by the friars as part of their corruption of society (B xx 274). Now, though, it is clearly being used in a favourable sense. Contemplation's willingness to suffer famine and want associates the term here with the ideal of poverty and asceticism voiced by Piers at the tearing of the Pardon and in the B version by Patience. A measure of how far the poem has come from the original spirit of the vision is the fact that in the A version the risk of hunger and privation was the mark of the idlers and recalcitrants who refused to work with Piers; the willingness to face that risk has now become a virtue and a necessary factor in the pursuit of Truth. Contemplation is re-enacting the commitment made earlier by Piers when tearing the Pardon.

The new passage thus invites the reader to question the idealisation of labour in the scenes that follow. In their main narrative outline those scenes remain largely unchanged. There is still the moral opposition between those who are prepared to work zealously for the community through their secular labours and the idlers and wasters. But one significant omission is Hunger's comment on work and the active and contemplative lives. In A (vii 231–3) Hunger had urged that all people had a natural and Christian duty to work, at teaching or tilling or labouring with hands, that is, he says, in the active life or the contemplative life. The lines are preserved in B (vi 247–9) except that the specific examples are now ditching or delving or labouring in prayer. In the C version the passage is dropped altogether. Presumably Langland felt that the passage was now an embarrassment, since Actif had refused to follow the path to Truth; perhaps also because he had come to see Contemplation as a willingness to accept hardship rather than a mode of activity.

The problem of work, idlers and beggars recurs again in a brief addition just a few lines later in Hunger's speech (C viii 278–89). The warning to Piers and his fellows to eat in moderation prompts Hunger to refer to Lazarus and Dives as contrasting examples; then, taking Piers (rather oddly) as a type of the rich man, he urges him to give food if he can to all the poor who beg at his gate, even the liars, thieves and idlers, but to leave these latter till last. This particular issue is then examined in much more detail in a long addition to the Pardon. In the A version the Pardon had included just fourteen lines on beggars, distinguishing between those in genuine need, who are therefore included in the Pardon, and false beggars who deceive benefactors and live a dissolute life. In the B version this is expanded, with a further eighteen lines urging that donors should give to all who ask and that the responsibility and sin lay with the beggars themselves if they were not in genuine need. In the C version Langland expands still further, replacing part of the B version's addition with a passage of about ninety lines that seeks to elaborate the distinction between worthy and unworthy beggars.[27] He gives a moving account of the genuinely needy, that is, our neighbours in their cottages who strive to make a living for themselves but fail through misfortune or incapacity and are ashamed to beg, and contrasts these with the unworthy – the idle and healthy beggars who could work and make a living but choose not to, though these in turn need to be distinguished from wandering lunatics who are healthy in body but incapable of supporting themselves. Langland seems in part to be trying to distinguish between the unobtrusive poor, who remain in their cottages among the other workers and struggle to survive, reluctant to ask for help, and the wandering 'professional' beggars who proclaim their needs at every man's gate, though he then needs to distinguish in turn the apparently similar wandering half-wits.

In the A and B versions the account of the Pardon is then completed with a few lines on those who cannot work – the old, the pregnant, the blind and the invalid. In the C version Langland expands this with other examples of those who do not contribute to society but accept misfortune or poverty patiently – lepers, prisoners, pilgrims, and those who have lost their possessions through theft, fraud, fire or flood. In citing pilgrims Langland is again drawing into the Pardon a category firmly excluded from the earlier dispensation, in the shape of the palmer. He then adds one line to include holy hermits in the Pardon, also absent in previous versions, and a further ninety-four lines largely on the problem of false hermits. The distinction which he attempts to draw, reminiscent of the earlier discussion of beggars, is between those who have given up wealth, status and comfort to become hermits and asked nothing of others, and those who had been labourers and artisans but gave up the hardships of the working life for the comforts and idleness of the hermit's life, begging their food from others. The passage ends with a sharp attack on bishops for their negligence in failing to deal with such problems.

The Pardon has thus been radically changed. In the A version it had run to just eighty-eight lines of which most had dealt with those who worked in their various ways for society and therefore merited Truth's Pardon; only the last twenty lines had dealt with the problem of beggars and the involuntary poor, and hermits and others who abjured the world had not been mentioned at all. In the C version it runs to 281 lines of which 220 deal with the problems of those who do not work for the community. In the process Langland often loses sight of the Pardon itself: the question becomes 'what should be done about beggars' rather than 'who is included in the Pardon'. By including more prominently in the Pardon those who do not help Piers in his activities, both hermits and the helpless poor, Langland is forced to confront the question of discriminating among the poor and the beggars and to drop work as his main criterion. The central concern of the passus is no longer the moral status of secular work in the scheme of salvation but the moral distinctions to be made among the vast section of the population who do not provide for themselves. The dominant virtue is no longer honest toil but the patient acceptance of hardship by those who cannot labour or have chosen poverty as their vocation – the virtue symbolised by Contemplation at the beginning of the plowing scene. At the same time as asceticism has been brought fully into the heart of the vision, so the presentation of the secular life has been modified to match it. One way in which this is done is the new emphasis on the religious duties of the laity, evident in an additional passage in the Pardon (C ix 227–39). But the main difference is the stress on the involuntary poor. Particularly in the moving description of the sufferings of the lower classes in the Pardon scene, Langland draws into the picture a group who might prefer to be successful workers contributing to the community but through misfortune find themselves destitute and forced to seek their salvation through the patient acceptance of suffering, a virtue initially associated with ascetics rather than the workers. The laity are thus drawn into the ambit of Contemplation through their acceptance of 'famine and defaute'.

It must have been largely because of this fundamental shift that Langland now deleted the tearing of the Pardon. In the A and B versions Piers had dramatically rejected the Pardon with its idealisation of labour and sworn to forsake his work as a plowman in pursuit of food for the life of prayer and asceticism. In the C version these lines are dropped altogether and we are left only with the very brief dispute between the priest and Piers before the vision ends. Clearly the renunciation of labour for the eremitic life no longer made sense in this context

begging for their negligence in failing to deal with such problems.
material things of this world has become only a minor element in the
Pardon. Though it might still be meaningful for Piers to renounce the
working life, it could no longer be represented by rejecting the Pardon
or indeed have much relevance to the Pardon at all. The alternative
way of life which was formerly represented by Piers' choice has now
been incorporated into the Pardon's scheme of salvation. It has indeed
been incorporated into the plowing too, since Contemplation is the
chief of Piers' followers.

The other, complementary meaning which the tearing of the Pardon
had appeared to have for Langland in the A and B versions was a movement away from a doctrine of salvation by merit according to strict justice and towards a reliance on divine mercy and grace. That had been
one manifestation of an oscillation that recurred repeatedly within the
poem, culminating in the final appeal for grace. In the C version there
is now no reply to the priest's claim that the Pardon amounts to no
more than an assurance that those who do good will go to Heaven and
those who do ill will go to Hell, though the dreamer's subsequent
musings on the relative importance of Do-wel, pardons and divine grace
remain. But in fact the reply is no longer necessary: the Pardon itself,
with its enlarged sympathy for the poor, the lunatic and the unfortunate,
has implicitly redefined Do-wel as the patient acceptance of poverty
and misfortune and ceased to offer a severe doctrine of merit and reward.

Two features then dominate the C revision of the second vision.
Firstly, there is an expansion of satire and an extension of its range,
notably in an intensification of the attack on the Church (one might
note the final addition to the Pardon as well as earlier passages).
Secondly, and more substantially, there is a major reconsideration of the
relationship of the active and contemplative lives and of the treatment
and status of beggars, both those who claim to be incapable of work
and those who claim an eremitic vocation. The later part of the B version had expressed a growing doubt about the moral status of the active life and an enthusiasm for the life of voluntary poverty, and these
views now find expression in the second vision. Yet while the life of
voluntary poverty or contemplation is still seen as the ideal, Langland
draws into the poem a concern with the complex reality of poverty as
it is lived.

The third vision

The third vision had been the great area of intellectual crisis for
Langland. It was the point at which he had abandoned the A version,
and (probably) a subsequent attempt to continue the poem. It was also
the point, in the B version, where he had agonised over the proper role

of the clerk and discussed the problems of the function and value of his own poetry . What marks the C text revision of this dream is the sense that the crisis has passed: the issues are still alive but Langland is no longer in the state of doubt which produced the bewildering tones and abrupt shifts of direction. The main discussion of his poetry (B xii 1ff) is now dropped altogether, some of the self-description is omitted, and the radical arguments of the dreamer are now distanced from the poet, and their status signposted, by reassigning them to a character called Recklessness.

In its original form the first part of the vision had described the dreamer's enquiries about the nature of Do-wel and the answers he received from a series of authority figures. In the B version there was already a shift from concerns with external society to a concern with more inward and spiritual definitions, and that is taken further in the C version. Wit's complaint about unkindness and the misuse of speech at B ix 71–108 is deleted; Study's critique of vulgar minstrels or jesters (B x 38–50) is dropped; so is her complaint of the decline of hospitality (B x 89–134); and Clergie's account of the failings of the clergy (B x 257–327), of which part is transferred to Reason's sermon at the beginning of the second vision. There is perhaps some endeavour here to concentrate the social criticism in the first two visions. Instead we have a sustained emphasis on the positive virtue of love, the virtue associated in the B version with Patience and reasserted by Kynde at the very end of the poem. It had already figured briefly in the speeches of Study and Trajan, but is now developed further by Wit, who urges that the clergy should have the courage to preach love to all the world (C ix 184–201), and by Imaginatif (C xiv 13ff).

In the A version the sequence of definitions of Do-wel by the friars, Thought, Wit, Study and Scripture had come to an abrupt crisis when the dreamer intervened with a series of provocative claims that doing well was irrelevant – because faith and baptism were sufficient in themselves, because predestination made merit irrelevant, because knowledge and study were more dangerous than helpful, and because pure simplicity was what counted. The poem then broke off, with the dream and the work itself apparently unfinished. In the B version Langland continued the poem with a dream within a dream at this point, in which the dreamer followed Fortune, met Lewte, Scripture and Trajan, and saw Middle Earth in all its wonders; the dreamer then awoke from his inner dream, discussed it with Imaginatif and finally awoke from the third vision. The issues of learning, predestination, baptism and the good life were debated anew, and partially resolved by Imaginatif. In the C version Langland drops the dreamer's argument with Scripture about the salvation of the rich and the importance of baptism and moves directly from the speech of Clergie (which is now a rather tame discussion of the Ten Commandments) into the inner dream of the narrator's life with Fortune. The dreamer's outburst on predestination and the perils of learning now comes at a later point in the narrative, within this inner dream, and is reassigned to the character Recklessness.

Recklessness is a perplexing figure. He had had only two lines in the B version but now emerges as a major character. He is introduced primarily as a figure of irresponsible carelessness. Elde warns the dreamer not to trust himself to Fortune, who will fail him in his old age, but Recklessness, said to be the kin of Wanhope (Despair), intervenes to urge him not to care and points out that at least if he goes to Hell he will be in good company, with all the rich (C xi 189–201). But as his speech develops Recklessness begins to be associated with the virtue of poverty and with taking no thought for the world, aligning himself with such figures as Patience. He seems at times a distinct character but the opening of C xii firmly identifies him with the dreamer, referred to both as 'me' and as Will:

> 'Allas, eye!' quod Elde and Holynesse bothe,
> 'That wit shal turne to wrechednesse for Wil hath al his wille!'
> Covetyse-of-yes conforted me aftur
> And saide, 'Rechelesnesse, reche the nevere . . .'.

The identification of Recklessness with the dreamer is equally evident later, at C xiii 131–3 and xiv 99–102.

The main effect of these changes is to 'place' the more radical arguments of the vision; they are still deployed with some energy but qualified by their context and speaker. This is particularly evident with the anti-intellectualism. Study's criticism of the pursuit of theological knowledge at B x 101–34 is dropped; so too is her account of the misuse of learning and the dangers of knowledge at B x 189–217. Recklessness blames on Clergie the extreme form of the doctrine of predestination which he expounds but his anti-intellectualism and his radicalism about salvation are then undermined by his return to the extravagant claim made by the dreamer in the A version, which Langland had dropped in the B version, that Aristotle and Solomon were damned for all their wisdom and their good works. He then qualifies his attack with an apology:

> Ac I countresegge the nat, Clergie, ne thy connyng, Scripture,
> That ho-so doth by youre doctrine doth wel, I leve.
> Ac me were levere, by oure lord, a lyppe of Goddes grace
> Thenne al the kynde wyt that ye can bothe and kunnyng of
>   youre bokes. (C xi 225–8)

The point is not, after all, that learning is dangerous or even unhelpful, but that divine grace is more important for salvation. Recklessness here voices casually the conclusion eventually reached in the B version after much anguish and debate. Again, Langland deletes a passage (B xi 211–29) in which as narrator he had argued that law and logic were of little help in salvation and claimed that faith alone could save, whatever the objections of clerks. Trajan himself becomes less an example of the uselessness of learning than a sign that baptism is not crucial: it is now *cristendom* rather than *clergie* that he discounts. Thus the great debate in the B version between the claims of learning and the arguments of the mystics and ascetics that learning was at best useless and at worst dangerous, gives way in the C version to the safer and more orthodox argument that learning is useful but grace superior, and the anti-intellectual position is reduced to a rebellious murmur. The whole vision is thus brought into accord with the reconciling speech by Imaginatif which ends it, showing that *clergie* is of great value in salvation, and superior to *kynde wit*, though grace itself is still mightier.

The major new concern of this vision is poverty, already seen as a dominant theme of the revision of the second vision. In the B version the topic had been raised in a digression by the narrator; the point was at first the virtue of caring for the poor, but with the mention of Martha and Mary the passage turned to the virtue of voluntary poverty. Here the question of poverty becomes a major element, expanded from about 100 lines in the B version to about 250 in C, and apparently spoken by Recklessness. The main concern is voluntary poverty. Recklessness begins with a series of biblical quotations on the duty to renounce the world to follow Christ (C xii 153–69) and cites the saints who suffered hardship for Christ's sake as examples of his ideal (l. 203). The discussion ends with a clear statement of poverty as an ideal for all the clergy:

Uch a parfit prest to poverte sholde drawe. (C xiii 99)

But much of the discussion, especially of the virtues of patiently enduring poverty, can apply to the ordinary poor as well. Recklessness goes on to tell a delightful story contrasting the merchants, who are weighed down by their burdens on their journeys and must travel an indirect way by the major roads, with the messenger who can ride unburdened wherever he wishes. He then explains that the merchants are the rich who have burdensome duties to the poor and suffer from the moral perils of wealth, while the messenger stands for 'these mendynaunts who live by mens alms'. The term *mendynaunt* or mendicant could mean either religious ascetics such as friars and hermits or ordinary beggars, and Recklessness seems in fact to include also those who work for a living – 'ne contiumax thogh he worche/Haly day or holy evene his mete to discerve' (ll. 84–5; that is, the mendicant will not be considered disobedient to authority if he works on a holy day or holy eve to earn his food). The speech thus propounds poverty both as the perfect way of life for the priesthood and a secure road to salvation for the laity.

The content of this discussion closely resembles the account of poverty as an ideal given by Patience and Anima in the B text, and largely preserved in the C version, but the tone and implications are hard to place. Recklessness's name, and the kinds of arguments he deploys earlier, are poor recommendations for his views, and parts of his apologia for poverty seem rather extravagant. The claim that the messenger may ride straight through the field of wheat because necessity has no law may be only an analogy but it recalls the more extreme claims made in B xx by Nede, himself a very dubious figure. Similarly Recklessness's argument that the poor are absolved from all religious observance, since for them faith and baptism are enough, seems tendentiously exaggerated. Yet in his denunciation of the complex carapace of the Church Recklessness has a kind of forthright vigour which attracts, and much of what he says contains elements of idealism, if overstated. Langland seems to be using Recklessness to express his own ambivalent feelings about the ideal and practice of poverty. The exemplars of voluntary poverty show a kind of holiness and merit in their simplicity and suffering, but also a kind of arrogant anarchy in their denial of authority (a point raised by Conscience in the Prologue to the second vision). Recklessness's account of poverty involves the same mixture of admiration for the ideal and wry acknowledgement of anarchic practice that is evident elsewhere in the C version. It is perhaps significant that both here and in the Prologue to the second vision Langland employs a figure of himself to speak these enthusiastic but somewhat unconvincing apologies for the ideal of poverty, as if reflecting on his own optimism when writing the B version.

Patience, Haukyn and the Tree of Charity

In the B version Langland had gone on to develop the theme of poverty in the fourth vision, with the story of Patience the hermit. Much of that episode remains, but with some significant differences. In the B version Patience is identified as a pilgrim and a hermit; here he is said to resemble a pilgrim and Piers:

And there cam Pacience as a pore thyng and preyede mete pur charite,
Ilyk Peres the ploghman, as he a palmere were,

Cravede and cryede, for Cristes love of hevene,
A meles mete for a pore man, or moneye, yf they hadde.

(C xv 33–6)

The substitution of 'a poor man' for 'a poor hermit' and the association with Piers the Plowman shifts Patience in the direction of the ordinary poor rather than specifically the voluntary poor or eremitic status. The implication that Piers is now to be seen as a kind of palmer or pilgrim is confirmed by Clergie a little later. Clergie excuses himself from defining Do-wel because Piers the palmer has impugned all learning and set up love alone:

> 'Have me excused,' quod Clergie, 'be Crist, but in scole,
> Shal no such motyef be meved for me, bote there,
> For Peres love the palmare gent, that inpugnede ones
> Alle kyne connynges and alle kyne craftes,
> Save love and leute and lowenesse of herte
> And no tixst ne taketh to preve this for trewe
> Bote *dilige deum et proximum*, and *domine, quis habitabit*,
> And preveth by puyre skile inparfyt alle thynges,
>   *Nemo bonus*,
> Bote lele love and treuthe, that loth is to be founde.'

(C xv 129–37)

(One might note in passing how far the poem has moved since the Z text when Piers was introduced as the very opposite of a palmer.) Piers himself proves to be present at the feast, alongside Patience, and replies to Clergie with a definition originally given by Patience in the B version:

> Quod Peres the ploghman: '*Pacientes vincunt*.
> Byfore perpetuel pees I shal preve that I saide
> And avowe byfore God, and forsaken hit nevere,
> That *disce, doce, dilige deum* . . . (C xv 138–41)

Piers then abruptly leaves the feast, followed by Reason but leaving Conscience, Clergie and Patience behind. (Reason is in fact the host for the meal in the C version, and his departure adds to the process of undermining Clergie and the *doctour*.) In the B version Conscience had talked in almost Messianic terms of the future coming of Piers, thus pointing forward to the identification of Piers with Christ made in B xv–xviii, and one might suppose that this is what his appearance in this scene in the C version should symbolise. But Conscience's words are now dropped and there is no hint of a Christ-like quality in Piers here,

195

as he speaks indeed of avowing his message before God (nor, as we shall
see, is there any longer a link between Piers and Christ in the equivalent
of B xv and xvi). Instead Piers is both plowman and palmer, and closely linked with Patience the poor man. There seems here a firm insistence on associating him with aspects of human life rather than the
divine, and attempting to link the poverty and austerity of the plowman
with the voluntary hardship and sacrifice of the palmer. Whereas in the
A and B version a sharp contrast is seen between the two ways of life –
Piers the Plowman is introduced as the opposite of the palmer, and he
subsequently forsakes plowing for the eremitic life – here his association as plowman with the values of Patience and the palmer seems to
suggest something like the linking of the working poor with voluntary
religious poverty that was evident in Langland's revision of the plowing and the Pardon scenes. The central issue of this scene remains the
rejection of learning for the life of austerity and ideal of love symbolised
by Patience, but the association of Patience with Piers rather than a hermit suggests a broadening of the scope of those values.

This suggestion is picked up in the following scene. In the B version
Conscience and Patience meet a personification of the active life called
Haukyn, who talks of his importance as a producer of food for others
but is seen to be wearing a coat on which his hopeless corruption is
revealed, with stains of all the deadly sins; Conscience proposes a
metaphorical penance which will transform his life, Patience describes
at great length the virtues of poverty and asceticism and Haukyn breaks
down and weeps over his sinfulness as the vision ends. In the C version
Haukyn is a man reborn. He loses his personal name and is called simply Actif, and all reference to his sinfulness disappears. So does the
penance proposed by Conscience and Haukyn's final lament for his sin.
(Much of the material on his sins is reused in the description of the sinners in the second vision.) The surviving account of Actif is indeed so
brief (41 lines in place of the 233 of the B version) that it is difficult to
be sure what he now represents. His role as minstrel becomes more
prominent than his status as a producer of food and agent of Piers; indeed the only reference to his activity as a waferer seems to point to the
religious use of wafers in the mass:

'As a waferer with wafres ay welcome Godes gestes' (C xv 199)

Possibly this was just a piece of tidiness on Langland's part: he had already condemned Actif in C vii, at the beginning of the plowing scene,
and already produced one lengthy account of the deadly sins in the
second vision. Yet the sheer spotlessness of Actif in the C version does
seem significant, particularly in contrast with the Actif of C vii. Actif
now seems to be simply a representative ordinary man used as an op-

portunity for Patience to articulate his ideal of patient poverty. That
great ideal still remains as in the B version, but it no longer depends on
destroying the claims of the active life of labour, and perhaps as a result
allows the virtue of poverty to spread its light over the laity more easily. Just as in the previous scene Patience can be linked with the plowman, so here he can be brought rather closer to the Actif Man. Langland
seems to be suggesting the possibility of an enhancement of Actif's life
through the virtues of Patience rather than the inescapable corruption
of the active life which he suggested in the B version.

The final indication of Haukyn's rehabilitation is that he is no longer
abandoned weeping and discredited with the end of the vision. In the
B version the dream had ended at this point, and a fifth vision began
with the character generally referred to as Anima. In the C version the
fourth vision continues, turning directly to Anima who is now called
Liberum Arbitrium (Free Will) and defined as Actif's leader or guide.

The dialogue with Anima in B xv had been long and rambling but
had seemed to be largely concerned with exploring further and discur-
sively some of the issues raised more dramatically in the previous dream,
especially issues of knowledge and love and the role of the clergy. This
seems still to be true in the C version, which remains rambling and apparently unstructured despite much rewriting. One case which shows
Langland still debating with himself over important issues and trying
to establish that balance and compromise which marks other revisions
is the addition of a passage (C xvii 136–58) arguing that love is only of
value if it is rooted in God's law. It is part of a discussion of Jews and
Saracens and would seem to refer back to the earlier arguments of the
righteous heathen Trajan, who had claimed love as an ideal in opposition to law. Liberum Arbitrium seems to be accepting the primacy of
love, a growing theme from passus x onwards, but attempting to har-
monise it with the opposing claims for the importance of Church and
baptism. As with Trajan, Jews and Saracens provide a test case for the
essentials of salvation, and love is not enough, Liberum Arbitrium
argues.

The most striking feature of Anima's teaching in the B version had
been a passage which seemed intrusive but acquired significance later
in the poem, a passage in which he identified Piers with God. The first
part of this remains:

> 'Where clerkes knowe hym [i.e. Charity] nat,' quod I, 'that kepen
>   holy churche?'
> 'Peres the plouhman,' quod he, 'moste parfitlyche hym knoweth.
>   *Et vidit deus cogitaciones eorum.*' (C xvi 336–7)

Yet the point of the identification has been lost. In the B version

Langland had argued, provocatively, that charity could not be identified in men by their words or their works but only by their thoughts or will, and hence could only be determined by God who can see into their hearts. Now he argues firmly that charity can be recognised by works; thus B xv 209–12

> 'Therfore by colour ne by clergie knowe shaltow hym nevere,
> Neither thorugh wordes ne werkes, but thorugh wil oone,
> And that knoweth no clerk ne creature on erthe
> But Piers the Plowman – *Petrus, id est, Christus.*'

is replaced by this:

> 'By clothyng ne by carpynge knowe shaltow hym nevere,
> Ac thorw werkes thow myhte wyte wher-forth he walketh.
> *Operibus credite*' [Trust in works]. (C xvi 338–9)

Langland clearly reverses here his earlier claim that issues of salvation and moral discrimination are mysteries known only to God, and as a consequence drops the identification of his authority-figure Piers with Christ – a change already hinted at in the feast scene earlier in the vision, where Piers is identified with the pilgrim Patience rather than with Christ.

It is this change which lies behind the radical transformation of the Tree of Charity episode. In the B version Anima's mention of Piers while describing the tree causes the dreamer to swoon with joy, and in an inner dream he sees Piers himself, who describes the tree and its props to him, shakes down some fruit, and throws one of the props at the devil to prevent him stealing the fruit, thus causing the Incarnation. It is an intensely imaginative but puzzling scene, and in the C version Langland thoroughly recasts it. Both in the preceding passus and in the episode of Patience he had removed the divine associations from Piers, and in this episode he carries this change of heart through and eradicates Piers altogether, replacing him with a variety of figures appropriate to his roles. It is Liberium Arbitrium or Free Will who describes the tree and its props, it is Elde or Old Age who shakes the fruit down, it is Libera-voluntas-dei (the free will of God) who throws the prop at the devil and Liberum Arbitrium again who teaches Christ leechcraft. The changes do have a logic. It is properly Liberum Arbitrium who takes the initial role, since this includes using the props to defend the fruit (that is, invoking the aid of the Trinity to protect man's good works and intentions) from the temptations of the world, the flesh and the devil, and this seems an appropriate function for man's free will. Elde is the right figure to pluck the fruit, since the plucking is an image of dying. And

though there is no particular rightness about Libera-voluntas-dei playing the role of initiating the Redemption of man, it should logically be
some aspect of God and the phrase suggests a kind of divine comp-
lement to Liberum Arbitrium. Even so one cannot help suspecting that
the impetus behind the change was the need to remove Piers rather
than to make a particular statement about free will. That triumphant
intervention of the numinous into human life which Piers had represented in the B version has now gone; hence, no doubt, the disap-
pearance of the dreamer's ecstatic swoon into an inner dream. Perhaps
the need to abandon the dramatic scene in which Piers tears up the Pardon sent by Truth made Piers no longer available as the universal guide
to salvation in Langland's imagination.

One further change to this scene connects it to the discussion of the
active life in the earlier part of the vision. In the B version Piers had
distinguished three kinds of fruit on the tree: the highest represented
virginity, the next chaste widowhood, the lowest matrimony. In the C
version Liberum Arbitrium first explains more clearly the concept of
different kinds of fruit or charity, a perplexing matter in the B version, and then goes on to repeat Piers' threefold distinction, but
identifies it simultaneously with the twofold distinction of active and
contemplative:

> Adam was as tre, and we aren as his apples,
> Somme of us soothfaste and some variable,
> Summe litel, somme large, ylik apples of oon kynde.
> As weddede men and wedewes and riht worthy maydones,
> The whiche the Seynt Spirit seweth, the sonne of al hevene,
> And conforteth hem in here continence that lyven in
>   contemplacoun,
> As monkes and monyals, men of holy churche;
> These haen the hete of the Holi Goost as hath the crop of tre
>   the sonne.
> Wedewes and wedewares, that here ownere wil forsaken
> And chaste leden here lyf, is lyf of contemplacioun,
> And more lykynde to oure lorde then lyve as kynde asketh
> And folewe that the flesche wole and fruyt forth brynge,
> That *Activa* lyf lettred men in here langage hit calleth.'
>
> (C xviii 68–80)

The identification of matrimony with the active life and chastity and
virginity with the contemplative life reflects Langland's continuing
concern with the active/contemplative distinction in the C version and
the development of its meaning. There are links with Haukyn, who in
the B version refers to the wife whose existence apparently stains his

life with sin, and more particularly with the character Actif in C vii, who has married a wife and therefore cannot come on the road to Truth. For Langland the active life has gradually come to mean not the zealous engagement in hard work for the material needs of society, as in the A version, but an inability to escape from corrupting engagement with the world and from the desires of the flesh and human nature. Contemplation has similarly developed from an engagement in prayer on behalf of the community (B vi) to a willingness to suffer poverty (C vii) and now to a willingness to dispense with the pleasures of the flesh. What is important is that the difference between the active and contemplative lives is now seen as one of degree rather than kind: matrimony and the active life are inferior but still good (C xviii 87), and the tree imagery and use of the word *kynde* hint that these are natural and innate distinctions. At the same time, the extension of the contemplative life to include not just the clergy but also some of the laity reflects the tendency elsewhere in the C version to extend the moral virtue of poverty and asceticism to the secular world.

The Passion

Although Langland eliminates the association of Piers with Christ and shows more concern with human nature and society in the fourth vision, the central argument of the Tree of Charity and Good Samaritan episodes – the need for a divine act of salvation rather than a human one – remains, and is taken up in the next vision (the fifth in the C version, the sixth in B). This was one of the great highlights of the B version of the poem, and remains little changed in substance in the C version, with the same powerful and imaginative description of the Passion and the Harrowing of Hell. Langland's failure to change the early references to 'Peres fruit the plowman' (C xx 18 and 32), which relate to the B version rather than C, might suggest some lack of close revision, but in fact a series of small additions throughout the passus show that his work on the poem continued. The longest is surprisingly uncharacteristic of the C text revision; a vigorous and dramatic passage in which Satan summons the other devils to his support, reminiscent in content and language of the mystery plays (C xx 281–94). There is a brief digression on lying at ll. 350–8, urging clerks and learned men not to beguile the unlearned, and several smaller additions that seek to explain further Langland's distinctive theology of redemption, especially the idea of Christ's *kynde*. The last identifiable revision to the poem is at C xx 434–5, where the reference in the B version to Purgatory being instituted to cleanse the wicked is replaced by lines in which Christ asserts his desire for vengeance on the wicked but acknowledges that his *kynde* or natural feelings for man will hold him back:

And so of alle wykkede I wol here take veniaunce.
And yut my kynde in my kene ire shal constrayne my will –
Domine, ne in furore tuo arguas me.

The tension between desire for justice and the pull of mercy, one of the
key themes of the whole poem, seems an appropriate note for Langland
to end his revision on. It had been the prime force behind the tearing
of the Pardon by Piers; its reconciliation had been one of the great tri-
umphs of passus xviii; and it was one of the tensions which disrupted
the society at the end of the B version. Once more, and for the last time,
Langland ponders the problem of reconciling a secular ideal of justice
and merit with a spiritual ideal of grace and mercy.

Taken together, Langland's revision of the poem to produce the C version remains a strange phenomenon. Some of it involves intensifying
or expanding, occasionally clarifying, elements already present in earlier versions of the poem: the expansion of the confession of the sins,
for example, or the criticism of authority in the first two visions. Other
changes show a major shift in Langland's thinking, sometimes amount-
ing to a critique of the earlier versions. Sometimes the rethinking is
carried through the poem in fairly comprehensive fashion, as with the
radical change in the role of Piers. At other times, the new arguments
are interpolated alongside the old ones which they counter, as with the
critique of labour in the second vision, or the old arguments are
preserved but undermined by a new context, as with the attack on learning by Recklessness. In matters of detail Langland sometimes entirely
reverses statements made in the B version, or returns to the arguments
which he had expressed in A but abandoned in B (see pp. 198 and 192).
Some of the changes seem at odds with each other: thus the sharp critique of Actif introduced in C vii contrasts with the more favourable view
of Actif introduced in C xv and xviii. The revision as a whole suggests
a poet responding vigorously to his earlier work in a spirit which was
both respectful and critical. The result is a poem which is in some respects easier to follow and often more logical, if less dramatic and imaginative, but which contains its own substantial share of inner conflicts
and at times almost explodes out of the framework created for it in earlier versions. In its own way it tells the story of its poet.

Notes and references

1. In *Chaucerian and Other Pieces*, ed. W. W Skeat (Oxford, 1897), pp. 1–145.
2. Ibid., pp. xxvii–xxviii.
3. Sister Mary Aquinas Devlin, 'The date of the C version of *Piers the*

Plowman', *Abstracts of Theses*, University of Chicago, Humanistic Series IV, 1925–6 (Chicago, 1928)*.

4. R. Bressie, 'The date of Thomas Usk's *Testament of Love*', *Modern Philology*, **26** (1928), pp. 17–29.

5. Cf. Pearsall, *Piers Plowman: an Edition of the C Text*, p. 9.

6. See Bressie, 'The date', p. 28. Bressie also casts doubt on Skeat's identification of borrowings by Usk from Chaucer's *Legend of Good Women*.

7. George Kane in a recent essay ('The Text', in *A Companion to Piers Plowman*, ed. J. A. Alford (Berkeley, 1988) pp. 175–200) says firmly that 'Langland was dead by 1387' (p. 185), alluding, presumably, to the theory that the John But who ended passus xii of the A version and refers there to the narrator's death was using reliable information of Langland's fate and can be identified with a particular John But who died in 1387. Both points of this theory are inevitably hypothetical.

8. A good example is C xii 370, an authentic-looking line which does not appear in any MSS of the B version, but is printed as part of the B text by both Kane–Donaldson and Schmidt. Cf. Kane–Donaldson, pp. 95 and 193n.

9. George Russell also raises the possibility that through some accident the ancestor of all surviving C version MSS had lost the last two passus, which were therefore supplied by a scribe from a B version MS, thus explaining the lack of difference between 'C' and B (see 'Some aspects of the process of revision in *Piers Plowman*', in *Piers Plowman: Critical Approaches*, ed. S. S. Hussey (London, 1969), p. 48). But the freedom of this last section from corruptions common to all surviving MSS of the B version indicates that if the source was a B MS it was one extremely close to Langland himself, and therefore probably supplied by someone in a position to know of any C version of the last part.

10. See S. S. Hussey, Introduction to *Critical Approaches*, ed. Hussey, p. 8; Russell, 'Some aspects' p. 48; and E. T. Donaldson, *Piers Plowman: The C-Text and its Poet* (New Haven and London, 1949), p. 28.

11. Donaldson, *The C-Text*, pp. 19–32.

12. Russell, 'Some aspects', pp. 36–9.

13. Ibid., pp. 39–40 . Kane–Donaldson (pp. 124– 7) appear to share this view.

14. Langland possibly intended the speech to continue to cover the succeeding lines from the B version, previously spoken in the narrator's own voice, so as to transfer the authoritative role to Conscience, but if so he has not revised the lines to make them fit.

15. C. M. Cipolla, *Before the Industrial Revolution: European Society and Economy 1000–1700* (New York, 1967), p. 15.

16. *The Ordinance of Labourers* 1349; in *Statues of the Realm* (London, 1810), I, 307–8.

17. B. Tierney, *The Medieval Poor Law* (Berkeley, 1959), pp. 47ff.

18. *Le Roman de la Rose*, ed. E. Langton (Paris, 1914–24), ll. 11223ff.

19. See R. W. Southern, *Western Society and the Church in the Middle Ages* (Harmondsworth, 1970), p. 320.

20. J. Thomson, *The Later Lollards* (Oxford, 1965), p. 78.

21. R. M. Clay, *The Hermits and Anchorites of England* (London, 1914), pp. 89ff.

22. *The Works of Sir Thomas Malory*, ed. E. Vinaver, 2nd edn (Oxford, 1967), II, 1076 (Book xviii, Chapter 13).

23. 'Lyeth' here has generally been taken to mean 'applies' but probably means 'lies, is untrue'; see M. R. Godden, 'Plowmen and hermits in Langland's *Piers Plowman*', *Review of English Studies*, **35** (1984), 155.

24. *Select English Works of John Wyclif*, ed. T. Arnold, 3 vols (Oxford, 1869–71), I, 5; *Cleanness*, eds A. C. Cawley and J. J. Anderson, *Pearl, Cleanness, Patience, Sir Gawain and the Green Knight* (London, 1976), ll.63–4.

25. Cf. Gregory the Great's homily in *Patrologia Latina*, ed. J-P. Migne, LXXVI, col. 1267.

26. Arnold, *Wyclif*, I, 5.

27. Mable Day, '*Piers Plowman* and poor relief', *Review of English Studies*, **8** (1932), 445–6, argues that Langland's deletion of the B text lines urging charity to all regardless of merit shows a hardening of attitudes towards beggars, but he makes a similar though more carefully formulated point in the new passage at C viii 278–89.

Epilogue

I have tried in this book to describe the richness and complexity of Langland's imaginative processes, and to show how the poem grew in response to his own development, gathering to itself like a snowball a steady accretion of themes and issues. Any summary of that gradual growth will inevitably simplify, but one can perhaps describe the general outlines of the story.

Looking back, we can see that *Piers* began as a relatively simple two-vision poem about the political and social issues of its time, rather like *Winner and Waster*, one of the works which probably influenced Langland. Although there was from the beginning a religious aspect too, voiced by Holy Church and Piers himself, this was used to validate a predominantly secular ideal at that stage. But when Langland resumed the poem, he did so with an action – the tearing of the Pardon – which both challenged all that had gone before and set the poet and his poem off on a long and tortuous journey. Henceforth the social and political themes were repeatedly to be opposed by more religious and spiritual ideals. In the third vision, added in the A version, Langland thus explored the problems of the good life and its relation to salvation, while at the same time increasingly registering a concern with issues of knowledge, learning and authority, issues which impinged on his own role as poet. It was perhaps because of such pressures and doubts that he then abandoned the poem a second time. His role as poet was one of the topics which Langland immediately took up when he eventually resumed the poem again, to produce the B version with its eight visions. That version is carried forward by a readiness to work out answers to the earlier dilemmas, as he challenged the emphasis on learning and work in favour of the ideals of simplicity and poverty. Yet what especially took hold of Langland as he wrote was the idea of a powerful and merciful king-figure who would render all human struggles and dilemmas irrelevant, and reconcile the claims of justice with an all-encompassing mercy and grace. This he explored and celebrated in the fifth and sixth visions of B. From that high point of his poetry, however, something forced him to turn back to the earthly community in the last two visions, back to the poem's roots in contemporary politics and society, in an attempt to relate the reality of redemption to the actuality of the contemporary world. There he saw the departure of the Messiah figure and his representatives, to be replaced by lesser authorities such as Conscience or by the powerful but ruthless figure of Kynde, and the recurrence of the conflict between justice and indulgence, and he ended the B version with a renewed plea for a Messianic power to restore a benevolent order to the world.

By the time Langland produced the C version the poem had already achieved some fame, and he seems to have written from a position of greater equanimity and detachment, accepting its main structure but adjusting it in various ways to later thoughts. He was now inclined to smooth out the dramatic poetry which had sprung from his own radical shifts of attitude – the tearing of the Pardon, the attack on learning, the repudiation of Haukyn, Piers' plucking of the fruit of the tree. The poem became in part a framework for the discussion of issues still preying on his mind – the social and political problems of the contemporary scene, the problems of beggars and false hermits – but a greater detachment prompted a balanced and less impassioned assertion of his ideals.

Certain themes and conflicts recur through the course of the poem's development: the notion of playing a useful part in the community and providing for oneself, as opposed to the religious ideal of trusting to God to provide; the opposition of justice and mercy; the need to strive for an achieved perfection, as opposed to the belief in simple innate qualities. Yet if one searches this complex history for the elusive essence of Langland's literary personality, it is perhaps to be found in the inner conflict between his yearning for a kind of oneness and simplicity and his intense and often excited awareness of plurality and complexity. This quality of unity and simplicity is often expressed visually in personifications and symbols: the tower of Truth on the hill; Holy Church in her white dress; the plowman in his simple garb of russet dedicated to labour and austerity; Piers himself, unifying the themes of the poem. It is also evident in the recurrent appeal to one great key to salvation which will unlock all the complexities of contemporary society: work in the second vision, love in the fourth and fifth, grace in the sixth and seventh. It is throughout contrasted with colour, complexity, plurality and conflict. We see this in the crowded anarchic society of the field, or the rich and varied lives of the sinners in the second vision. The colour and multiplicity are often associated directly with sin, as in the stains of corruption which mar Haukyn's coat or the rich colours and jewels of Mede's costume which contrasts with Holy Church's white linen. But they are sometimes associated with doctrinal and intellectual complexity, as when the simple and compelling image of the Tree of Charity develops into a multiple one with three different props, and with fruits which shift from one variety to three and then to a multiplicity of individuals; or, in the reverse direction, when the four wenches who come from opposite corners and engage in vigorous debate end by joining hands and dancing in a circle. As these examples suggest, although Langland's idealising aspiration was drawn to unity and simplicity, his imagination was caught by multiplicity. He could not contemplate an image of unity for long without making it dissolve into a spectrum of many colours, and it was in the complexity of the real world that his wit and imagination were generally engaged. As his representative confesses of the colourful Lady Mede, 'her array me ravished'. It is perhaps after all fitting that his last substantial piece of writing was Satan's call to his fellow-devils to rally to the defence of Hell:

'Ac arise up, Ragamoffyn, and areche me all the barres
That Belial thy beel-syre beet with thy dame,
And I shal lette this lord and his liht stoppe.
Ar we thorw brihtnesse be blente, go barre we the gates.
Cheke we and cheyne we and uch a chine stoppe
That no liht lepe in at lover ne at loupe.
Astarot, hoot out, and have out oure knaves,
Coltyng and al his kyn, the castel to save.
Brumstoon boylaunt brennyng out cast hit
Al hoot on here hedes that entrith ney the walles.
Setteth bowes of brake and brasene gonnes
And sheteth out shot ynow his sheltrom to blende.
Set Mahond at the mangenel and mullestones throweth
And with crokes and kalketrappes acloye we hem uchone!'

(C xx 281–94)

Like Blake's Milton, Langland was imaginatively drawn to the Satanic side.

Bibliography

The list includes all the works cited in this book, apart from those which are only of very peripheral interest for the poem, together with a few other studies of *Piers* which are particularly relevant to the argument.

Editions of *Piers Plowman*

The Vision of William concerning Piers the Plowman, in Three Parallel Texts, ed. W. W. Skeat (2 vols, Oxford, 1886).

William Langland: Piers Plowman, the Z Version, eds A. G. Rigg and C. Brewer (Toronto, 1983).

Piers the Plowman: a Critical Edition of the A-Version, eds T. A. Knott and D. C. Fowler (Baltimore, 1952).

Piers Plowman: the A Version, ed. G. Kane (2nd edn, London, 1988).

Piers Plowman: the B Version, eds G. Kane and E. T. Donaldson (2nd edn, London, 1988).

Langland, Piers Plowman: the Prologue and Passus i–vii of the B Text, ed. J. A. W. Bennett (Oxford, 1972).

The Vision of Piers Plowman: a Complete Edition of the B Text, ed. A. V. C. Schmidt (London, 1978).

Piers Plowman by William Langland: an Edition of the C Text, ed. D. A. Pearsall (London, 1978).

Other primary texts

The Riverside Chaucer, ed. L. D. Benson (Oxford, 1988).

Cursor Mundi, ed. R. Morris (Early English Text Society OS 57, 59, 62, 66, 68, 99, 101, London, 1874–93).

The Earliest English Translations of the De Imitatione Christi, ed. J. K. Ingram (Early English Text Society ES 64, London, 1893).

The Gospel of Nicodemus, ed. H. C. Kim (Toronto, 1973).

The English Works of John Gower, ed. G. Macaulay (Early English Text Society OS 81, London, 1900).

The Middle English Translations of Robert Grosseteste's Château d'Amour, ed. K. Sajavaara (Helsinki, 1967).

The Harley Lyrics, ed. G. L. Brook (Manchester, 1948).

Historical Poems of the XIVth and XVth Centuries, ed. R. H. Robbins (New York, 1959).

The Lanterne of Liȝt, ed. L. M. Swinburn (Early English Text Society OS 151, London, 1915).

The Lay Folks' Catechism, eds T. F. Simmons and H. E. Nolloth (Early English Text Society OS 118, London, 1901).

The Macro Plays, ed. M. Eccles (Early English Text Society 262, London, 1969).

The Middle English Harrowing of Hell and Gospel of Nicodemus, ed. W. H. Hulme (Early English Text Society ES 100, London, 1908).

Middle English Religious Prose, ed. N. F. Blake (London, 1972).

Mum and the Sothsegger, eds M. Day and R. Steele (Early English Text Society OS 199, London, 1936).

The Northern Passion, ed. F. A. Foster (Early English Text Society OS 145, 147, 183, London, 1913–30).

Old English Homilies of the Twelfth Century, ed. R. Morris (Early English Text Society OS 53, London, 1873).

Pierce the Ploughmans Crede, ed. W. W. Skeat (Early English Text Society OS 30, London, 1867).

The Pilgrimage of the Lyf of the Manhode, ed. Avril Henry, vol. 1 (Early English Text Society 288, Oxford, 1985).

The Recluse, ed. J. Pahlsson (Lund, 1911).

Le Roman de la Rose, ed. E. Langton (Paris, 1914–24).

St Erkenwald, ed. Ruth Morse (Cambridge and Totowa, 1975).

Thomas Usk, *The Testament of Love* in *Chaucerian and Other Pieces*, ed. W. W. Skeat (Oxford, 1897), pp. 1–145.

Winner and Waster, ed. I. Gollancz (London, 1920).

Select English Works of John Wyclif, ed. T. Arnold, 3 vols (Oxford, 1869–71).

The English Works of Wyclif hitherto unprinted, ed. F. Matthew (Early English Text Society OS 74, London, 1880).

Iohannis Wyclif Sermones, ed. J. Loserth, 4 vols (London, 1887–90).

Historical and critical studies

R. Adams, 'The nature of Need in *Piers Plowman* XX', *Traditio*, **34** (1978), 273–301.

R. Adams, 'The reliability of the rubrics in the B-Text of *Piers Plowman*', *Medium Ævem*, **54** (1985), 208–31.

J. Alford (ed.), *A Companion to Piers Plowman* (Berkeley, 1988).

Hope Emily Allen, *Writings ascribed to Richard Rolle, and Materials for his Biography* (New York and London, 1927).

Anna Baldwin, *The Theme of Government in Piers Plowman* (Cambridge, 1981).

J. A. W. Bennett, 'The date of the B-text of *Piers Plowman*', *Medium Ævum*, **12** (1943), 55–64.

J. A. W. Bennett, 'Chaucer's contemporary', in Hussey, *Piers Plowman: Critical Approaches*, pp. 310–24.

M. Bloomfield, '*Piers Plowman* and the three grades of chastity', *Anglia*, **76** (1958), 227–53.

R. Bressie, 'The date of Thomas Usk's *Testament of Love*', *Modern Philology*, **26** (1928), 17–29.

A. H. Bright, *New Light on Piers Plowman* (London, 1928).

J. A. W. Burrow, 'The audience of *Piers Plowman*', *Anglia*, **75** (1957), 373–84, reprinted in his *Essays in Medieval Literature* (Oxford, 1984), pp. 102–16.

J. A. W. Burrow, 'The action of Langland's second vision', *Essays in Criticism*, **15** (1965), 247–68, reprinted in his *Essays in Medieval Literature* (Oxford, 1984), pp. 79–101 .

J. A. W. Burrow, *Ricardian Poetry* (London, 1971).

C. M. Cipolla, *Before the Industrial Revolution: European Society and Economy 1000–1700* (New York, 1967).

R. M. Clay, *The Hermits and Anchorites of England* (London, 1914).

N. Coghill, 'Two notes on *Piers Plowman*', *Medium Ævum*, **4** (1935), 83–7.

N. Coghill, 'The Pardon of Piers Plowman', *Proceedings of the British Academy*, **30** (1944), 303–57.

N. Coghill, 'God's wenches and the light that spoke', in *English and Medieval Studies presented to J. R. R. Tolkien*, eds N. Davis and C. L. Wrenn (London, 1962), pp. 200–18.

N. Cohn, *The Pursuit of the Millennium* (London, 1977).

J. Coleman, *Piers Plowman and the Moderni* (Rome, 1981).

E. Colledge, 'A Lollard interpolated version of the *Ancren Riwle*', *Review of English Studies*, **15** (1939), 1–15, 119–45.

Florence Converse, *Long Will: a Romance* (London, 1903).

C. Dawson, 'William Langland', in *The English Way*, ed. M. Ward (London, 1933).

Mable Day, '*Piers Plowman* and poor relief', *Review of English Studies*, **8** (1932), 445–6.

Sister Mary Aquinas Devlin, 'The date of the C version of *Piers the Plowman*', *Abstracts of Theses*, University of Chicago, Humanistic Series IV, 1925–26 (Chicago, 1928).

E. T. Donaldson, *Piers Plowman: the C-Text and its Poet* (New Haven, 1949).

E. T. Donaldson, 'MSS R and F in the B-tradition of Piers Plowman', *Transactions of the Connecticut Academy of Arts and Sciences*, **39** (1955), 179–212.

T. P. Dunning, *Piers Plowman: an Interpretation of the A Text* (Dublin and London, 1937), 2nd edn revised by T. P. Dolan (Oxford, 1980).

R. W. Frank, 'The Pardon scene in *Piers Plowman*', *Speculum*, **26** (1951), 317–31.

R. W. Frank, *Piers Plowman and the Scheme of Salvation* (New Haven, 1957).

W. Gaffney, 'The allegory of the Christ-Knight in *Piers Plowman*', *Publications of the Modern Language Association of America*, **46** (1931), 155–68.

M. R. Godden, 'Plowmen and hermits in Langland's *Piers Plowman*', *Review of English Studies*, **35** (1984), 129–63.

M. Goldsmith, *The Figure of Piers Plowman* (Cambridge, 1981).

J. F. Goodridge, *Langland, Piers the Ploughman* (Harmondsworth, 1959).

Pamela Gradon, 'Langland and the ideology of dissent', *Proceedings of the British Academy*, **66** (1980), 179–205 and separately.

Anne Hudson, *The Premature Reformation: Wycliffite Texts and Lollard History* (Oxford, 1988).

J. Huizinga, *The Waning of the Middle Ages*, trans. F. Hopman, 2nd edn (Harmondsworth, 1972).

S. S. Hussey, 'Langland, Hilton and the three lives', *Review of English Studies*, NS **7** (1956), 225–37.

S. S. Hussey (ed.), *Piers Plowman: Critical Approaches* (London, 1969).

George Kane, *Piers Plowman: the Evidence for Authorship* (London, 1965).

George Kane, 'The text', in Alford, *A Companion to Piers Plowman*, pp. 175–200.

J. N. King, 'Robert Crowley's editions of *Piers Plowman*: a Tudor apocalypse', *Modern Philology*, **73** (1976), 342–52.

E. D. Kirk, *The Dream Thought of Piers Plowman* (New Haven, 1972).

M. D. Lambert, *Franciscan Poverty* (London, 1961).

J. Lawlor, 'The imaginative unity of *Piers Plowman*', *Review of English Studies*, NS **8** (1957), 113–26.

J. Lawlor, *Piers Plowman: an Essay in Criticism* (London, 1962).

G. Leff, *Medieval Thought* (London, 1959).

G. Leff, 'John Wyclif: the path to dissent', *Proceedings of the British Academy*, **52** (1966), 143–80.

G. Leff, *Heresy in the Later Middle Ages*, 2 vols (Manchester, 1967).

C. S. Lewis, *The Allegory of Love* (Oxford, 1936).

L. K. Little, *Religious Poverty and the Profit Economy in Medieval Europe* (London, 1978).

J. M. Manly, '*Piers Plowman* and its sequence', *The Cambridge History of English Literature*, eds A. W. Ward and A. R. Waller (Cambridge, 1908), II, 1–42.

Jill Mann, *Chaucer and Medieval Estates Satire* (Cambridge, 1973).

M. E. Marcett, *Uhtred de Boldon, Friar William Jordan and Piers Plowman* (New York, 1938).

A. Middleton, 'The idea of public poetry in the reign of Richard II', *Speculum*, **53** (1978), 94–114.

Anne Middleton, 'The audience and public of *Piers Plowman*', in *Middle English Alliterative Poetry and its Literary Background*, ed. D. A. Lawton (Cambridge, 1982), pp. 101–23 .

Anne Middleton, 'Making a good end: John But as a Reader of *Piers Plowman*', in *Medieval English Studies presented to George Kane*, eds E. D. Kennedy, R. Waldron and J. S. Wittig (Wolfeboro and Woodbridge, 1988), pp. 243–63.

D. Mills, 'The role of the dreamer in *Piers Plowman*', in Hussey, *Piers Plowman: Critical Approaches*, pp. 180–212.

S. Moore, 'Studies in *Piers Plowman*', *Modern Philology*, **12** (1914), 19–50.

A. R. Murray, *Reason and Society in the Middle Ages* (Oxford, 1978).

T. F. Mustanoja, 'The suggestive use of Christian names in Middle English poetry', in *Medieval Literary and Folklore Studies in Honor of F. L. Utley*, eds J. Mandel and B. A. Rosenberg (New Brunswick, 1970), pp. 51–76.

J. Norton-Smith, *William Langland* (Leiden, 1983).

H. A. Oberman, 'Fourteenth-century religious thought: a premature profile', *Speculum*, **53** (1978), 80–93.

D. Owen, *Piers Plowman: a Comparison with some Earlier and Contemporary French Allegories* (London, 1912).

G. R. Owst, *Literature and Pulpit in Medieval England* (Cambridge, 1933; 2nd edn Oxford, 1961).

B. Palmer, 'The guide convention in *Piers Plowman*', *Leeds Studies in English*, NS **5** (1971), 13–27.

G. Pantin, *The English Church in the Fourteenth Century* (Cambridge, 1955).

D. A. Pearsall, *Old English and Middle English Poetry* (London, 1977).

T. Renna, 'Wyclif's attacks on the monks', in *From Ockham to Wyclif*, eds A. Hudson and M. Wilks (Oxford, 1987), pp. 267–80.

G. Russell, 'Some aspects of the process of revision in *Piers Plowman*', in Hussey, *Piers Plowman: Critical Approaches*, pp. 27–49.

M. L. Samuels, 'Dialect and grammar', in Alford, *A Companion to Piers Plowman*, pp. 201–22.

A. V. C. Schmidt, *The Clerkly Maker* (Cambridge, 1987).

G. Shepherd, 'The nature of alliterative poetry in late medieval England', *Proceedings of the British Academy*, **56** (1970), 57–76.

W. J. Shiels (ed.), *Monks, Hermits and the Ascetic Tradition* (Studies in Church History, vol. XXII, Oxford, 1985).

W. J. Shiels and D. Wood (eds), *The Church and Wealth* (Studies in Church History, vol. XXIV, Oxford, 1988).

R. W. Southern, *The Making of the Middle Ages* (London, 1953).

R. W. Southern, *Western Views of Islam in the Middle Ages* (Cambridge, Mass., 1962).

R. W. Southern, *Western Society and the Church in the Middle Ages* (Harmondsworth, 1970).

P. Szittya, *The Anti-Fraternal Tradition in Medieval Literature* (Princeton, 1986).

J. J. Thomson, *The Later Lollards* (Oxford, 1965).

B. Tierney, *The Medieval Poor Law* (Berkeley, 1959)

H. Traver, *The Four Daughters of God* (Bryn Mawr, 1907).

E. Vasta, *The Spiritual Basis of Piers Plowman* (The Hague, 1965).

R. A. Waldron, 'Langland's originality: the Christ-Knight and the Harrowing of Hell', in *Medieval English Religious and Ethical Literature: Essays in Honour of G. H. Russell*, eds G. Kratzmann and J. Simpson (Cambridge, 1986), pp. 66–81.

H. W. Wells, 'The construction of *Piers Plowman*', *Publications of the Modern Language Association of America*, **44** (1929), 123–40 .

H. R. B. White, 'Langland's Ymaginatif, Kynde and the *Benjamin Minor*', *Medium Ævum*, **55** (1986), 241–8.

H. R. B. White, *Nature and Salvation in Piers Plowman* (Cambridge, 1988).

Helen C. White, *Social Criticism in Popular Religious Literature of the Sixteenth Century* (New York, 1944).

R. Woolf, 'The theme of Christ the lover-knight in medieval English literature', *Review of English Studies*, **13** (1962), 1–16.

R. Woolf, 'The tearing of the Pardon', in Hussey, *Piers Plowman: Critical Approaches*, pp. 50–75.

J. A. Yunck, *The Lineage of Lady Meed: the Development of Medieval Venality Satire (Notre Dame, 1963).*

Index

213